NewTalentDesignAnnual1998

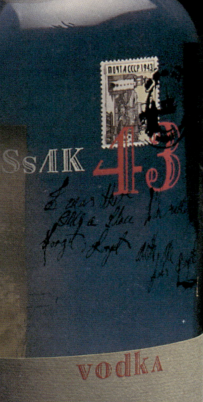

NewTalentDesignAnnual1998

The International Annual of Design and Communication by Students

Das internationale Jahrbuch über Kommunikationsdesign von Studenten

Un répertoire international de projets d'expression visuelle d'étudiants

Publisher and Creative Director: B. Martin Pedersen

Art Director: Massimo Acanfora
Graphic Designer: Mei Yee Yap
Editors: Clare Hayden, Heinke Jenssen
Associate Editors: April Heck, Allison Xantha Miller

Published by Graphis Inc.

(opposite) Label and package design by Hilario Vila Pouca, University of Ballarat, Australia

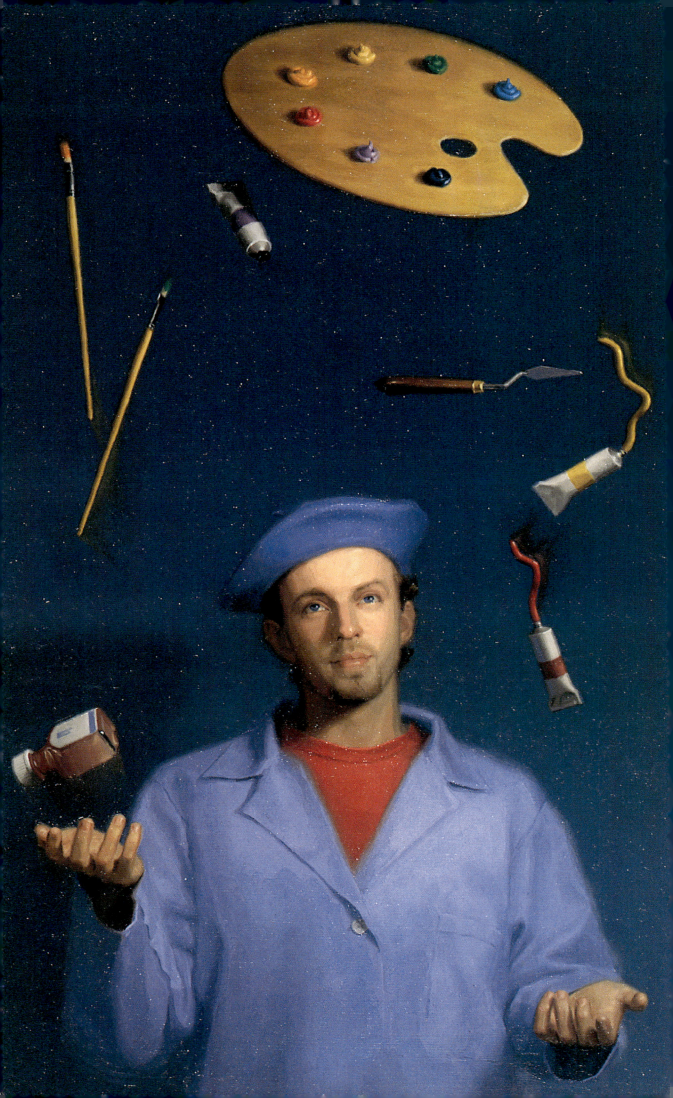

Contents Inhalt Sommaire

Remarks: We extend our heartfelt thanks to contributors throughout the world who have made it possible to publish a wide and international spectrum of the best work in this field. Entry instructions for all graphis books may be requested from: **Graphis Inc.**, 141 Lexington Avenue, New York, NY 10016-8193 or visit our web site: www.graphis.com

Ammerkungen: Unser dank gilt den einsendern aus aller welt, die es uns möglicht haben, ein breites, internationales specktrum der besten arbeiten zu veröfentlichen. Teilnahmebedingungen für die graphis-bücher sind erhältlich beim: **Graphis Inc.**, 141 Lexington Avenue, NewYork, NY 10016-8193. Besuchen sie uns im World Wide Web: www.graphis.com

Remerciements: Nous remercions les participants du monde entier qui ont rendu possible la publication de cet ouvrage offrant un panorama complet des meilleurs travaux. les modalités d'inscription peuvent être obtenues auprès de: **Graphis Inc.**, 141 Lexington Avenue, New York, NY 10016-8193. Rendez-nous visites sur notre site web: www.graphis.com

(opposite) Manveet Saluja, School of Visual Arts *(next spread)* Damian Heinisch, GH Essen, Folkwang *(page 256)* John Grande, School of Visual Arts

CommentaryKommentarCommentaire

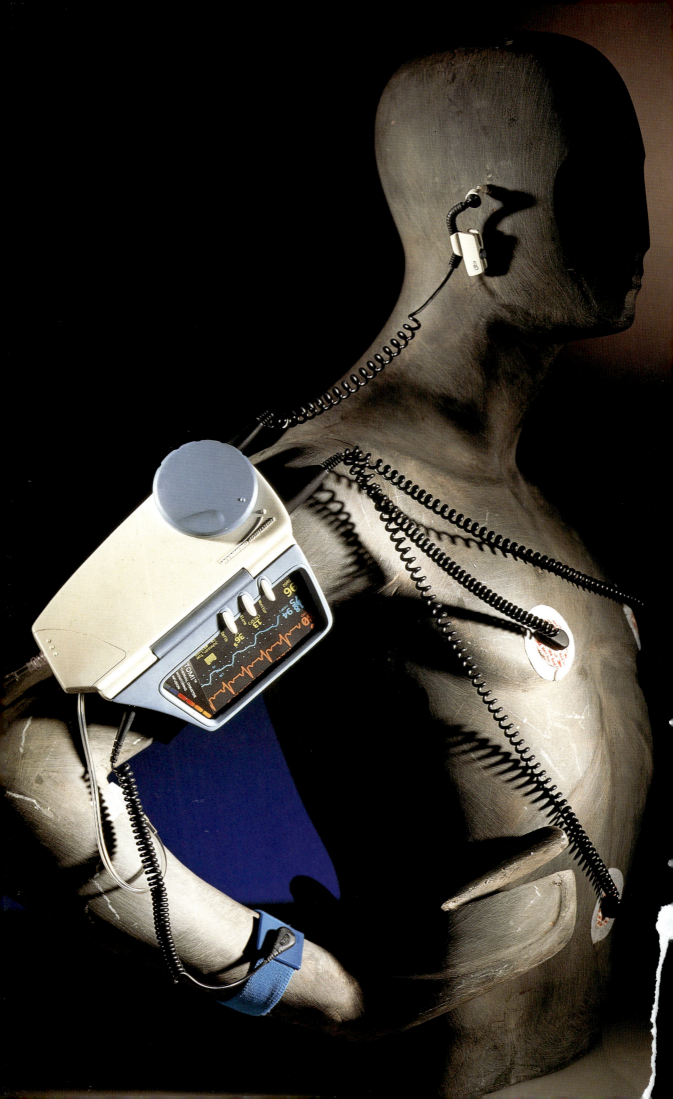

What They Never Taught You in Design School:
A Survey by Steven Skov Holt & Craig Janik

Design education doesn't stop when school ends. As a designer and teacher of design at Stanford University, this is something Craig Janik knows and seeks to communicate to his students. Recently, to give graduating seniors the benefit of the knowledge of those in whose footsteps they follow, Janik asked a group of 30 designers in the San Francisco Bay area to respond to the question: "What were you not taught in design school?" Steven Skov Holt, contributing editor to Student Design Annual 1998, was one of the designers surveyed.

He suggested that they expand the survey, making it interdisciplinary and global and that they share the results with the wider audience of *Student Design Annual 1998*. While only a portion of the replies could be reproduced here, next year the project will be expanded into a book. The rich variety of responses received is testament to the often tacit wisdom, strength and diversity of the design community.

John Armitage *Aaron Marcus and Associates:* In school, we're taught that a Mercedes performs better than a Chevy, so we're taught to design Mercedes. But the problem is that many people find the Chevy a better value. Schools might consider acknowledging that, in the real world, judging quality is far more complex than judging performance.

Bob Aufuldish *Aufuldish & Warinner, and CCAC:* The Swiss Modern–oriented program that I graduated from implied that there was one perfect solution to each problem; if you were good enough, you'd find it. Since then, there has been a cultural shift from modernist universality to postmodernist plurality. For those of us who didn't fit into the one-size-fits-all mentality, this was a welcome relief. My least favorite canard is "form follows function." I believe "form follows failure"; see Henry Petroski's *The Evolution of Useful Things*. Design is an inherently critical act based on the realization that the status quo is inadequate. New design is built on the failure of old design—a look at any mid-1970s design annual will confirm this…I've come to realize that "design school" is a lifetime curriculum. Otherwise, I'm dead.

Ken Cato *Cato Design Inc.:* My biggest design-based "life lesson" was figuring out that what we do affects both our client's profitability and other people's lives. Our skills are not an end in themselves, but the tools that allow us to do this as a job.

Chris Cavello *Design Edge:* A common misperception that design school perpetuates is that you have to contribute across the entire creative spectrum. What I've learned is just the opposite: there are valued roles for everyone. For example, the most common scenario you'll likely face after graduation is that you will be part of a team trying to design together. I've found that the magic is in the grouping, and that my role centers on encouraging everyone to cooperate. I've realized that I'm not a great aesthete, but what I add is invaluable. Trying to discover where your talents emerge effortlessly will take time and a broad range of experiences, but once you get it, you won't be burdened by having to create opportunities. Alas, they'll find you.

Bülent Erkmen *Istanbul, Turkey:* No one taught me that graphics are a spatial construction; that text is image and image is text; that it's important to oppose the "pretty–not pretty" dichotomy; that a good form comes with a good idea; that resorting to decoration when a good idea can't be found is a poor escape; that it's necessary to include the viewer and seek his participation; that style can't be chosen—it can only evolve; that it's better to foster new ways of comprehension and perception than it is to foster new forms or images; and, finally, that smell can be sculpture, that a creaking door can be music, that standing still can be dancing, that eating is not simply filling one's self, and that making love is not just reaching an orgasm.

Milton Glaser *Milton Glaser Design:* The most significant thing not taught in design school is that it's the audience that shapes the solution. Schools focus on the visionary talents of the student, and while those can't be overlooked, they're secondary. Talent has to be mutable, adaptive and receptive. We have to get off the idea that the world is waiting for our personal ability. We have to get away from the Ayn Randian notion that all-powerful visions prevail. Maybe they happen once in awhile, but they're so rare as to not be a factor. It comes down to this: students need to start thinking about how to be attentive to the world.

Fritz Gottschalk *Gottschalk & Ash International:* School gave me first-class training, but it never taught me that designs have to be considered as part of a strategy, that content and form have to convey a message and be treated equally, that teamwork is a prerequisite, that there's nothing negative about the "economics of design," that a passion for what's new in the world matters, and that I should be frank, relentless and have a positive attitude.

Jessica Helfand *Jessica Helfand/William Drenttel:* When I was in ninth grade, I took a class called environmental science whose curriculum was built around daily visits to a creek. I kept a journal to record changes in environment, climate, insect population and so forth. Looking back, this study may have had more to do with my decision to become a graphic designer than anything else. At graduate school at Yale, I resisted such rigor. Strict visual problems with formal restrictions prevailed: plaka, gouache and ruling pens were the common currency. If I'd approached those assignments with the same open-mindedness I had at the creek, I might have seen them as liberating. But at the time, all I could think of was how stifling they were. I longed to see my work informed by history and philosophy, so I spent every free moment in the library. I produced a densely written thesis, and I wrote a 194-page book on the history of the square. I designed it in the last two weeks before gradua–

tion—and it looked like it—but the good news was that I knew Paul Rand would read it. I regret that there wasn't a better way to merge my studio life with my library time. Perhaps if Rand had gone with me to the library and then back to the studio, there might have been a way to join the observational thinking I'd discovered as a ninth-grader with the resources of the university. At the very least, I learned how to scrutinize the questions as much as the answers—a very good thing for any designer to know how to do.

Andy Hodge *Ideo Product Development:* You can be proactive in creating the client's expectations. You have to hunt for the right information. It's like a Charlie Chan movie: you know enough to find the answer, but there's a lot of information that misleads you. The same comment applies to the people who use your designs: they're not experts at telling you what they want, so you need to read them like tea leaves.

Craig Janik

Steven Skov Holt *Frogdesign & CCAC:* Design school failed to communicate anything about the necessity of (and the beauty and pleasure one can take in) incessantly searching for what Gregory Bateson called "the pattern that connects." That pattern is what makes design real, and a sense of "the real" is what makes the whole thing called "life" meaningful. And no one taught me how hard I'd have to fight for my inalienable rights to creativity, discovery and the self-identification of my own guiding meme. No one taught me that we need a new kind of cultural hero, and that a role in the new information economy exists for designers "beyond design." But I expect to see a new breed of leaders and entrepreneurs who, because of their design training, refuse to compartmentalize when they can synthesize.

Tony Hu *Primal Products:* The patent library is choked with designs that never made it. But late-night infomercial products net their creators millions. The lesson? Building a better mousetrap doesn't automatically lead to riches. For example, you need a salesperson to pitch the mousetrap to a thousand jaded buyers. You need a P.R. firm to stick it into ten million Happy Meals. You need an attorney to fight the copycats. You need a lobbyist to make your mousetrap mandatory restaurant equipment.

Craig Janik *Speck Product Design:* I wasn't taught about the relentless pursuit of your individual "sweet spot." Design schools often don't acknowledge that individuals vary greatly in their innate talents. I believe you have to work toward incremental, but relentless improvement. You need to constantly reflect on what you've learned, what you want to learn and what you still need to learn. I also wasn't taught that working within a group doesn't necessarily mean committee decision-making; it means never underestimating the power of lots of thoughts.

Scott Klinker *Ideo Product Development:* How about: "Who's a designer?" So many people call themselves designers that even practitioners don't know what it means. I wish someone would have pointed out to me the distinctions between design as "cultural project" and design as "product development."

Peter Krämer *Peter Krämer Illustration:* Design school is a place where you define yourself. If it's a good school, you learn how to do this for the rest of your life. The best thing that school gave me was four years of time, and to come back to the original question, I was hardly taught anything in school, but I got the chance there to teach myself something.

Flemming Ljorring *Flemming Ljorring Design & Photography International:* I didn't learn anything about the business of design. For example: how to get a job, how to explain my work, how to express myself in writing or speech, how to promote myself and present my work, how to deal with CEOs and other designers within a client company, how to calculate the worth of my services, that there is a world outside my own country, and that others might not understand my rules, habits or tastes.

Ken Martin *Immersion Corporation:* "Craftsmanship" is just as important in CAD as it is in woodworking. The ability to make changes up to the final hour—to fix the "oh shit!"s—depends on having a stable model that won't blow up when you push it. Every design has an Achilles' heel, and every designer is afraid to tackle it because they're afraid their "grand concept" will fall apart. But the key is to look for it—and then attack it. It takes a while to start hitting on all cylinders as a designer. When you start out, you're surprised that you made a mistake. Later, you "plan" to make a mistake so that when it happens, you're not upset. Still later, you're surprised when you don't screw up. But everybody who's good does it a little (or a lot) differently. Figure out your way, and trust it.

Michael McDonough *Michael McDonough Architect: Start with what you know.* Start by drawing what you already understand. If you're designing a chair, for example, its dimensions, angle of repose and loading requirements can be determined—so draw them. Forget about what you don't know, and focus on what you do. Solve the unknowns one at a time. This is the most important rule in design; in Zen Buddhist terms, "Be where you are." ■ *Talent is one-third of success.* Talent is important, but it's no guarantee of success. Hard work and luck are equally important. Hard work means discipline and sacrifice, and luck means access to powerful contacts or money. Even if you're not talented, you can still succeed via the other two, and if you think I'm kidding, just look around. ■ *Ninety-five percent is "shit work."* In school you focus on the five percent of design that is actually fun. But in real life, it's about paperwork, research, paying taxes and so forth. You can't succeed without learning to accept—if not love—the shit work; it's all part of the whole. ■ *Don't overthink a problem.* Once in graduate school, a critic said to me after one week on a ten-week problem, "OK, you solved it—draw it up." My other critics had always tried to prolong the problem, even if it was

Craig Janik is a founding partner at Speck Product Design, a Palo Alto, California-based firm specializing in the development of products and intellectual property for clients in the areas of computing, medicine, sports and fitness. He earned a B.F.A. in design from Carnegie Mellon University, and a

Master's in product design from Stanford. He is currently a lecturer at Stanford University's Mechanical Engineering Design division and has taught graduate and undergraduate classes for the past five years. Steven Skov Holt has been a designer at frogdesign, inc. in Sunnyvale, California, since 1992. Since already solved. This was a revelation. When a thing is done, move on. Do something else. ■ *Be who you are.* I remember a student who tried to impress a visiting professor. With great facility, he imitated her work. When he finished, he proudly displayed his drawings, and the professor looked at everything and said, "This is how I'd do it. But how would you do it?" Then she failed him. ■ *Don't forget your goal.* As a teacher, I have seen students approach a problem with brilliance, only to let it slip away in wasted effort. They forget their goals and make up new ones as they go along. Write your idea down on a piece of paper and place it in front of you. Refer to it as often as possible. ■ *It's all about output.* No matter how cool your design is, if you can't output it and share it, it doesn't exist. Therefore, orient yourself to scheduling, thinking and producing output. If you want someone to "show you the money," then "show them the output." ■ *Master the basics.* Students show me

Steven Skov Holt

their digital doodles all the time, but most don't know their PCs. They can't administer a network, set up a directory or perform any of the other myriad routines required for smooth running. Never underestimate the power of the basic stuff. ■ *The rest of the world counts.* No matter how good your design is, someone has to make, assemble, ship and sell it. Respect these people. They can perform their jobs as well as you perform yours—and you need them.

Catherine Montalbo *Addison Design:* They didn't teach much about design as a business. Or how to sell our work and put visual ideas into words since most of our clients aren't visually astute, poor dears.

David Moore *The Design Company:* It was never made clear to me how much design is a "social study." You have to look at who's on the receiving end. You can't design your way through a project—you have to feel and live it. You ever get the feeling there's something going on here we don't know about? A design education can only give you the tools. You have to learn how to apply them in ways no one else has. I'm constantly surprised at how design has pushed me in so many directions, asked me to create things I'd never imagined and encouraged me to take as many risks as possible.

Finn Nygaard *Finn Nygaard Graphic Design:* They didn't teach me that becoming a designer is not only completing four years of education, but embarking on a never-ending educational journey; that I would have to be open and continuously conscious of bringing something unique to each assignment; and that I would need to see clearly into the future.

Chris Pullman *WGBH Boston and visiting critic, Yale University:* You'll never realize how much you didn't learn in school until you try to teach in one. I learned a lot about typography, for example, but it wasn't until I was teaching that I realized I didn't have a simple way to communicate its value to my students. Compared with the rich inflections, nuances and rhythms of oral speech—not to mention the crucial context of facial

expression and body language—typographic expression is relatively arid and abstract. But with the introduction of time, motion and sound as part of the graphic designer's palette, the potential for typographic expression that approaches the richness of spoken language has increased dramatically. Now, how will we teach this in design school?

Michael Sainato Art Center's approach was to keep students in their own little departments. There were few opportunities to get to know the other students, and there was almost no interdisciplinary teaching. But design is design—graphic designers work on interiors and industrial design people do graphics—so why not introduce this early in the education process? Art school never mentioned anything about the "business" of design. It was assumed that everyone was going to get a corporate job and live happily ever after. But with more interesting work going to free-lancers, art schools (which aren't cheap!) should teach the basics of self-promotion and client and vendor relationships.

Leslie Speer *Praxis:* They don't teach you that the frustration and confusion that you experience are a lesson to be learned from, expanded upon and applied to all the other areas of your life.

Michael Vanderbyl *Vanderbyl Design:* What they taught me in college was that "form follows function." What they meant was that "form follows modernism." What they didn't teach me—and what took years for me to understand—was that pluralism is what makes both design and life interesting.

John Wadsworth *S.G. Hauser:* The purpose of it all is to produce something, and someone is going to assemble that something for eight hours per day. That means assembly design has to be idiot-proof, which is hard, because most idiots are so damned creative. For that reason alone, precision, draft and tolerances matter.

Lorraine Wild *California Institute of Art:* The two design schools I attended both applied a great deal of energy to the pursuit of ideas as a conceptual, aesthetic and sociopolitical practice. But almost no energy was spent teaching how those ideas might be translated to the client. It was assumed that "good design" would triumph, and if it didn't, it was due to the small-mindedness of your client. This was communicated implicitly in the language that we used to discuss our work, and in the way that language was circumscribed by inward-turned professionalism. In the mid- to late-1970s, when design offices weren't geared to self-promotion, schools that emphasized presentation were looked down on. Attention to sales techniques allegedly took time away from the serious pursuit of the art of design. But it takes trust to make design work, and an atmosphere of genuine collaboration between you, the client and your audience. It was easy to write that off as a student, and as a faculty member it's still easy to write it off. But it must be approached at school because it's so critical to the outcome of any design.

1995, he has also been chair of the industrial design program at California College of Arts and Crafts in San Francisco. He is a former partner of Zebra Design (Cologne, Germany), a former designer at Smart Design (New York), and former editor of ID magazine. A co-founder of the Department of Product Design at Parsons School of Design in New York, Holt is a regular contributor to magazines such as Axis, Metropolitan Home, and Graphis. Born and raised in Connecticut, Holt received an A.B. in Cognitive science from Brown University and an M.F.A. in design studies from Stanford University.

«Was hat man Ihnen an der Design-Schule nicht beigebracht?»
Redigiert von Steven Skov Holt und Craig Janik

Die Design-Ausbildung endet nicht mit dem Abschluss einer entsprechenden Schule. Als Designer und Lehrer an der Stanford University weiss Craig Janik das und versucht, es seinen Studenten zu vermitteln. Um seine Schüler der Abschlussklasse von den Erfahrungen der Praktiker profitieren zu lassen, stellte Janik einer Gruppe von 30 Designern aus der Gegend von San Francisco die Frage: «Was hat man Ihnen an der Design-Schule nicht beigebracht?» Steven Holt, Contributing Editor von Graphis Student Design, war einer der Befragten.

Er kam auf die Idee, die Umfrage auf eine interdisziplinäre, globale Ebene auszulegen. Während hier nur ein Teil der Antworten weidergegeben werden kann, ist für nächstes Jahr ein ganzes Buch zu diesem Thema geplant. Die ganz unterschiedlichen Antworten zeugen von der Reife, Stärke und Vielfalt der Branche.

John Armitage *Aaron Marcus and Associates:* In der Schule erzählen sie einem, dass ein Mercedes besser sei als ein Chevrolet, also lernen wir, einen Mercedes zu entwerfen. Das Problem ist, dass viele Leute finden, dass beim Chevy das Preis-Leistungsverhältnis eher stimmt. An den Schulen sollte man vielleicht darüber nachdenken, dass in der Realität die Beurteilung von Qualität viel komplexer ist und nicht nur die Leistung betrifft.

Bob Aufuldisch *Aufuldish & Warinner und CCAC:* Der Studiengang, den ich absolvierte, war ganz dem modernen Schweizer Stil verpflichtet, der implizierte, dass es für jedes Problem eine perfekte Lösung gibt; wenn man gut genug war, würde man sie finden. Seitdem hat sich ein kultureller Wandel vollzogen, weg von der modernistischen Allgemeingültigkeit hin zur postmodernistischen Pluralität. Für alle, die nichts mit dieser Auffassung von nur einer richtigen Lösung anfangen konnten, war das eine willkommene Erlösung. Mir gefällt der Leitsatz «Form folgt Funktion» überhaupt nicht. Ich glaube, dass «Form Scheitern folgt» – siehe Henry Petroskis *The Evolution of Useful Things.* Design ist naturgemäss ein kritischer Akt, der auf der Erkenntnis beruht, dass der Status quo unzureichend ist. Neues Design baut auf dem Scheitern vorhandenen Designs auf – ein Blick auf ein Design-Jahrbuch aus dem Jahre 1970 wird das bestätigen....Mir ist bewusst geworden, dass Design-Schule ein lebenslanger Lernprozess ist. Sonst wäre ich tot.

Ken Cato *Cato Design Inc:* Die wichtigste Design-Lektion, die mir das Leben erteilt hat, war die Erkenntnis, dass das, was wir machen, sowohl die Rentabilität des Kunden als auch das Leben anderer Leute beeinflusst. Unser handwerkliches Können ist lediglich das Werkzeug, das uns erlaubt, unsere Arbeit in diesem Sinne zu tun.

Chris Cavello *Design Edge:* An vielen Design-Schulen herrscht die irrige Annahme vor, dass man das gesamte kreative Spektrum beherrschen muss. Aber ich habe das Gegenteil erfahren: es gibt für jeden eine bestimmte Rolle. Nach dem Verlassen der Schule wird man meistens Teil einer Designgruppe, die gemeinsam Aufgaben zu lösen hat. Ich habe herausgefunden, dass es allein um die Frage der richtigen Zusammensetzung geht und dass meine Rolle vor allem darin besteht, alle zur Zusammenarbeit zu ermuntern. Ich habe festgestellt, dass meine Stärke nicht in der Ästhetik liegt, dass aber das, was ich beitrage, wertvoll ist. Herauszufinden, wo die eigenen besonderen Talente liegen, braucht Zeit und auch viel Erfahrung, aber wenn man es einmal weiss, wird man sich nicht damit abmühen müssen, Aufträge zu bekommen. Sie werden dich schon finden.

Bülent Erkmen *Istanbul, Türkei:* Niemand erklärte mir, dass Graphik eine räumliche Konstruktion ist; dass Text gleich Bild ist und Bild gleich Text; dass es wichig ist, sich gegen die Ausschliesslichkeit von 'hübsch' oder 'nicht hübsch' zu wehren; dass eine gute Idee eine gute Form mit sich bringt; dass Dekoration statt einer guten Idee eine armselige Ausflucht ist; dass es notwendig ist, den Betrachter teilhaben zu lassen und ihn einzubeziehen; dass man einen Stil nicht wählen, sondern dass er sich nur ergeben kann; dass es besser ist, neue Wege des Verständnisses und der Auffassung zu fördern statt neue Formen oder Bilder; und schliesslich, dass Geruch Skulptur sein kann, dass eine quietschende Tür Musik sein kann, dass stillstehen tanzen sein kann, dass essen nicht nur sich vollstopfen bedeutet und dass lieben nicht nur bedeutet, einen Orgasmus zu haben.

Milton Glaser *Milton Glaser Design:* Das Wichtigste, das ich nicht an der Design-Schule gelernt habe, ist die Tatsache, dass das Zielpublikum die Lösung einer Aufgabe bestimmt. Die Schulen konzentrieren sich auf die visionären Talente der Studenten, und wenn diese auch nicht vernachlässigt werden dürfen, so sind sie doch von sekundärer Bedeutung. Talent muss variabel, anpassungs- und aufnahmefähig sein. Wir müssen die irrige Auffassung, dass die Welt auf unsere persönlichen Fähigkeiten wartet, vergessen. Wir müssen wegkommen von der Behauptung Ayn Randians, dass sich allmächtige Visionen durchsetzen. Es gibt sie vielleicht hin und wieder, aber sie sind so selten, dass sie kein Kriterium sind. Das heisst im Klartest: Studenten müssen anfangen, darüber nachzudenken, wie sie der Welt Beachtung schenken.

Fritz Gottschalk *Gottschalk + Ash International:* Was ich von der Schule bekam, war eine erstklassige, solide Ausbildung, aber man lehrte mich nicht, dass Gestaltung als Teil einer Strategie zu sehen ist; dass Inhalt und Form die Botschaft transportieren müssen und dass sie gleichberechtigt sind; dass Teamwork eine Voraussetzung ist; dass Wirtschaftlichkeit nichts Negatives ist; dass Begeisterung für alles Neue wichtig ist und dass man offen, dass man

(opposite)
Architectural form study by Travis Rogers,
Rhode Island School of Design

positiv sein und Durchhaltevermögen haben muss.

Jessica Helfand *Jessica Helfand/William Drenttel:* Als ich in der neunten Klasse war, entschied ich mich für ein Wahlfach, das Umwelt-Wissenschaft hiess. Die Basis des Lehrprogramms bestand aus täglichen Besuchen eines Baches. Ich führte Buch über Veränderungen der Umwelt, des Klimas, der Insektenpopulation und so weiter. Wenn ich zurückblicke, dann hat dieser Unterricht vielleicht mehr als alles andere zu meinem Beschluss geführt, Gestalterin zu werden. In den letzten Semestern des Design-Studienganges in Yale wollte ich von solchem Aufwand nichts wissen. Hier ging es um rein visuelle Probleme mit formalen Beschränkungen: Plaka, Gouache und Feder waren das tägliche Brot. Wenn ich jene Aufgaben so offen wie damals am Bach angegangen wäre, hätte ich sie vielleicht als befreiend empfunden. Damals aber dachte ich nur darüber nach, wie einengend sie waren. Ich wollte, dass Geschichte und Philosophie meine Arbeit prägen und verbrachte jede freie Minute in der Bibliothek. Ich produzierte eine umfassende schriftliche Abschlussarbeit, und ich schrieb ein 194 Seiten starkes Buch über die Geschichte des Quadrates. Ich gestaltete es in den letzten beiden Wochen vor der Abschlussprüfung − und so sah es auch aus −, aber immerhin wusste ich, dass Paul Rand es lesen würde. Ich bedaure, dass ich die beiden Dinge, Atelier und Bibliothek, nicht auf andere Art verbinden konnte. Wenn Rand mit mir in die Bibliothek und dann zurück ins Atelier gegangen wäre, hätte es vielleicht einen Weg gegeben, das beobachtende Denken, das ich in der 9. Klasse entdeckt hatte, mit den Möglichkeiten der Universität zu verbinden. Aber wenigstens lernte ich die Fragen so genau zu untersuchen wie die Antworten − , und das sollte jeder Designer können.

Andy Hodge *Ideo Product Development:* Man muss herausfinden, was der Auftraggeber eigentlich will. Man muss sich um die richtige Information bemühen. Es ist wie in einem Film von Charlie Chan: Du weisst genug, um die Antwort zu finden, aber es gibt eine Menge Informationen, die dich irreführen können. Das trifft auch auf die Leute zu, die deine Designs benutzen: Sie können nicht klar formulieren, was sie von dir wollen, also muss man sich um eine Deutung ihrer Äusserungen bemühen, so als würde man aus dem Kaffeesatz lesen.

Steven Skov Holt *Frogdesign & CCAC:* An der DesignSchule hat man uns nichts von der Notwendigkeit (und der Freude und Schönheit) der unaufhörlichen Suche nach dem erzählt, was Gregory Bateson «das verbindende Muster» nennt. Eben dieses Muster macht Design real, und ein Gefühl des «Realen» gibt dem, was man «Leben» nennt, Sinn. Und niemand hat mir gesagt, wie hart ich für mein unbestreitbares Recht auf Kreativität, Entdeckung und Identität zu kämpfen haben würde. Niemand hat mir erzählt, dass wir eine neue Art kulturellen Wegbereiter brauchen und dass ein Designer interdisziplinär denken und sich für mehr interessieren muss als nur für Design. Ich glaube jedoch, dass eine neue Generation von führenden Leuten und Unternehmern aufgrund ihrer Designausbildung Ausgrenzungen nicht zulassen werden, wenn sie die Möglichkeit einer Verschmelzung sehen.

Tony Hu *Primal Products:* Das Archiv des Patentamts ist vollgestopft mit Entwürfen, die nie umgesetzt wurden. Aber Produkte, die spätnachts in den Infomercials (als Informationen verkleidete Spots) angepriesen werden, bringen ihren Herstellern Millionen ein. Die Moral von der Geschichte? Die Gestaltung einer besseren Mausefalle führt nicht zwangsläufig zu Reichtum. Zum Beispiel braucht man einen Verkäufer, der die Mausefalle Tausenden von übersättigten Kunden schmackhaft macht. Man braucht eine PR-Firma, um die Werbung zehn Millionen Packungen Katzenfutter beizulegen. Man braucht einen Anwalt, um sich gegen illegale Nachahmungen zu wehren. Man braucht einen Lobbyisten, der diese Mausefalle zur Pflichtausstattung von Restaurants macht.

Craig Janik *Speck Design:* Ich lernte nichts über die ständige Suche nach den eigenen besonderen Talenten. An den Design-Schulen wird oft nicht erkannt, dass die einzelnen Schüler sich in ihren angeboren Talenten stark unterscheiden. Man muss unablässig an sich arbeiten. Man muss ständig darüber nachdenken, was man gelernt hat, was man lernen möchte und was man noch lernen muss. Mir wurde auch nichts darüber gesagt, dass das Arbeiten in der Gruppe nicht unbedingt etwas mit Konsenspolitik zu tun hat, sondern dass man das Potential vieler verschiedener Gedanken nicht unterschätzen darf.

Scott Klinker *Ideo Product Development:* Was ist mit der Frage: «Wer ist ein Designer?» Mittlerweile nennen sich so viele Leute Designer, dass nicht einmal die Praktiker wissen, was der Begriff bedeutet. Ich wünschte, jemand hätte mir erklärt, worin sich Design als «kulturelles Projekt» und Design als «Produktentwicklung» unterscheidet.

Peter Krämer *Peter Krämer Illustration:* Ich sehe die Schule als einen Ort, sich zu definieren. Wenn es eine gute Schule ist, lernt man, wie man sich ein Leben lang weiter definiert. Das Beste, was mir die Schule gegeben hat, waren 4 Jahre Zeit. Um auf die Frage zurückzukommen: In der Schule hat man mir kaum etwas beigebracht, aber mir wurde die Chance gegeben, mir selbst etwas beizubringen.

Flemming Ljorring *Flemming Ljorring Design + Photography International:* Ich lernte nichts über die geschäftliche Seite des Designs. Zum Beispiel: wie man einen Auftrag bekommt; wie ich meine Arbeit anderen erkläre; wie ich mich mündlich oder schriftlich ausdrücken muss; wie ich für mich werbe und wie ich meine Arbeit präsentiere; wie ich mit der Geschäftsführung und anderen Designern in einer Firma umgehen muss; wie ich meine Dienstleistungen berechne. Wir lernten nicht, dass es eine Welt ausserhalb unseres Landes gibt, dass andere unsere Regeln, Gewohnheiten oder Vorlieben vielleicht nicht verstehen.

(opposite)
Timepiece design by Jim Doan, Victor Fernandez, and Elliot Hsu of the University of Illinois.

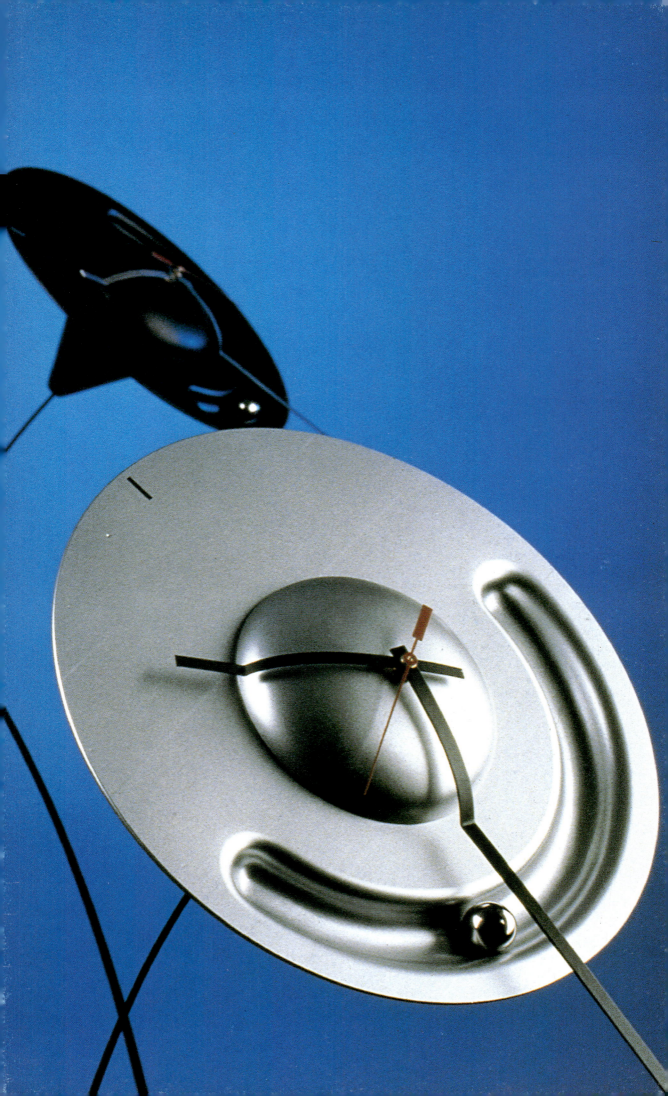

Ken Martin *Immersion Corporation:* Handwerkliches Können ist beim CAD genauso wichtig wie beim Holzschnitzen. Die Fähigkeit, bis zum Schluss Änderungen vorzunehmen − all die Ausrutscher zu beheben − hängt ganz davon ab, ob man ein solides Modell hat, das nicht explodiert, sobald man es bewegt. Jedes Design hat eine Achilles-Ferse, und jeder Designer hat Angst, daran zu rühren, weil er fürchten muss, dass sein «prächtiges Konzept» zusammenbrechen wird. Aber man muss die Schwachstelle suchen, um sie dann zu beheben. Man braucht als Designer einige Zeit, bevor man alle Register ziehen kann. Am Anfang ist man überrascht, wenn man einen Fehler gemacht hat. Später «plant» man, einen Fehler zu machen und regt sich nicht auf, wenn es passiert. Noch später ist man überrascht, wenn man's nicht vermasselt. Aber jeder, der gut ist, macht es ein bisschen (oder völlig) anders. Man muss für sich den richtigen Weg finden und darauf vertrauen.

Michael McDonough *Michael McDonough Architect Beginn' mit dem, was du kannst.* Zeichne etwas, das du schon verstehst. Wenn du zum Beispiel einen Stuhl entwirfst, können seine Dimensionen, der Neigungswinkel der Lehne und die Belastbarkeit bestimmt werden − also zeichne sie. Denk' nicht an das, was du nicht weisst, und konzentriere dich auf das, was du tust. Löse die Unbekannten eine nach der anderen. Das ist die wichtigste Regel der Gestaltung; in der Sprache des Zen Buddhismus: «Sei wo du bist.» ■ *Talent ist 1/3 des Erfolgs.* Talent ist wichtig, aber es ist keine Erfolgsgarantie. Harte Arbeit und Glück sind ebenso wichtig. Harte Arbeit heisst Disziplin und Entbehrung, und Glück bedeutet Zugang zu Leuten mit Macht oder Geld. Selbst wenn man kein Talent hat, kann man dank der anderen beiden Faktoren durchaus Erfolg haben, und ich meine das ernst − man schaue sich nur um. ■ *95% der Arbeit sind unangenehm.* In der Schule konzentriert man sich auf die 5% des Designs, die wirklich Spass machen. Aber in der Realität geht es um Papierkrieg, Nachforschungen, Steuerzahlungen und so weiter. Man kann keinen Erfolg haben, wenn man nicht lernt, die unangenehme Arbeit zu akzeptieren, wenn schon nicht zu lieben − sie gehört dazu. ■ *Mach' nicht zuviel aus einer Aufgabe.* In der Schule ging es einmal um ein 10-Wochen-Projekt, und nach einer Woche sagte mir ein Gutachter: «Okay, du hast die Aufgabe gelöst − zeichne sie.» Die anderen Gutachter hatten immer versucht, die Aufgabe auszudehnen, auch wenn sie bereits gelöst war. Deshalb war dieses Erlebnis eine Offenbarung. Wenn eine Sache getan ist, wende dich etwas anderem zu. ■ *Sei du selbst.* Ich erinnere mich an einen Studenten, der versuchte, bei einer Gastprofes-sorin Eindruck zu machen. Mit grosser Leichtigkeit imitierte er ihre Arbeit. Als er fertig war, zeigte er stolz seine Zeichnungen. Die Professorin schaute sich alles sorgfältig an und sagte: «So hätte ich es gemacht. Aber wie würdest Du es machen?» Sie liess ihn durchfallen. ■ *Verliere nicht dein Ziel aus den Augen.* Als Lehrer habe ich Studenten beobachtet, die ein Problem brillant angingen und es dann aus den Augen verloren. Sie vergessen ihre Ziele und verfolgen im Verlauf der Arbeit andere. Man sollte seine Ideen auf ein Stück Papier schreiben und dieses immer vor sich haben. Und dann sollte man so oft wie möglich draufschauen. ■ *Es geht um Resultate.* Wie 'cool' auch immer der Entwurf sein mag, wenn man ihn nicht umsetzen kann, vermitteln kann, dann existiert er nicht. Man sollte sich deshalb an Termine halten, denken und etwas Greifbares produzieren. Wenn du Geld sehen willst, musst du ihnen etwas vorlegen können. ■ *Man muss die Grundlagen beherrschen.* Die Studenten zeigen mir ständig ihre digitalen Spielereien, aber die meisten von ihnen kennen ihre PCs nicht. Sie können weder eine Vernetzung herstellen, noch eine Richtschnur aufstellen oder irgendeine der unendlichen anderen Routinearbeiten verrichten, die einen problemlosen Ablauf garantieren. Man sollte nie die Bedeutung der Grundlagen unterschätzen. ■ *Der Rest der Welt zählt.* Wie gut dein Entwurf auch sein mag, jemand muss ihn ausführen, zusammenbauen, verschiffen, verkaufen. Respektiere diese Leute. Sie machen ihre Jobs so gut wie du deinen − und du brauchst sie.

Catherine Montalbo *Addision Design:* Sie haben uns nicht viel über die geschäftliche Seite des Designs erzählt, wie man seine Arbeit verkauft oder visuelle Ideen in Worte fasst, denn die meisten unserer Kunden sind in visueller Hinsicht nicht gerade auf der Höhe.

David Moore *The Design Company:* Man hat mir nicht klargemacht, in welchem Ausmass Design eine «soziale Studie» ist. Man muss darauf achten, wer der Empfänger ist. Man kann sich nicht einfach auf die Gestaltung eines Projektes konzentrieren − man muss es erfühlen, es leben. Haben Sie je das Gefühl, dass hier etwas vor sich geht, von dem Sie keine Ahnung haben? Eine Schule kann einem nur das Werkzeug mit auf den Weg geben. Man muss lernen, es auf eine völlig neue Art einzusetzen. Ich wundere mich immer wieder darüber, in wieviele neue Richtungen mich die Arbeit geführt hat, wie ich dazu kam, Dinge zu schaffen, an die ich nie gedacht hätte, und alle möglichen Risiken einzugehen.

Finn Nygaard *Finn Nygaard Graphic Design:* Sie lehrten mich nicht, dass vier Jahre Ausbildung nicht bedeuten, dass man ein Designer wird, sondern dass man eine nie endende Ausbildung vor sich hat; sie sagten nichts darüber, dass ich offen sein muss, so dass ich bewusst bei jedem Auftrag etwas Einzigartiges zustande bringe, und ich lernte nicht, dass ich mir ein klares Bild von der Zukunft machen muss.

Chris Pullman *WGHB Boston und Gastgutachter an der Yale University:* Man wird nie realisieren, wie viel man an der Design-Schule nicht gelernt hat, bis man versucht, selbst Unterricht zu geben. Ich habe zum Beispiel viel über Typographie gelernt, aber erst als ich zu unterrichten begann, stellte ich fest, dass ich nicht in der Lage war, den Studenten die Bedeutung der Typographie auf einfache Art zu vermitteln.

Craig Janik ist Mitbegründer von Speck Product Design, einer Firma in Palo Alto, Kalifornien, die sich auf die Entwicklung von Produkten und geistigem Eigentum für Kunden in den Bereichen Computer, Medizin, Sport und Fitness spezialisiert hat. Er erwarb den Titel B.F.A. in Design an der Carnegie Mellon University und den M.F.A. in Produkt-Design an der Universität von Stanford. Zurzeit unterrichtet er an dieser Universität im Bereich Maschinenbau-Design. *Steven Skov Holt* arbeitet seit 1992 als Designer bei frogdesign inc. in Sunnyvale, Kalifornien. Seit 1995 hat er auch einen Lehrstuhl für Industrie-

Verglichen mit den vielfältigen Tonlagen, Nuancen und Rhythmen der mündlichen Sprache – ganz abgesehen von dem vielsagenden Zusammenspiel von Gesichtsausdruck und Körpersprache, – ist der typographische Ausdruck relativ nüchtern und abstrakt. Aber nachdem auch Zeit, Bewegung und Ton zu den Möglichkeiten des Designers gehören, sind die typographischen Ausdrucksmöglichkeiten der Vielfalt der gesprochen Sprache bedeutend näher gekommen. Wie werden wir das den Studenten in der Design-Schule vermitteln?

Michael Sainato Das Art Center lässt die Studenten in kleinen Klassen arbeiten. Es gab kaum Möglichkeiten, andere Studenten kennenzulernen, und es gab kaum einen interdisziplinären Unterricht. Aber Design ist Design – Graphik-Designer arbeiten auch an Inneneinrichtungen und Innenarchitekten machen auch Graphik – warum macht man die Studenten also nicht schon früh damit vertraut? Über die geschäftliche Seite des Designs wurde überhaupt nicht gesprochen. Man nahm an, dass jeder Schüler in einer Firma landen und dort für den Rest seiner Laufbahn glücklich sein würde. Da aber die interessanteren Arbeiten an Freelancer vergeben werden, sollten die Kunstschulen (die nicht gerade billig sind!) den Schülern die Grundlagen der Eigenwerbung und des Umgangs mit den Auftraggebern vermitteln.

Leslie Speer *Praxis:* Sie bringen einem nicht bei, dass der Frust und die Irritation, die man verspürt, eine Lektion sind, von der man lernen kann und die man verarbeiten und auf alle anderen Bereiche des Lebens anwenden muss.

Michael Vanderbyl *Vanderbyl Design:* Am College habe ich gelernt, dass Form Funktion folgt. Gemeint war damit, dass «Form dem Modernismus» folgt. Was sie mir nicht beigebracht haben – und ich brauchte Jahre, um es zu begreifen – ist, dass Pluralismus sowohl Design als auch das Leben an sich erst interessant macht.

John Wadsworth *S.G. Hauser:* Der Sinn des Ganzen liegt darin, etwas zu produzieren, und jemand wird acht Stunden am Tag damit verbringen, dieses Etwas zusammenzusetzen. Das bedeutet, dass Montage-Design idiotensicher sein muss, und das ist schwer, denn die meisten Idioten sind so verdammt kreativ. Nur aus diesem Grund kommt es auf Präzision, Skizzen und Toleranzen an.

Lorraine Wild *California Institute of Art:* An den beiden Design-Schulen, die ich besucht habe, wurde grosser Wert auf die Verfolgung von Ideen als eine konzeptuelle, ästhetische und soziopolitische Übung gelegt. Aber wie man diese Ideen dem Auftraggeber vermitteln sollte, wurde so gut wie nicht behandelt. Es wurde angenommen, dass sich «gutes Design» durchsetzen würde, und wenn das nicht der Fall war, so war das auf die Engstirnigkeit des Kunden zurückzuführen. Wir benutzten eine eigene Fachsprache, um unsere Arbeiten zu diskutieren, eine introvertierte Fachsprache, die andere ausschloss. Gegen Mitte bzw. gegen Ende der siebziger Jahre, als Design-Studios noch keine Eigenwerbung machten, wurden Schulen, die Wert auf Präsentationen legten, von oben herab angesehen. Verkaufstaktik war etwas, das nur Zeit raubte, die doch der Kunst der Gestaltung vorbehalten war. Aber man braucht Vertrauen, damit Design funktioniert und eine Atmosphäre echter Zusammenarbeit zwischen Gestalter, Auftraggeber und dem Zielpublikum. Als Student konnte man das leicht übergehen, und auch als Lehrer kann man das noch immer ohne weiteres. Aber es wäre dringend notwendig, das Thema an den Schulen aufzunehmen, weil es für den Erfolg jeglichen Designs ausschlaggebend ist.

Design am California College of Arts and Crafts in San Francisco. Früher war er Partner von Zebra Design, Köln, Designer bei Smart Design, New York, und Redakteur der Zeitschrift ID. *Er ist Mitbegründer des Studienganges Produkt-Design an der Parsons School of Design in New York und schreibt regelmässig für Zeitschriften wie* Axis, Metropolitan Home *und* Graphis. *Er wurde in Connecticut geboren und ist dort aufgewachsen. Den B.A. (Bachelor of Arts) in kognitiven Wissenschaften erwarb er an der Brown University und den M.F.A.(Master of fine Arts) in Design an der Stanford University.*

Ce que vous n'avez pas appris dans votre école de design:
par Steven Skov Holt et Craig Janik

Une formation en design ne s'achève pas avec la fin de l'école. En tant que designer et professeur, Craig Janik en est conscient et essaie de sensibiliser ses étudiants à ce problème. Pour faire profiter sa classe de diplôme des expériences des praticiens, Janik a posé la question suivante à un groupe de 30 designers établis dans la baie de San Francisco: «Qu'est-ce que vous n'avez pas appris dans votre école de design?» Parmi les personnes interrogées figurait Steven Skov Holt, rédacteur en chef adjoint de Graphis Student Design,

qui a eu l'idée d'étendre cette enquête à d'autres disciplines et d'en publier les résultats dans *Graphis Student Design*. Bien que seule une partie des réponses soit présentée dans cette édition, un livre consacré à ce thème est en préparation pour l'année prochaine. Les réponses apportées témoignent de la maturité, de la force et de la diversité de la branche.

John Armitage *Aaron Marcus and Associates:* A l'école, on nous a appris qu'une Mercedes est plus performante qu'une Chevrolet. Nous avons donc concentré nos efforts sur la Mercedes. Mais toujours est-il que, pour la plupart des gens, la Chevrolet offre un meilleur rapport qualité/prix. Les écoles devraient en tirer une leçon et reconnaître que, dans la réalité, juger la qualité est beaucoup plus complexe que juger la performance.

Bob Aufuldish *Aufuldish & Warinner et CCAC:* Axé sur le style moderne typiquement suisse, le cursus que j'ai suivi impliquait qu'il y avait une solution optimale à chaque problème; si tu étais assez bon, tu la trouvais. Depuis, un changement culturel s'est produit, l'universalité moderniste ayant cédé la place à la pluralité postmoderniste. Pour tous ceux d'entre nous qui n'arrivaient pas à entrer dans le moule, ce fut un grand soulagement. Parmi les poncifs qu'on a voulu nous inculquer, la «forme suit la fonction» est celui que je désapprouve le plus. Je crois plutôt que «la forme suit l'échec» – cf. *The Evolution of Useful Things* de Henry Petroski. Le design est un acte foncièrement critique dès lors qu'on a pris conscience que le *statu quo* n'est jamais satisfaisant. Le nouveau design naît de l'échec de l'ancien – un coup d'œil sur n'importe quel livre de design des années 70 le confirme. J'en suis arrivé à la conclusion qu'une formation en design dure toute une vie. Sinon, je serais déjà mort.

Ken Cato *Cato Design Inc:* La plus grande leçon que j'ai reçue en tant que designer a été de me rendre compte que le fruit de notre travail influence les revenus du client mais aussi la vie d'autres personnes. Nos aptitudes ne sont pas une fin en soi, mais des outils qui nous permettent de faire notre travail.

Chris Cavello *Design Edge:* Nombre d'écoles perpétuent cette tradition qui veut que l'on maîtrise toutes les facettes du design. Mon expérience m'a démontré le contraire: chacun a un rôle précis à jouer. Une fois diplômés, la plupart des designers se retrouvent au sein d'une équipe, et chacun d'entre eux va contribuer à sa manière à la résolution d'un problème. Je me suis rendu compte que la magie vient de la bonne composition du groupe, et ma principale fonction consiste à encourager chacun à collaborer. J'ai réalisé que je n'étais pas un grand esthète, mais que mon apport au groupe n'en était pas moins précieux. Trouver la nature de son talent requiert beaucoup de temps et de multiples expériences, mais une fois que c'est fait, on ne doit plus s'évertuer à décrocher des contrats. Ils viennent à toi.

Bülent Erkmen *Istanbul, Turquie:* Personne ne m'a enseigné que le graphisme est une construction spatiale; que le texte est image et que l'image est texte; qu'il est important de s'opposer à des considérations telles que «joli – pas joli»; qu'une bonne forme naît d'une bonne idée; que s'en remettre à la décoration lorsque l'idée fait défaut est une solution bon marché; qu'il est nécessaire d'intégrer l'observateur et de rechercher sa participation; que l'on ne choisit pas son style mais qu'il évolue seulement; qu'il vaut mieux rechercher de nouveaux moyens de compréhension et de perception que de nouvelles formes et images; et, finalement, qu'une odeur peut être une sculpture, qu'une porte qui grince peut être une musique, qu'être immobile peut être une danse, que manger ne se limite pas à se gaver de nourriture et que faire l'amour ne se limite pas à atteindre l'orgasme.

Milton Glaser *Milton Glaser Design:* La chose la plus importante qui ne nous a pas été enseignée, c'est que c'est le public qui détermine la solution d'un problème. Les écoles s'intéressent avant tout aux talents visionnaires des étudiants, et si ceux-ci ne doivent pas être ignorés, ils demeurent néanmoins secondaires. Le talent doit être adaptable et réceptif. Nous devons arrêter de penser que le monde entier attend notre contribution personnelle. Nous devons nous distancer de la conception d'Ayn Randian qui veut que toutes les visions puissantes s'imposent. Elles existent peut-être, mais elles sont si rares qu'il ne faut pas en faire un critère. L'important se résume à ceci: les étudiants doivent apprendre à se demander comment ils peuvent être attentifs au monde.

Fritz Gottschalk *Gottschalk & Ash International, Switzerland:* J'ai reçu une excellente formation, mais on ne m'a pas appris à considérer le design comme faisant partie d'une stratégie; que forme et contenu doivent véhiculer un message et qu'ils doivent être placés sur un pied d'égalité; que le travail d'équipe est une condition de base; que l'économie de moyens n'est pas négative; qu'il est important de s'enthousiasmer pour tout ce qui est nouveau et qu'il faut être ouvert, positif et persévérant.

Jessica Helfand *Jessica Helfand/William Drenttel:* En neuvième année, je me suis inscrite à un cours intitulé «Science de l'Environnement» dans le cadre

(opposite)
Illustration by Chris Torres,
School of Visual Arts

duquel nous nous rendions chaque jour à un ruisseau. A l'époque, je tenais un journal pour y consigner mes observations sur les changements de l'environnement, du climat, de la population d'insectes, etc. Cette étude m'a sans doute décidée, plus que tout autre chose, à devenir designer graphique. Durant les dernières années passées à Yale, je me suis farouchement opposée à une telle rigueur, car nous nous attachions à résoudre des problèmes purement visuels avec des restrictions formelles: plaka, gouache et plume constituaient les moyens du bord. Si j'avais appréhendé ces problèmes avec la même ouverture d'esprit que j'avais dans le cadre du cours sur l'environnement, je les aurais peut-être trouvés libérateurs, mais là, ils étaient uniquement astreignants. J'aspirais à documenter mon travail avec des considérations historiques et philosophiques. Aussi, je passais chaque minute de mon temps libre à faire des recherches dans la bibliothèque. J'ai donc rédigé une thèse très dense et un livre de 194 pages sur l'histoire du carré que j'ai conçu durant les deux dernières semaines avant l'examen final – et il ressemblait à un carré! Je savais que Paul Rand le lirait et cette idée me réconfortait. Je regrette pourtant que je ne sois pas parvenue à mieux concilier mes recherches à la bibliothèque et le travail effectué dans mon atelier. Si Paul Rand m'avait accompagnée à la bibliothèque et à mon atelier, nous aurions peut-être pu établir un lien entre mes réflexions nées de l'observation et les possibilités offertes par l'université. Au moins, j'ai appris à disséquer les questions autant que les réponses – une bonne chose pour tout designer.

Andy Hodge *Ideo, Product Development:* L'une des tâches du designer consiste à cibler les attentes du client, à rassembler les bonnes informations. C'est comme dans un film de Charlie Chan: tu en sais assez pour trouver la réponse, mais quantité d'informations peuvent t'induire en erreur. La même remarque s'applique aux personnes qui utilisent tes designs: elles n'arrivent pas à formuler clairement leurs attentes, c'est donc à toi de donner un sens à leurs propos, comme si tu lisais dans le marc de café.

Steven Skov Holt *Frogdesign & CCAC:* Dans mon école, personne n'a jamais évoqué la nécessité – ni la joie et la beauté qui en résultent – de rechercher inlassablement ce que Gregory Bateson nomme «le motif qui connecte». Car c'est justement ce motif qui rend le design réel, et cet aspect «réel» donne un sens à ce qu'on appelle la «vie». Personne ne m'a prévenu que je devrais me débattre comme un beau diable pour avoir le droit inaliénable à la créativité, à la découverte et la possibilité de respecter ce qui s'impose à moi comme une évidence. Personne ne m'a dit qu'on avait besoin d'une sorte de nouveau héros culturel et qu'à l'époque où la diversification représente une condition *sine qua non*, les designers ont un rôle à jouer au-delà du spectre du design. Je suis pourtant d'avis qu'une nouvelle génération de leaders et d'entrepreneurs va refuser, en raison de la formation en design reçue, le cloisonnement alors que la synthèse est possible.

Tony Hu *Primal Products:* Les archives du bureau des brevets regorgent de designs restés à l'état d'esquisse. Par contre, les produits qui sont vantés tard la nuit dans les spots 'informatifs' rapportent des millions à leur fabricant. La leçon? Concevoir une souricière améliorée ne mène pas forcément à la fortune. Vous avez besoin, par exemple, d'un représentant qui se chargera de la promotion de votre produit auprès des consommateurs blasés. Vous avez besoin d'une société de RP pour intégrer votre publicité à dix millions d'emballages de 'Happy Meals'. Vous avez aussi besoin d'un avocat pour vous protéger des contrefaçons et d'un groupe de pression qui se chargera de rendre votre souricière obligatoire dans les équipements de base d'un restaurant.

Craig Janik *Speck Product Design:* Je n'ai rien appris sur la quête incessante de mon propre talent. Dans les écoles de design, les enseignants ne tiennent pas compte du fait que les talents des étudiants varient énormément d'une personne à l'autre. Je crois que, pour cette raison, il convient de mener une réflexion continue sur ce qu'on a appris, ce qu'on aimerait apprendre et ce qu'on doit encore apprendre. Cette approche n'a rien à voir avec une politique de consensus, mais vise plutôt à ne jamais sous-estimer l'impact d'une réflexion, la force des idées.

Scott Klinker *Ideo Product Development:* Et qu'en est-il de la question: Qui est designer? Tant de personnes se disent designers que même les praticiens en ont oublié la signification. J'aurais aimé que quelqu'un m'explique ce qui différencie le design en tant que 'projet culturel' et en tant que 'développement de produits'.

Peter Krämer *Peter Krämer Illustration:* Une école de design est un endroit où l'on se définit soi-même. Si c'est une bonne école, vous apprendrez à faire cela pour le reste de votre vie. La meilleure chose que m'ait donnée l'école, ce sont quatre années durant lesquelles j'ai eu le temps. Et pour en revenir à la question, je n'ai presque rien appris durant ma formation, mais j'ai eu la chance d'apprendre par moi-même.

Flemming Ljorring *Flemming Ljorring Design & Photography International:* Je n'ai rien appris sur tous les aspects commerciaux du design. Par exemple, comment décrocher un job? Comment expliquer mon travail? Comment m'exprimer par écrit ou verbalement? Comment faire ma promotion et présenter mes travaux? Comment me comporter avec les directeurs et les designers travaillant au sein d'une même société? Comment calculer le prix de mes services? Nous n'avons pas appris qu'il y a un monde au-delà des frontières de notre pays, que les autres ne comprendraient peut-être pas nos règles, nos habitudes et nos préférences.

Ken Martin *Immersion Corporation:* Au CAD, les aptitudes manuelles revêtent la même importance

Craig Janik est cofondateur de Speck Product Design, une agence de Palo Alto, Californie, spécialisée dans le développement de produits et la propriété intellectuelle dans des domaines tels que l'informatique, la médecine, le sport et le fitness. Licencié en design de la Carnegie Mellon University,

il a aussi décroché un MFA de design de produits à l'université de Stanford où il enseigne dans la section «Design d'ingénierie mécanique».
Steven Skov Holt Né dans le Connecticut où il a grandi, travaille depuis 1992 en tant que designer pour frogdesign inc., Sunnyvale, Californie.

que dans le domaine de la sculpture sur bois par exemple. La possibilité d'opérer des changements de dernière minute – d'éliminer toutes les erreurs – dépend du modèle que l'on a créé, il doit tenir la route et ne pas tomber en morceaux dès qu'on y apporte une modification. Chaque design a son talon d'Achille, et chaque designer a peur d'y toucher parce qu'il craint que son «grand concept» ne s'effondre. Mais c'est justement ce qu'il faut rechercher pour s'y attaquer ensuite. Un designer a besoin d'un certain temps pour maîtriser tous les registres. Au début, on est surpris quand on a commis une erreur. Plus tard, on planifie l'erreur et on ne s'énerve plus quand elle se produit. Plus tard encore, on est surpris de ne plus commettre d'erreur. Chaque designer a sa façon de procéder. Le tout est de trouver la bonne méthode et de s'y tenir.

Michael McDonough *Michael McDonough Architect: Commence par ce que tu sais faire.* Commence par dessiner ce que tu comprends. Si tu dessines une chaise par exemple, ses dimensions, l'angle d'inclinaison du dossier et sa capacité de charge peuvent être déterminés – donc, tu les dessines. Oublie ce que tu ne sais pas et concentre-toi sur ce que tu fais. Résous les inconnues une à une. C'est la règle la plus importante en design – en termes zen: «Sois là où tu es!» ■ *Le talent représente un tiers du succès.* Le talent est important, mais il ne garantit pas le succès. Le labeur et la chance revêtent la même importance. Par labeur, j'entends la discipline et le sacrifice et, par chance, le fait d'avoir de bonnes relations, de connaître des gens riches et puissants. Même en étant dépourvu de tout talent, on peut avoir du succès en recourant aux deux autres moyens, il suffit de regarder ce qui se passe autour de nous. ■ *Le travail est à 95% inintéressant.* A l'école, on se concentre sur les 5% qui procurent du plaisir. Mais dans la vie, on doit se débattre avec la paperasserie, la recherche, les impôts, etc. On ne peut pas avoir de succès si l'on n'apprend pas à accepter – voire à aimer – le travail inintéressant, il fait partie d'un tout. ■ *Ne pousse pas la réflexion jusqu'à l'extrême.* Tandis que j'étais encore étudiant, un expert m'a dit un jour, après que j'avais passé une semaine à peine sur un projet de longue haleine, «C'est bon, tu as trouvé la solution, dessine-la maintenant!». Les autres experts ont toujours essayé de faire durer le problème, même lorsqu'il était déjà résolu. Pour moi, cette expérience a été une révélation. Quand une chose est faite, passe à autre chose! ■ *Sois toi-même.* Je me souviens d'un étudiant qui voulait impressionner un professeur invité. Avec une grande facilité, il a imité son travail. Une fois ses dessins terminés, il les a fièrement montrés au professeur qui les a examinés avec le plus grand soin et a dit: «C'est ce que j'aurais fait. Mais vous, comment feriez-vous?» Résultat des courses: le professeur l'a recalé. ■ *N'oublie pas ton objectif.* En tant que professeur, j'ai vu des élèves appréhender un problème avec brio pour s'en écarter ensuite au prix d'efforts inutiles. Ils oublient

leurs objectifs et en créent de nouveaux au fil de leur travail. Ecris ton idée sur un bout de papier, place-le devant toi et regarde-le aussi souvent que possible. ■ *L'essentiel, c'est la concrétisation.* Peu importe la qualité d'un design, si on n'arrive pas à le traduire, à le transposer, il n'est rien. C'est pourquoi, il convient de planifier dans le temps, de penser et de donner corps à ses esquisses. Si tu veux qu'on te donne de l'argent, donne leur quelque chose de concret. ■ *Maîtrise les bases.* Les étudiants me montrent tout le temps leurs griffonnages numériques, mais la plupart d'entre eux ne connaissent pas leur ordinateur. Ils sont incapables d'administrer un réseau, de créer un répertoire ou d'exécuter les autres opérations de base qui garantissent un déroulement optimal du travail. Ne sous-estime jamais l'importance des outils de base. ■ *Le reste du monde compte.* Peu importe la qualité du design, quelqu'un devra l'exécuter, l'assembler, le promouvoir et le commercialiser. Respecte ces personnes. Elles font leur travail aussi bien que toi – et tu as besoin de leurs services.

Catherine Montalbo *Addison Design:* Nous n'avons pas beaucoup appris sur l'aspect commercial du design, comment vendre notre travail ou traduire des idées visuelles en mots, ce qui est regrettable, la plupart de nos clients n'étant pas très à l'aise dans le domaine visuel.

David Moore *The Design Company:* On ne m'a jamais vraiment expliqué à quel point le design est une «étude sociale». Vous devez toujours garder à l'esprit qui se trouve à l'autre bout de la chaîne. Vous ne pouvez pas faire votre petit bonhomme de chemin sans jamais lever la tête de votre projet – il faut le ressentir, le vivre. Avez-vous déjà eu l'impression qu'il se passe quelque chose sous vos yeux que vous n'arrivez pas à saisir? Une école peut uniquement vous donner les outils. Et c'est à vous d'apprendre à les utiliser de façon inédite. Je suis toujours surpris de voir où le design m'a mené, tous les chemins que j'ai empruntés, comment j'en suis arrivé à créer des choses que je n'aurais jamais imaginées et à prendre tous les risques possibles et imaginables.

Finn Nygaard *Finn Nygaard Graphic Design:* Ils ne m'ont pas appris que, lorsqu'on aspire à devenir designer, il ne suffit pas de suivre une formation de quatre ans, mais qu'il faut se former une vie entière, être ouvert, apporter à chaque travail quelque chose d'unique et anticiper clairement le futur.

Chris Pullman *WGBH Boston et expert invité à l'université de Yale:* On prend seulement conscience de tout ce que l'on n'a pas appris dans une école de design le jour où l'on essaie d'enseigner soi-même. Par exemple, j'ai beaucoup appris sur la typographie, mais le jour où je me suis retrouvé devant une classe d'étudiants, j'ai réalisé que je ne parvenais pas à leur communiquer de façon simple la signification de la typographie. Comparée aux riches inflexions de l'expression verbale, à ses nuances et à ses rythmes – sans oublier l'importance cruciale de la mimique et de la gestuelle –, l'expression

Depuis 1995, il est également titulaire d'une chaire de design industriel au California College of Arts and Crafts à San Francisco. Par le passé, il a été l'un des associés de Zebra Design à Cologne, designer au sein de l'agence Smart Design, New York, et rédacteur du magazine ID. *Cofondateur de la* section «Design de produits» à la Parsons School of Design de New York, il rédige régulièrement des articles pour des magazines tels que Metropolitan Home, Axis et Graphis. Il a obtenu une licence en sciences cognitives à la Brown University et un MFA de design à la Stanford University.*

typographique est relativement aride et abstraite. Pourtant, depuis que le temps, le mouvement et le son sont venus enrichir la palette du designer graphique, le potentiel de l'expression typographique a fait une avancée spectaculaire et approche aujourd'hui la richesse du langage. Désormais la question qui se pose est de savoir comment nous allons enseigner cela dans les écoles de design?

Michael Sainato L'approche de l'Art Center consistait à confiner les gens dans leur domaine. Peu d'occasions se présentaient pour nouer des contacts avec d'autres étudiants, et l'enseignement interdisciplinaire était quasiment inexistant. Mais le design étant ce qu'il est – les designers graphiques font aussi de l'architecture intérieure et les architectes, du graphisme –, pourquoi ne pas en tenir compte dès le début de la formation? Quant à l'aspect commercial du design, ce n'était pas notre tasse de thé. Les enseignants partaient du principe que chaque étudiant trouverait un job dans une entreprise et y coulerait des jours heureux jusqu'à la fin de sa vie. Les travaux les plus intéressants étant confiés à des indépendants, les écoles spécialisées (qui ne sont tout de même pas bon marché!) devraient nous apprendre à faire notre propre promotion et nous inculquer le b.a.-ba des relations client/vendeur.

Leslie Speer *Praxis:* Ils ne vous enseignent pas que vous pouvez tirer une leçon de toutes les frustrations et irritations que vous allez endurer, que vous devez les digérer en effectuant un travail sur vous-même pour appliquer ensuite le fruit de vos expériences à tous les autres aspects de votre vie.

Michael Vanderbyl *Vanderbyl Design:* A l'école, ils m'ont appris que «la forme suit la fonction». Par là, ils entendaient que «la forme suit le modernisme». Par contre, ils ne m'ont pas appris – et il m'a fallu des

années pour comprendre cela – que c'est le pluralisme qui rend à la fois le design et la vie intéressants.

John Wadsworth *S.G. Hauser:* Le but, c'est de produire quelque chose, et quelqu'un va passer huit heures par jour à assembler ce quelque chose. Cela signifie que l'assemblage doit être d'une simplicité enfantine même pour un idiot et c'est là que réside la principale difficulté parce que la plupart des idiots font preuve d'une créativité surprenante. Voilà pourquoi précision, esquisses et tolérance constituent des aspects décisifs.

Lorraine Wild *California Institute of Art:* Dans les deux écoles où j'ai suivi ma formation, la recherche d'idées en tant qu'exercice conceptuel, pratique et sociopolitique occupait la majeure partie de notre temps. Mais les enseignants ne nous ont que peu ou prou appris à transmettre ces idées au client. Ils partaient du principe qu'un «bon design» s'imposerait de toute façon à moins que le client ne soit trop étroit d'esprit. Cette façon de voir les choses était communiquée implicitement dans le langage que nous utilisions pour parler de nos travaux, un jargon propre à notre profession et incompréhensible pour les non-initiés. A partir de la seconde moitié des années 70, lorsque les agences de design ne s'attachaient pas encore à faire leur autopromotion, les écoles qui mettaient l'accent sur la présentation étaient mal vues. S'intéresser aux techniques de vente aurait empiété sur le temps consacré au vrai design. Pour qu'un design fonctionne, il est pourtant nécessaire d'instaurer un climat de confiance et une véritable collaboration entre le concepteur, le client et le public cible. Pour un étudiant, c'était facile de passer outre ces aspects et pour un membre de la faculté, c'est toujours le cas. Néanmoins, ce thème devrait être abordé dans les écoles parce qu'il est décisif pour le succès de tout design.

NewTalentDesignAnnual1998

At The End Of The Night, The Ugly People Will Still Be Ugly.

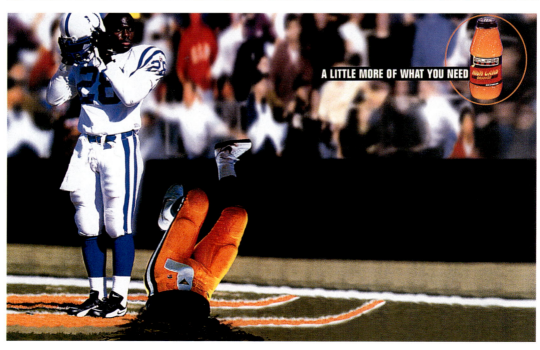

(opposite top, bottom)
Heather Plansker
School of Visual Arts

(opposite middle)
Shane Nearman
School of Visual Arts

(this page)
Sung Woo Hong
School of Visual Arts

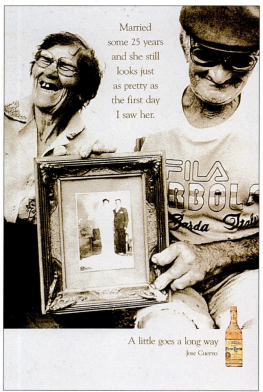

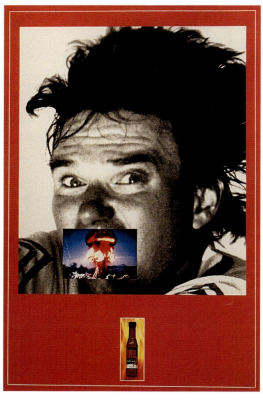

(top)
Harold German
School of Visual Arts

(bottom)
Jay Howard
California State Polytechnic
University, Pomona

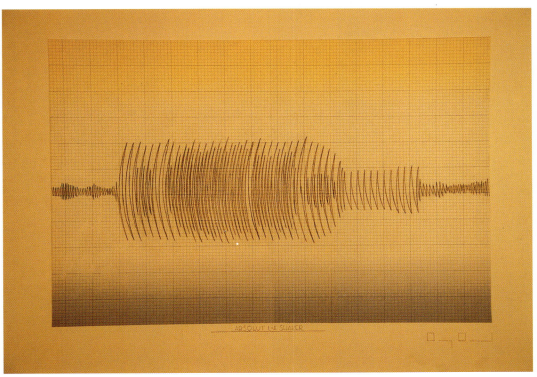

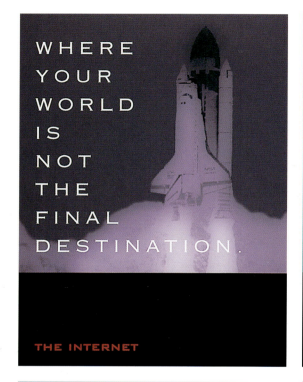

WHERE YOUR WORLD IS NOT THE FINAL DESTINATION.

THE INTERNET

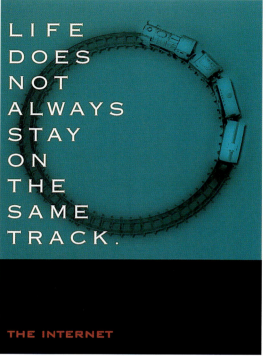

LIFE DOES NOT ALWAYS STAY ON THE SAME TRACK.

THE INTERNET

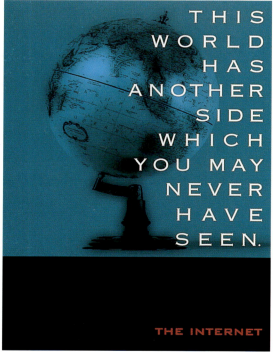

THIS WORLD HAS ANOTHER SIDE WHICH YOU MAY NEVER HAVE SEEN.

THE INTERNET

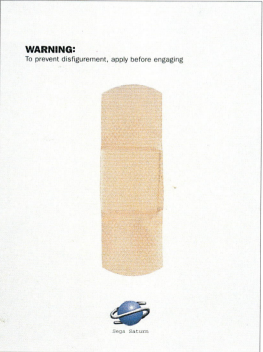

WARNING:
To prevent disfigurement, apply before engaging

Sega Saturn

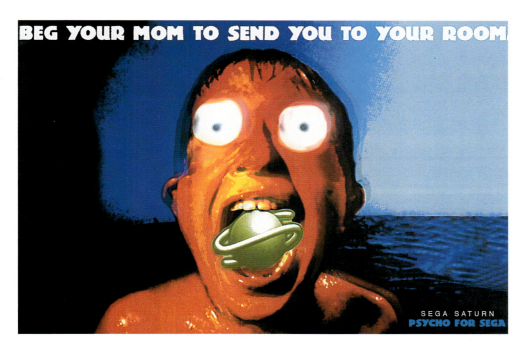

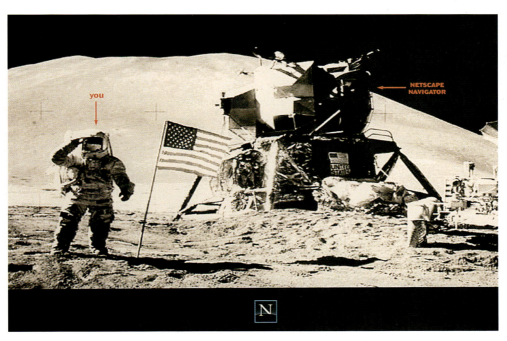

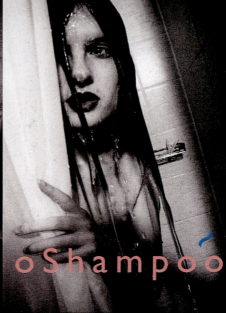

(top)
Michael Czako
School of Visual Arts

(bottom)
Salomon Sainvil Jr.
School of Visual Arts

(oppostire top, bottom)
Joseph Ferrazano
School of Visual Arts

(oppostie middle)
Christine Baffa
School of Visual Arts

Recommended by your doctor, with over 12,000 second opinions.

The NordicTrack cross country ski machine is used by over 12,000 doctors daily. According to fitness experts, cross country skiing is one of the best aerobic exercises you can get. So in as little as 20 minutes a day, three days a week, you'll start looking and feeling better than ever. The new NordicTrack, it's just what the doctor ordered. **NordicTrack**

This is no time to be bringing up last night's dinner.

LISTERMINT
ARTICULATE.

A   B

The easiest way to get from point A to point B.

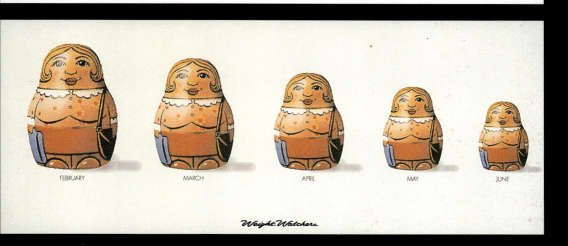

FEBRUARY   MARCH   APRIL   MAY   JUNE

Weight Watchers

We see less of our clients every week.

(top)
Mark Cook
Portfolio Center

(bottom right)
Rafael Soberal
School of Visual Arts

(bottom left)
Alexis Rodriguez
School of Visual Arts

(opposite)
Marco Morgella
School of Visual Arts

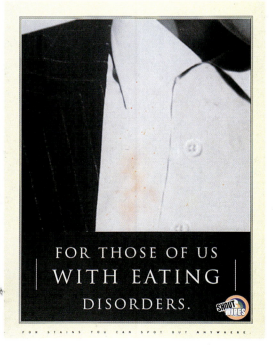

DO YOURSELF A FAVOR, VISIT YOUR LOCAL TORO SNOWBLOWER DEALER OR CALL 1 800 NO-PAIN

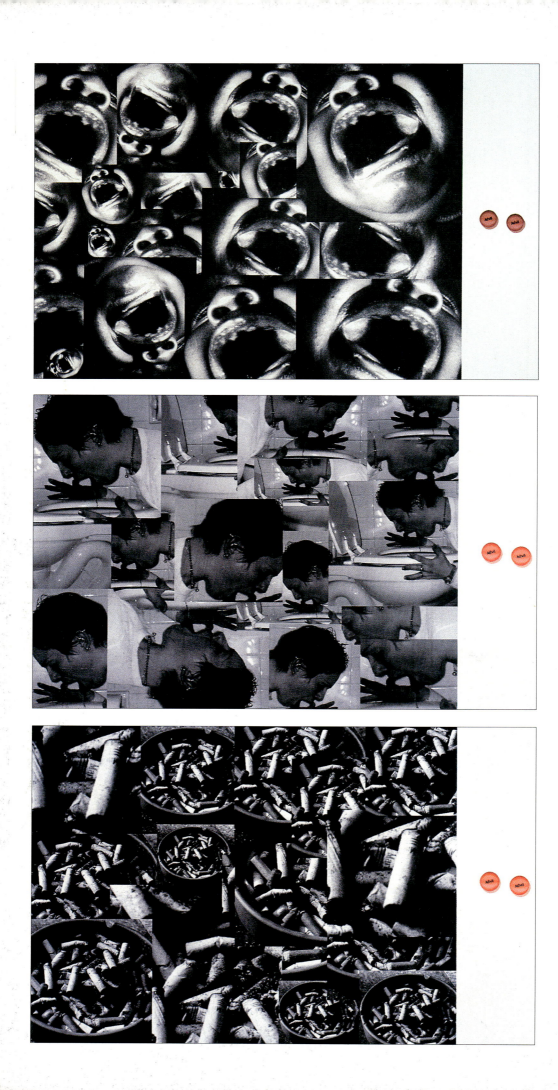

AS LONG AS THERE ARE PEOPLE, THERE WILL BE HEADACHES.

This is the right answer for your headache.

Advil®
60 IBUPROFEN 200mg TABLETS, USP

AS LONG AS THERE ARE PEOPLE, THERE WILL BE HEADACHES.

(opposite top, bottom)
Alice Butts
School of Visual Arts

(opposite middle)
Sung Woo Hong
School of Visual Arts

(this page)
James Helms
University of Delaware

Ever wonder how the guy who drives to the snowplow gets to his car?

winter proof boots

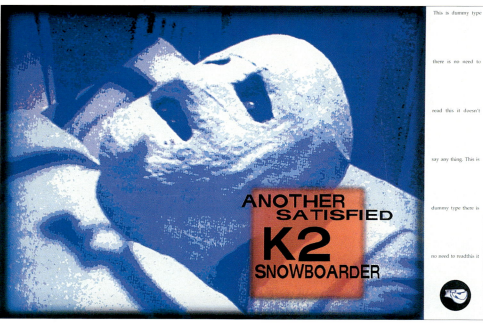

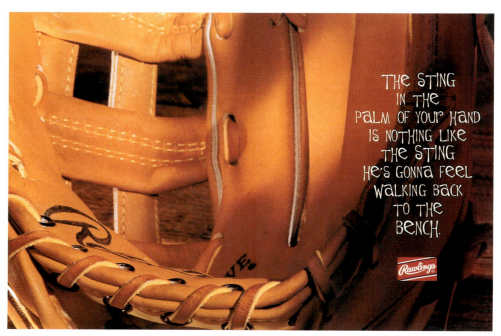

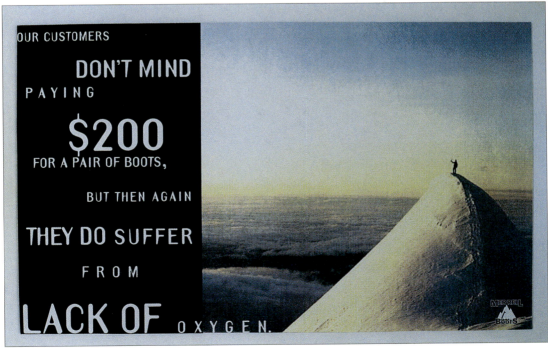

WHAT YOU COULD BE WEARING INSTEAD OF A BAND AID.

BAND-AID®

Right now millions of bacteria are trying to get inside your body and attack your immune system. So next time you accidentally hurt yourself, put on a Band Aid to cover your cut, before a few thousand germs beat you to it.

IT'S A DIRTY WORLD

Just a reminder, it's tax season.

(opposite top)
Michael Czako
School of Visual Arts

(opposite middle)
Dana Betgilan
School of Visual Arts

(opposite bottom)
Cora Flaster, Heather Plansker
School of Visual Arts

(this page, top right)
Grant Holland,
Jerry Underwood
The Creative Circus

(this page, top left)
Marco Morsella
School of Visual Arts

(this page, bottom left)
Rafael Soberal
School of Visual Arts

(this page, bottom right)
Emmanuel Santos
School of Visual Arts

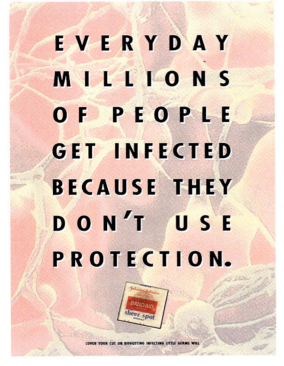

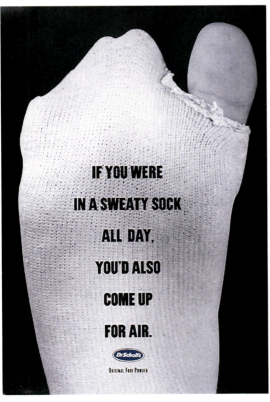

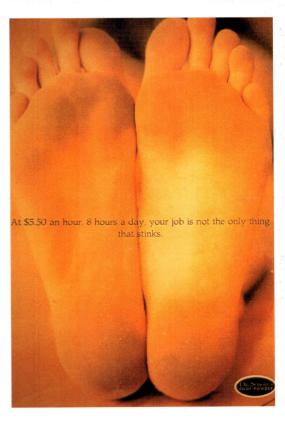

We design our hair pieces
to stay on,
in some intense environments.

NEW MAN
TOUPEE SHOP

Fear of Flying?

THE
TOUPEE
SHOP

THE LAST TIME YOU HAD THIS PROBLEM YOU WERE CUTE ENOUGH TO GET AWAY WITH IT.

NEW MAN
TOUPEE SHOP

(opposite top, bottom)
Eric Shutte
School of Visual Arts

(this page)
Henry Belfor
School of Visual Arts

(opposite middle)
Shayne–Alexis Humphrey
School of Visual Arts

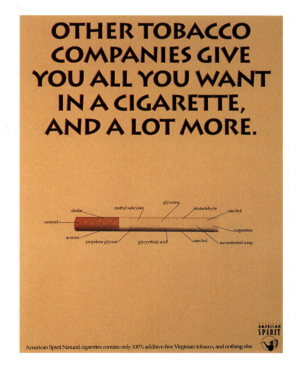

FOR THAT CONSTANT

SORE, AND PULLING ACHE

IN YOUR LOWER BACK

TAKE TWO OF THESE

Rockport

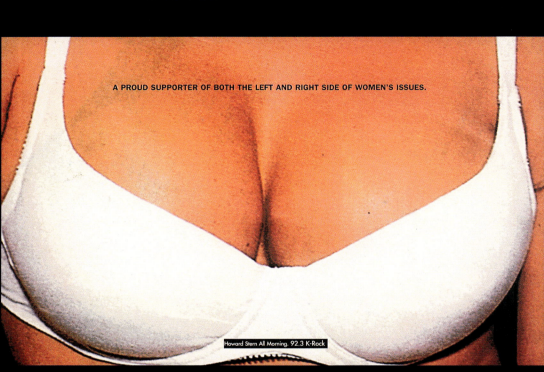

A PROUD SUPPORTER OF BOTH THE LEFT AND RIGHT SIDE OF WOMEN'S ISSUES.

Howard Stern All Morning. 92.3 K-Rock

NO ONE HAD HIM IN MIND WHEN THEY WROTE THE FIRST AMENDMENT.

HOWARD STERN
92.3 K-ROCK

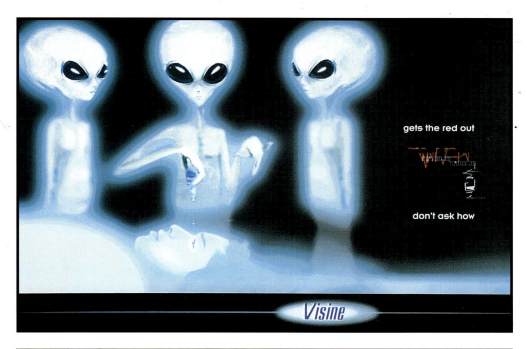

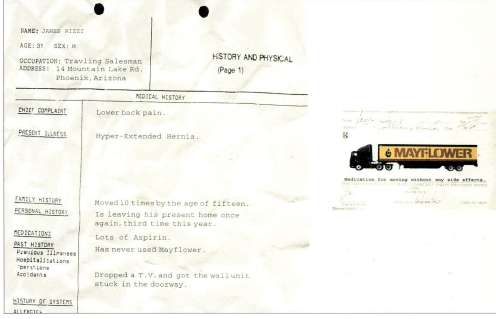

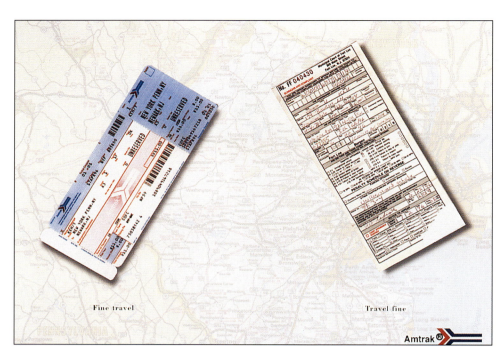

Fine travel   Travel fine

Amtrak

It's Tax Season Again.

Brace yourself or call us. H&R BLOCK

Legal speeding tickets

Amtrak

(opposite top, bottom)
Yong H. Keh
School of Visual Arts

(this page, left)
Jaydee Jana
School of Visual Arts

(opposite middle)
Shawn Brown
Portfolio Center

(this page, right)
Wendell Woodford
The Creative Circus

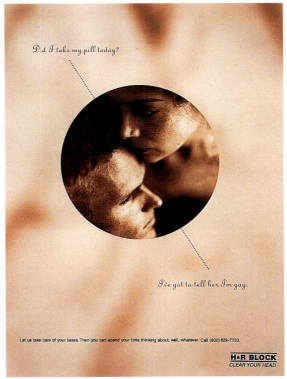

(top left)
Dana Betgilan
School of Visual Arts

(bottom left)
Michael Czako
School of Visual Arts

(top right)
Jennie Lee
School of Visual Arts

(bottom right)
Sung Woo Hong
School of Visual Arts

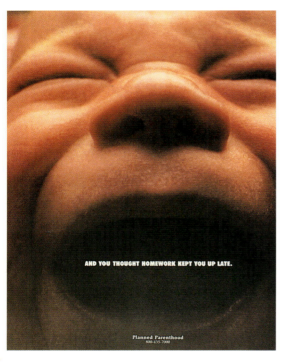

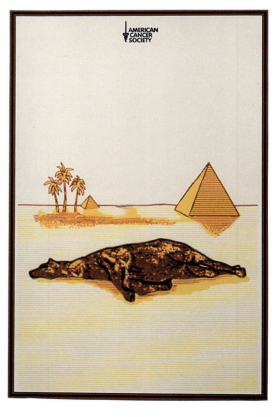

(top)
Eric Schutte
School of Visual Arts

(bottom)
Shayne-Alexis Humphrey
School of Visual Arts

Minus 20 Grad
Celsius, eine

KÄLTEWELLE

ist vorhergesagt

Klirrende Kälte,
eine schwarze Piste
liegt vor Dir,
der Anblick läßt Dein

BLUT

gefrieren.

Minusgrade,
und Du
hast eine

40

Kilometer
lange Abfahrt
vor Dir

Redsox-WärmeGel

Die in die Schuhsohle integrierte REDSOX-Einheit,
verfügt über ein Reservoir an WärmeGel.

plus 40 Grad Celsius

Das WärmeGel wird aktiviert, sobald Druck
auf die Schuhsohle ausgeübt wird, und erwärmt
sich dabei auf +40°C.

wasserresistent

Die Redsox-Einheit ist ein abgeschlossenes System
und dadurch gegen Nässe resistent.
Weiter Informationen zu dem REDSOX-Schuh
erhalten Sie bei Ihrem Fachhändler.

jetzt sind
Schuhe mit
HITZEWELLE
angesagt.

REDSOX

Das
BLUTROTE
WärmeGel
taut
es wieder auf.

REDSOX

Redsox-WärmeGel

Die in die Schuhsohle integrierte REDSOX-Einheit,
verfügt über ein Reservoir an WärmeGel.

plus 40 Grad Celsius

Das WärmeGel wird aktiviert, sobald Druck
auf die Schuhsohle ausgeübt wird, und erwärmt
sich dabei auf +40°C.

wasserresistent

Die Redsox-Einheit ist ein abgeschlossenes System
und dadurch gegen Nässe resistent.
Weiter Informationen zu dem REDSOX-Schuh
erhalten Sie bei Ihrem Fachhändler.

Plus
40 GRAD
Celsius
in Deinem Schuh,
lassen der Kälte
keine Chance

Redsox-WärmeGel

Die in die Schuhsohle integrierte REDSOX-Einheit,
verfügt über ein Reservoir an WärmeGel.

plus 40 Grad Celsius

Das WärmeGel wird aktiviert, sobald Druck
auf die Schuhsohle ausgeübt wird, und erwärmt
sich dabei auf +40°C.

wasserresistent

Die Redsox-Einheit ist ein abgeschlossenes System
und dadurch gegen Nässe resistent.
Weiter Informationen zu dem REDSOX-Schuh
erhalten Sie bei Ihrem Fachhändler.

REDSOX

BELL

Who said nothing lasts forever?

COURAGE FOR YOUR HEAD.

BELL

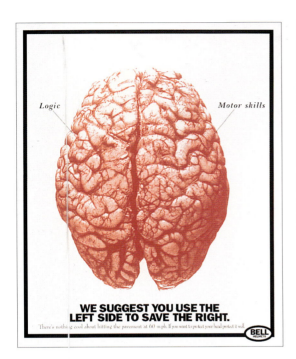

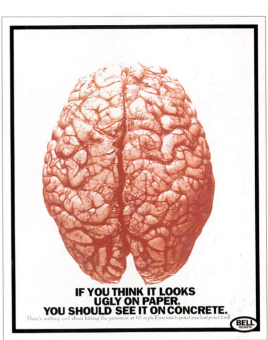

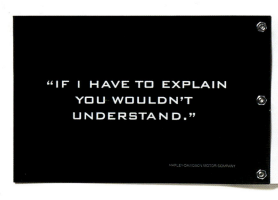

"IF I HAVE TO EXPLAIN YOU WOULDN'T UNDERSTAND."

HARLEY-DAVIDSON MOTOR COMPANY

INTRODUCING
THE 1997 HERITAGE SPRINGER

HARLEY-DAVIDSON 1997
ANNUAL REPORT

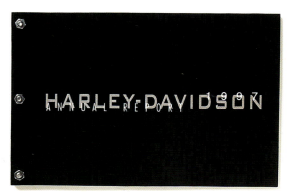

WHAT YOU WANT. WHEN YOU WANT IT. GET IT. THE HARLEY CARD.

HARLEY-DAVIDSON CREDIT INTRODUCES THE HARLEY CARD, YOUR OPEN ROAD TO THE WORLD OF HARLEY-DAVIDSON.

THE HARLEY CARD GIVES YOU THE FREEDOM TO PURCHASE WHAT YOU WANT, WHEN YOU WANT IT: BOOTS, HELMETS, SHIRTS, LEATHERS, COLLECTIBLES, PARTS AND ACCESSORIES, REPAIRS AND MAINTENANCE, INSURANCE AND EVEN YOUR H.O.G. MEMBERSHIP RENEWAL. ALMOST ANY PRODUCT OR SERVICE OFFERED BY YOUR LOCAL DEALER. WITH NO ANNUAL FEE AND A GRACE PERIOD TO PAY FOR YOUR PURCHASES WITH NO FINANCE CHARGE.

ITCHING TO BUY THAT LEATHER JACKET TODAY? YOUR HARLEY-DAVIDSON DEALER CAN TAKE YOUR APPLICATION AND HAVE YOUR CARD APPROVED IN AN HOUR OR LESS — READY TO USE

THE HARLEY CARD LOOKS LIKE LEATHER, SPENDS LIKE GOLD.

IMMEDIATELY. AND IF YOU FINANCE YOUR MOTORCYCLE WITH HARLEY-DAVIDSON CREDIT, INFORMATION ABOUT YOUR MOTORCYCLE LOAN AND YOUR CARD PURCHASES WILL BE PROVIDED ON THE SAME CONVENIENT MONTHLY BILLING STATEMENT.

THE HARLEY CARD IDENTIFIES YOU AS A PREFERRED MEMBER OF THE HARLEY-DAVIDSON FAMILY. YOU'LL BE AMONG THE FIRST TO HEAR OF SPECIAL SALES AND EVENTS AND NEW HARLEY-DAVIDSON PRODUCTS AND SERVICES.

FOR MORE INFORMATION, ASK YOUR DEALER OR CALL HARLEY-DAVIDSON CREDIT AT 800-544-1137.

How are we doing?
Here's a brief review of our long-term strategic plan—Plan 2003—along with a progress report.

Objective: Establish Harley-Davidson as a recognized leader in the development and participation of its people, to maximize each employee's potential.

Status: We invested more resources in employee training in 1996 than at any other time in our history, the results of which can clearly be seen in our improved operating efficiencies. Also, we now have formal Partnership Agreements with each of our four local unions. These agreements call for the involvement of our people in information exchange, problem solving and decision-making processes to a far greater extent than in the past. With the ratification of a new contract early in 1997 by our York union-represented employees, all of our local unions now have five year

MAKING A STATEMENT: TO HELP HARLEY OWNERS EXPRESS THEIR INDIVIDUALITY, WE OFFER LIMITLESS CREATIVE OPTIONS THROUGH MOTORCLOTHES ITEMS LIKE OUR NEW 1340 JACKET AND MORE THAN 19,000 P&A ITEMS AT $9,995. BUELL'S NEW 1997 M2 CYCLONE, LIKE ALL BUELL MOTORCYCLES, IS A PACKAGE OF EMOTIONS WAITING TO BE RELEASED.

contracts (up from three year contracts in the past).

Objective: Grow and maintain demand for over 200,000 motorcycle unit sales by 2003 by providing exceptional product styling, performance, quality, reliability and customer service at prices our customers can afford.

Status: The styling of our new Heritage Springer and new Buell Cyclone—and the favorable market attention they've received—speaks for itself. Our new Product Development Center will serve to speed the flow of exciting new products to the market—

better meet dealer and customer needs. Our average increase in suggested retail prices for our domestic 1997 model year motorcycles was only 2.0 percent.

Objective: Meet the demand for over 200,000 motorcycles by 2003 by

place in 1997 and beyond. Quality and reliability, as measured internally as well as through customer audits, is continuing to improve beyond our already excellent levels. We reorganized our Customer Service functions into "specialty" teams with expertise in specific product areas, to

expanding our existing distribution and manufacturing capacity, and, where necessary, adding new production and retail distribution points.

Status: In 1996, we began the construction of our new facility in Kansas City. We also acquired additional engine and transmission manufacturing space in the Milwaukee area and moved to our new P&A Distribution Center. Expansion within our existing facilities in Wauwatosa and Tomahawk, Wisconsin, and York, Pennsylvania, are continuing without delays. At retail, we're adding some new dealerships.

Objective: Improve information services capabilities to enable all stakeholders to easily do business with Harley-Davidson, though the creative integration of information technologies.

Status: In 1996, our primary emphasis was dealer

HARLEY-DAVIDSON, INC.
CONSOLIDATED STATEMENTS OF OPERATIONS

(In thousands, except per share amounts)			
Years ended December 31,	1996	1995	1994
Net sales	$1,531,227	$1,350,466	$1,158,887
Cost of goods sold	1,041,133	939,067	800,548
Gross profit	490,094	411,399	358,339
Operating income from financial services	7,801	3,620	
Selling, administrative and engineering	(269,449)	(234,223)	(204,777)
Income from operations	228,446	180,796	153,562
Interest income	3,309	1,446	2,363
Interest expense		(1,350)	(481)
Other—net	(4,123)	(4,903)	1,196
Income from continuing operations before provision for income taxes	227,632	175,989	156,640
Provision for income taxes	84,213	64,939	60,359
Income from continuing operations	143,429	111,050	96,221
Discontinued operations:			
Income from operations, net of applicable income taxes			
Gain on disposition of discontinued operations, net of applicable income taxes	22,619	1,430	8,051
Net income	$166,028	$112,480	$104,272
Per common share:			
Income from continuing operations	$1.90	$1.48	$1.26
Income from discontinued operations	.30	.02	.11
Net income	$2.20	$1.50	$1.37
Cash dividends per common share	$.22	$.18	$.16

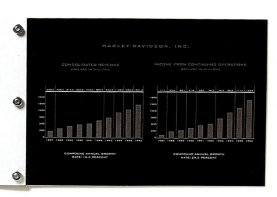

HARLEY-DAVIDSON, INC.

CONSOLIDATED REVENUE
DOLLARS IN MILLIONS

INCOME FROM CONTINUING OPERATIONS
DOLLARS IN MILLIONS

COMPOUND ANNUAL GROWTH RATE: 16.2 PERCENT

COMPOUND ANNUAL GROWTH RATE: 29.2 PERCENT

THANKS FOR YOUR SUPPORT

WITH OUR COMPLIMENTS
HARLEY-DAVIDSON, INC.

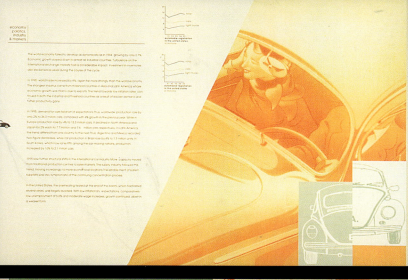

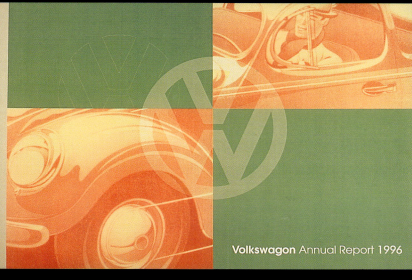

(opposite)
Beverly M. Kasman
Austin Community College

(this page)
Paul Neely
Monash University

economy,
politics,
industry
& markets

The world economy failed to develop as dynamically as in 1994, growing by only 2.7%. Economic growth slowed down in almost all industrial countries. Turbulence on the international exchange markets had a considerable impact. Investment in inventories also slackened as usual during the course of the cycle.

In 1995, world trade increased by 8%, again far more strongly than the world economy. The strongest impetus came from the export countries in Asia and Latin America whose economic growth was mainly due to exports. The trend towards low inflation rates continued in both the industrial and threshold countries as a result of slacker demand and further productivity gains.

In 1995, demand for cars fell short of expectations. Thus, worldwide production rose by only 2% to 36.3 million cars, compared with 8% growth in the previous year. While in Europe production rose by 4% to 13.3 million cars, it declined in North America and Japan by 2% each to 7.7 million and 7.6 million cars respectively. In Latin America, the trend differed from one country to the next. Thus, Argentina and Mexico recorded two-figure decreases, while car production in Brazil rose by 4% to 1.3 million units. In South Korea, which now ranks fifth among the car-making nations, production increased by 10% to 2.1 million cars.

1995 saw further structural shifts in the international car industry. More capacity moved from traditional production centres to sales markets. The supply industry followed this trend, moving increasingly to more economical locations. The establishment of system suppliers was also symptomatic of the continuing concentration process.

In the United States, the overheating feared at the end of the boom, which had lasted several years, was largely avoided. With low inflation, expectations, comparatively low unemployment of 5.6% and moderate wage increases, growth continued, albeit in a weaker form.

Volkswagon Annual Report 1996

economic
review of the
Volkswagen
Group

Depreciation on intangible and tangible fixed assets increased by 12% to DM2.9 billion and thus once again, more strongly than the total value of production. Its share rose to 6.1%. The rise in depreciation is due to the marked increase in the level of investment in the previous year.

With DM1,367 million, the result from ordinary business activities in the Volkswagen Group remained at the previous year's level. Net income amounted to DM692 million, compared with DM687 million in the previous year.

The Board of Management and the Supervisory Board propose to the Annual General Meeting that Volkswagen's unappropriated profit available for distribution, amounting to DM267 million, be used to pay a dividend of DM12.50 per ordinary share and DM 18.50 per preference share with a nominal value of DM50 each on the share capital (DM935 million in ordinary shares and DM96 million in preference shares).

In 1995 the Volkswagen Group purchased goods and services worth DM87 billion. This expenditure was mainly on production materials and capital goods. While the strength of the D-mark and continuing rationalization in the supply industry checked the growth of the cost of materials, the high wage settlements throughout the German supply industry and shorter working hours in the metal industry increased costs. The upsurge in world market prices for industrial raw materials, recorded in previous years, came to an end. Some prices even began to decrease slightly.

By the end of 1995, the workforce of the Volkswagen Group had increased by 5,400 employees to 115,765 employees. Additional employees were required mainly at the Dingolfing plant where the new sedan's cars are manufactured and at the Spar, Hamburg plant. At the new 65 point, the workforce increased by almost 1,300 to 1,568 associates in the course of the pre-production start-up.

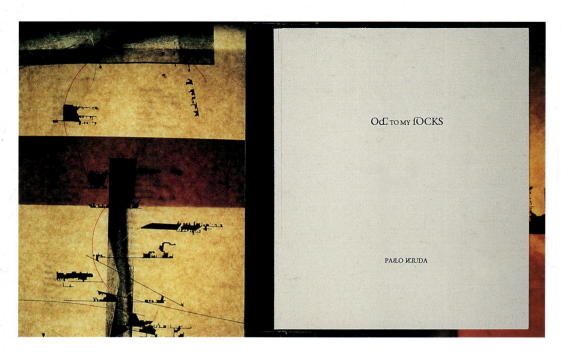

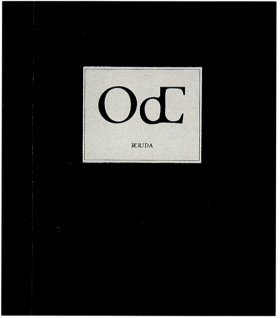

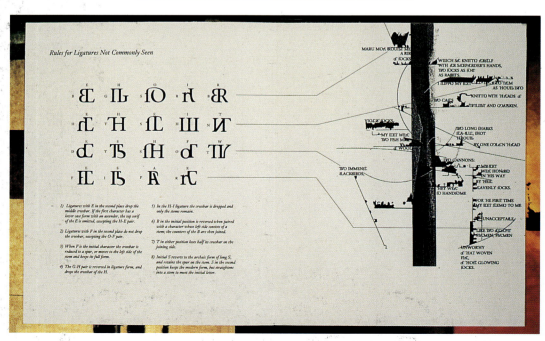

(this page)
Cliff Jew
California College of
Arts & Crafts

(opposite)
James Tung
School of Visual Arts

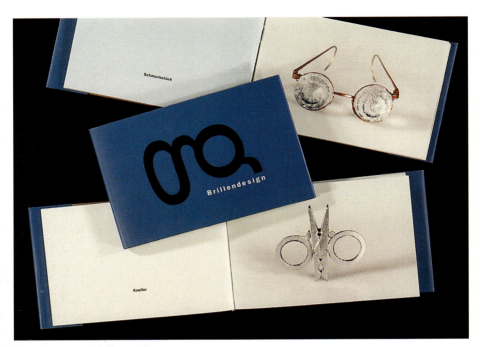

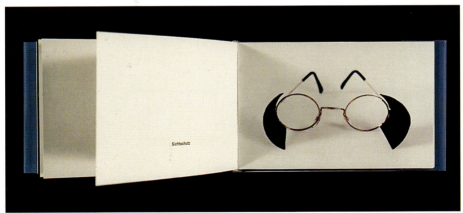

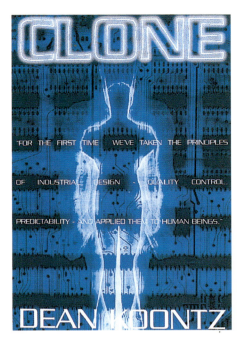

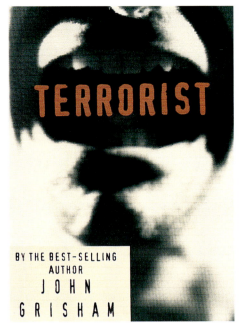

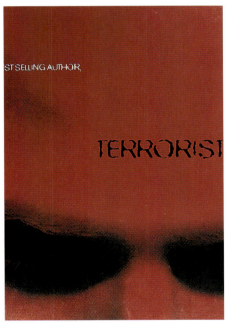

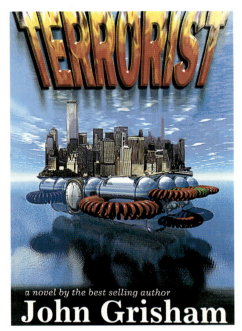

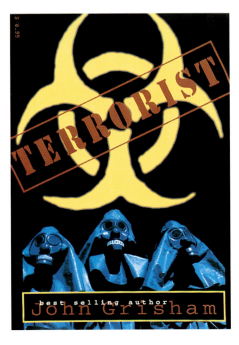

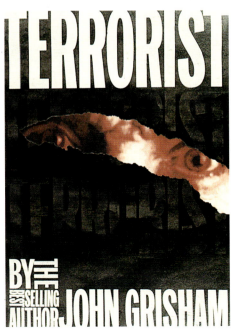

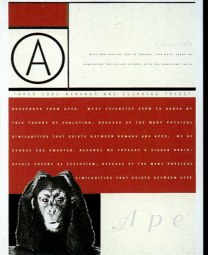

Ⓐ

"APES LOVE BANANAS AND CLIMBING TREES"

DESCENDED FROM APES. MOST SCIENTIST SEEM TO AGREE BY
THIS THEORY OF EVOLUTION. BECAUSE OF THE MANY PHYSICAL
SIMILARITIES THAT EXISTS BETWEEN HUMANS AND APES. WE OF
COURSE ARE SMARTER. BECAUSE WE POSSESS A BIGGER BRAIN.
OF THIS THEORY OF EVOLUTION. BECAUSE OF THE MANY PHYSICAL
SIMILARITIES THAT EXISTS BETWEEN APES

A p e

my first PICTURE
DICTIONARY

THIS IS A DICTIONARY BOOK THAT SETS OUT FIRST TO CAPTURE
ATTENTION FOR ITS IMPECCABLE DESIGN, FROM BOTH ADULTS AND
CHILDREN. THE COMPLEXITY, AND SOPHISTICATION TREATS
CHILDREN AS YOUNG ADULTS WHILE INCREASING THEIR APPRECIA-
TION FOR WHAT IS BEAUTIFUL. THIS IS A DICTIONARY BOOK
THAT SETS OUT FIRST TO CAPTURE ATTENTION FOR ITS IMPECCA-
BLE DESIGN, FROM BOTH ADULTS AND CHILDREN. THE COMMENT

my first

PICTURE

DICTIONARY

BY

RAFAEL SOBERAL

three

DARWIN'S THEORY OF EVOLUTION SUGGESTS THAT
HUMANS DESCENDED FROM APES. MOST SCIENTIST
SEEM TO AGREE BY THIS THEORY OF EVOLUTION.

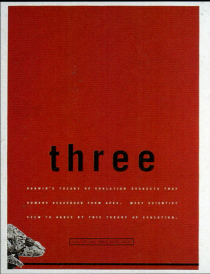

CHAMELEON

C

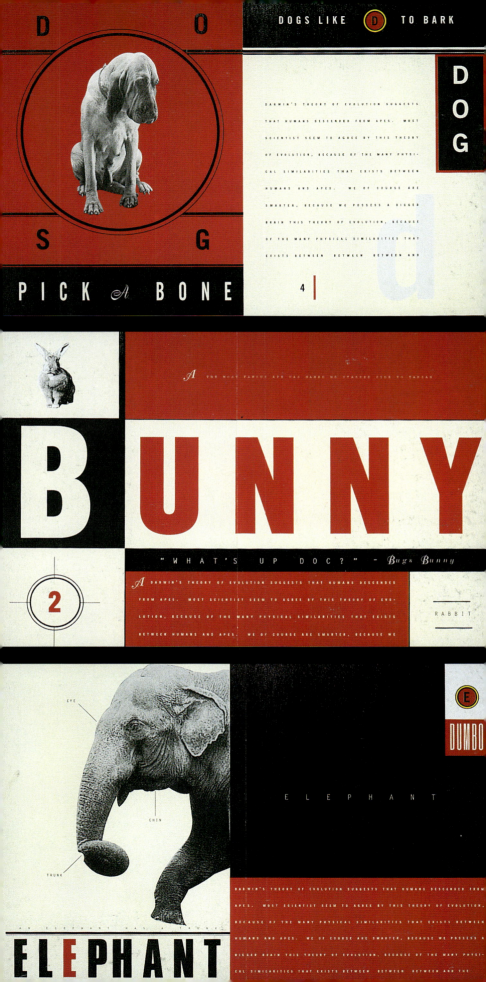

James Winagle
School of Visual Arts

Claudia Oelert
Hochschule der Künste

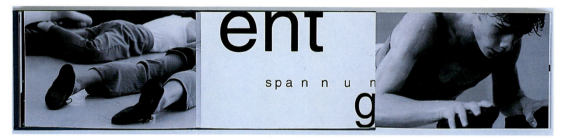

1938

Bericht des Lt. Faber vom 11. August 1942

Um 3 Uhr 45 in der Frühe griff 3 km nördlich von Paschkowskaja. Die erste Brücke über einen Altwasserarm des Kuban nahm Hpt. Sätzler stürmend als erster in Besitz. Der Widerstand in den ersten Häuserzeilen wurde gebrochen. Am Südrand von Paschkowskaja statt des Kuban ein Obstgut von, wie sich nachher zeigte, etwa 3 km Länge. Dort wurde der Feindwiderstand ungeheuer. In meiner ganzen Kriegszeit habe ich keinen solchen Beschuß erlebt. Wir hatten große Verluste. Nach ungefähr 2 km kamen Häuser mit Strohhaufen, die angezündet worden als Zeichen für die Artillerie. Dort lag auch der Bat. Gefechtsstand. Vom Kuban war nichts zu sehen. Keine Verbindung mit dem I. Bat., das rechts der Straße vorgehen sollte. (Später stellte sich heraus, daß es zurückkonnte.) Auch die 6. Komp. gleich links der Straße lag etwas zurück. Hpt. Sätzler, Lt. Faber und ein Melder gingen nach rechts auf die Straße

durch das Obstgut und vorwärts, eine kleine Steigung überwindend, an zwei kleinen Häusern vorbei. Und da lag nur der Kuban, etwa 100 bis 150 m flach deckungslos abfallend. Auf der Brücke Russen, die sich zurückzogen. Da müssen Sturmgeschütze her, sagte Hpt. Sätzler. Auf der Straße ging es zurück und im Baumgut wieder vor, immer unter starkem Infanterie und Artilleriebeschuß. Herr Hauptmann sagte, auf einos der beiden Häuser zeigend: Da heraus schießt es, sehen Sie mal nach. Wir gingen, schossen mit der Maschinenpistole, darauf saßen zwei Botschewisten mit erhobenen Armen heraus. Als wir uns umdrehten, das ganze hat höchstens ein bis zwei Minuten gedauert, sehen wir zwei Soldaten um jemanden bemüht. Es war Herr Hauptmann. Er war schon tot. Den Schuß hatte einer der beiden Kerle abgegeben. Er ging durch den Mund. Der Ausschuß war an der Hirbeisäule.

beim rechten, dessen Kdr. ebenfalls schwer verwundet wurde, vorläufig nichts mehr zu tun ist. Immer Aisne aufwärts, Kompad vor der Nase. Unterwegs schnappe ich mir eine Maschinenpistole von einem Gefallenen. Man kann nie wissen. Einige Gestalten im Nebel. Ich lege mich hin und rufe sie an. Antwort ein geflüstertes „a bas" und schon rauscht mir's um die Birne. Also doch Franzosen. Ein Rahmen Munition in die Richtung und nichts wie verdünnisieren. Mit einer Mordsangst, die Franzosen könnten die Lücke im Regiment bemerken, gehts in einem respektvollen Bogen um die Burschen herum weiter stromaufwärts. Der Nebel lichtet sich. Ich laufe zufällig zwei Krad-Meldern vom linken Batl. in die Hände. Gott sei Dank! Sie berichten: Das linke Batl. ist beim Nachbarregiment über den Bach und bereits über dem Kanal. Der eine Melder wird mit der Meldung über die Franzosen in der Lücke und dem Befehl, das feindliche Höhengelände unbedingt in Besitz zu nehmen und zu halten, zum linken Batl. gehetzt. Dann eine teile Fahrt mit dem Krad durchs französische Sperrfeuer zur Division.

Das Reserve-Regiment wird eingesetzt. Wieder vor zum Regiment. Der Nebel ist weg. Nun sieht man, wies reingelutzt hat. Das ganze Tal im gezielten MG-Feuer (Baumschützen), ausgebaute Ortschaften, die man umgangen hatte usw.) Wie auf dem Übungsplatz – hinlegen, auf! Marsch, Marsch. Ehe der MG-Schütze einen im Visier hat, muß man wieder im Gras liegen. Noch 100 m bis zur Aisne, da gibts Deckung. Eine Fuchs- und Has-Jagd. Man freut sich bereits, wie man das „Anderen" immer wieder aufs Ärmchen nimmt. Doch das Grinsen ist verfrüht. Plötzlich Feuer von rechts hinten. Verfluchte Sauerei, wo sommst das her? Und schon hat's geschnappelt! Ein glühend heißer Schlag auf die Kehrseite, daß es einen hochwirrt. Heiß rie seits den Schenkel herunter. Gott sei Dank! Schlagader ganz, also noch nicht hin. Aber der Oberschenkelknochen hat eine weggekriegt. Nun gehts um die Wurscht. Hier holt dich doch kein Schwein bei dem Feuer, also liegen bleiben bis es Nacht wird? Es ist 11 Uhr. Drüben am Feindhang klettern die weißen Leuchtkugeln immer höher. Gott sei Dank. Das ist unser rechtes Batl. Wir habens also geschafft. Es war ein Kampf bis aufs

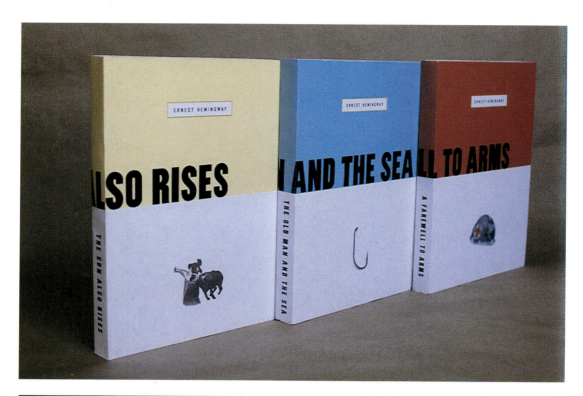

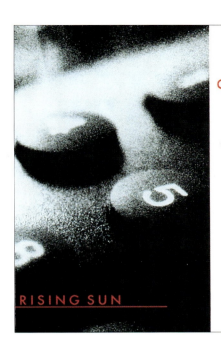

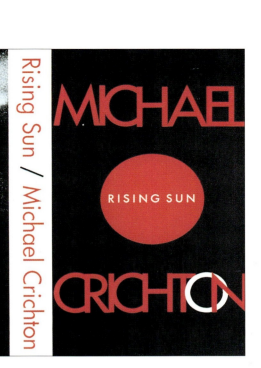

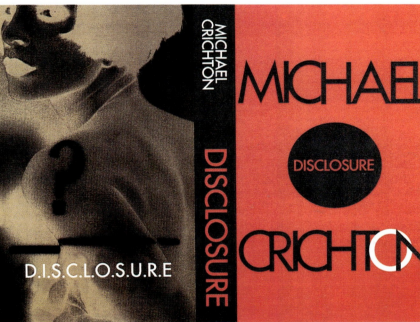

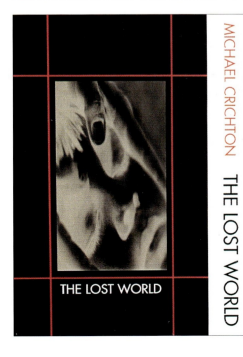

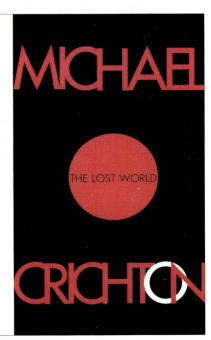

Cliff Jew
California College of Arts & Crafts

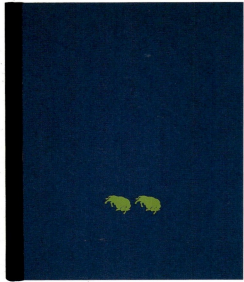

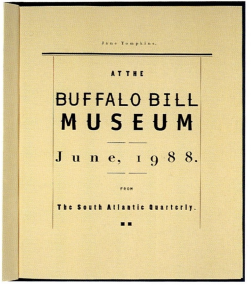

Nancy Smith
School of Visual Arts

In whatever form my work is finally presented, by a drawing, by a painting, by a photograph or by the object itself in its original material and dimensions, it is designed to amuse, bewilder, annoy or to inspire reflection, but not to arouse admiration for any technical excellence usually sought for in works of art. The streets are full of admirable craftsmen, but so few practical dreamers.

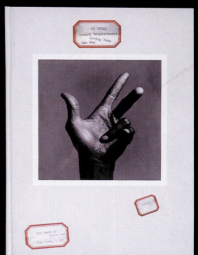

Jack · In · The · Pulpit , 1988

Mapplethorpe

Poppy

"PLASTIC SOUL"

+

"AVANT GARDE DISCO"

=

BOWIE

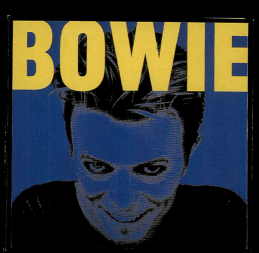

FAME

AUGUST 1975 FAME BECOMES BOWIE'S FIRST NUMBER ONE RECORD IN THE U.S.

"ZIGGY, PARTICULARLY, WAS CREATED OUT OF CERTAIN ARROGANCE. BUT, REMEMBER, AT THAT TIME I WAS YOUNG AND I WAS FULL OF LIFE , AND THAT SEEMED LIKE A VERY POSITIVE ARTISTIC STATEMENT. I THOUGHT THAT WAS A BEAUTIFUL PIECE OF ART, I REALLY DID."

Jesse Wan
Academy of Art

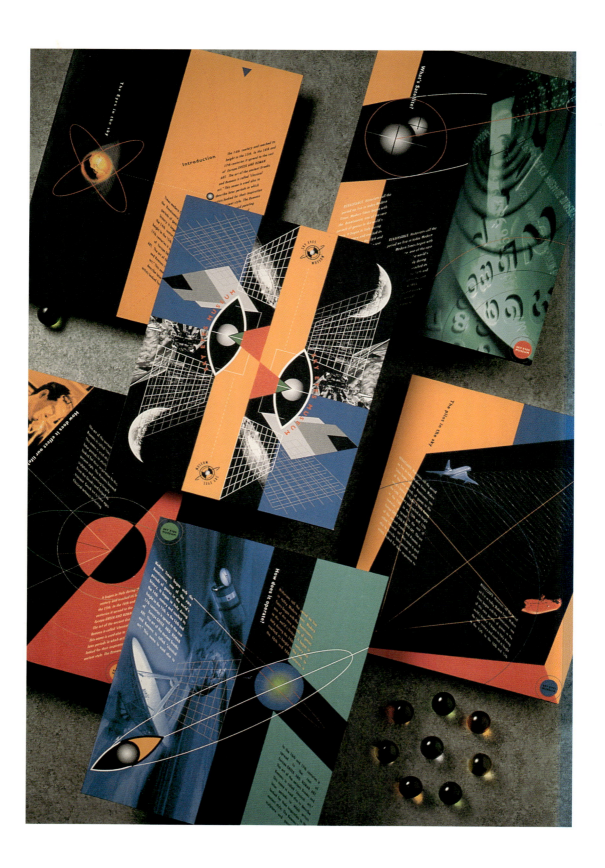

Pei-Chun Hsu
Academy of Art

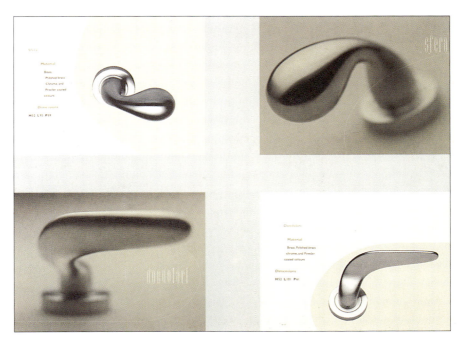

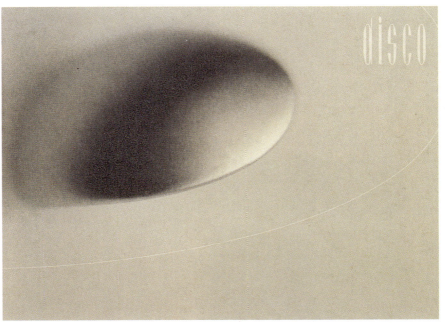

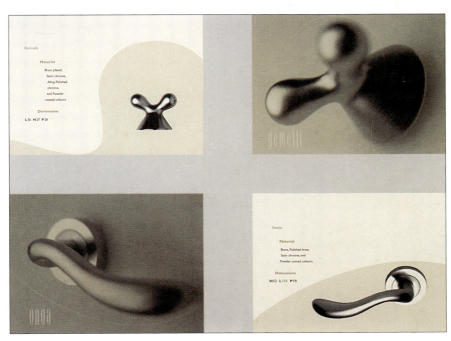

(this spread)
Annett Göhlich, Michael Kempf
Fachhochschule Mainz

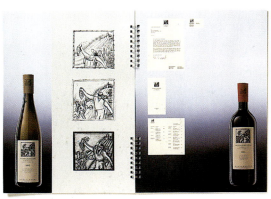

Ines Oehlmam
School of Visual Arts

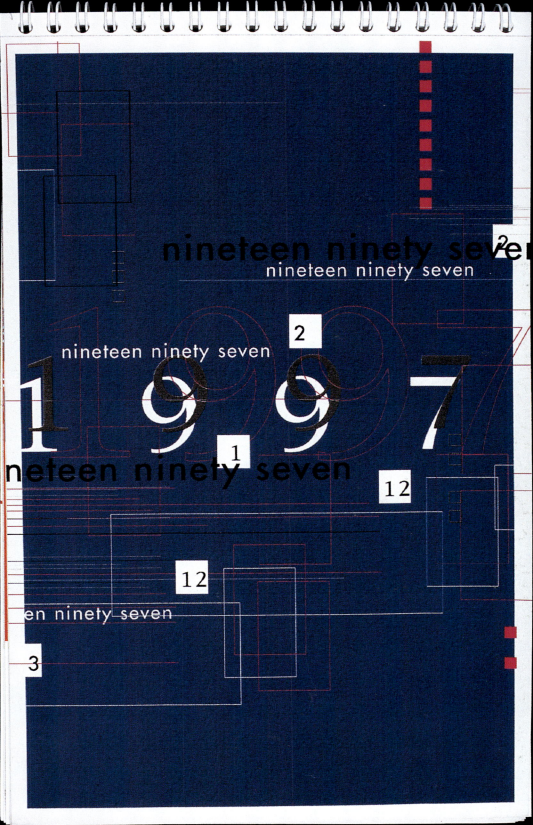

(this spread)
Marcel Teine
Fachhochschule Mainz

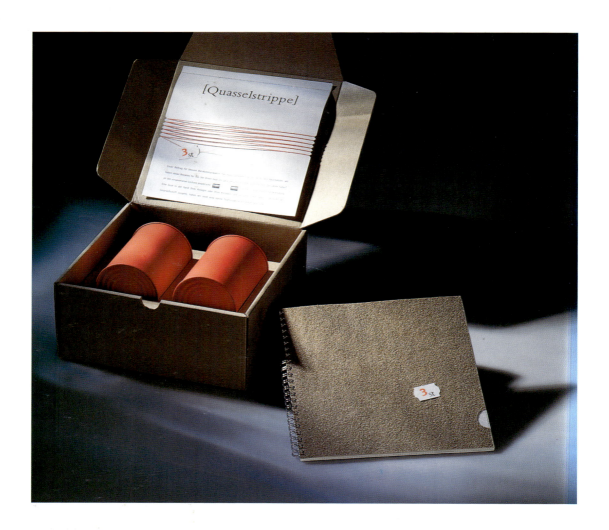

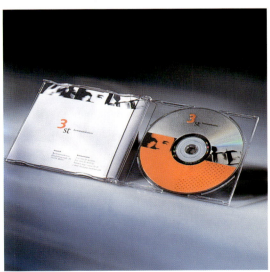

Joey Fong
Academy of Art

Roger Siu
Academy of Art

Bundesverband
Unfallversicherungsträger der öffentlichen Ha

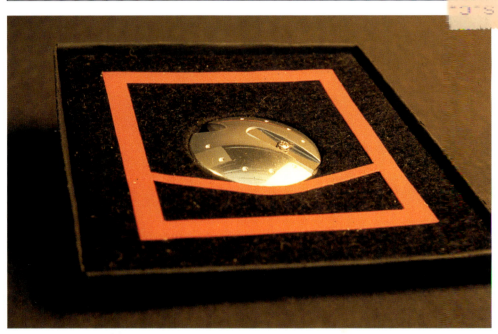

Bundesverband
Unfallversicherungsträger der öffentlichen Hand

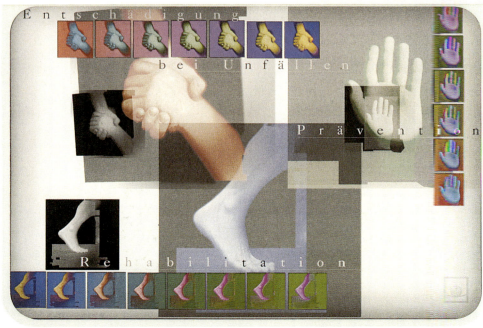

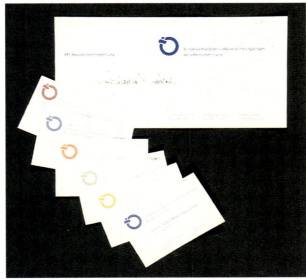

(this page, top)
Nancy Smith
School of Visual Arts

(this page, bottom)
Mark Wong
Academy of Art

(opposite)
Gertrud Nolte
Bergische Universität GH
Wuppertal

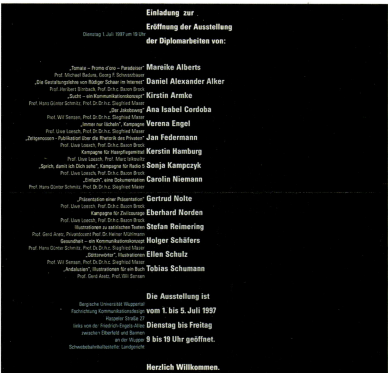

Einladung zur

Eröffnung der Ausstellung

Dienstag 1. Juli 1997 um 19 Uhr

der Diplomarbeiten von:

„Tomate – Promo d'oro – Paradeiser" **Mareike Alberts**
Prof. Michael Badura, Georg F. Schwarzbauer
„Die Gestaltungslehre von Rüdiger Schaar im Internet" **Daniel Alexander Alker**
Prof. Heribert Birnbach, Prof. Dr.h.c. Bazon Brock
„Sucht – ein Kommunikationskonzept" **Kirstin Armke**
Prof. Hans Günter Schmitz, Prof. Dr. Dr. h.c. Siegfried Maser
„Der Jakobsweg" **Ana Isabel Cordoba**
Prof. Wil Sensen, Prof. Dr. Dr. h.c. Siegfried Maser
„Immer nur lächeln", Kampagne **Verena Engel**
Prof. Uwe Loesch, Prof. Dr. Dr. h.c. Siegfried Maser
„Zeitgenossen - Publikation über die Rhetorik des Privaten" **Jan Federmann**
Prof. Uwe Loesch, Prof. Dr. h.c. Bazon Brock
Kampagne für Haarpflegemittel **Kerstin Hamburg**
Prof. Uwe Loesch, Prof. Marc Izikowitz
„Sprich, damit ich Dich sehe", Kampagne für Radio 5 **Sonja Kampczyk**
Prof. Uwe Loesch, Prof. Dr. h.c. Bazon Brock
„Einfach", eine Dokumentation **Carolin Niemann**
Prof. Hans Günter Schmitz, Prof. Dr. Dr. h.c. Siegfried Maser

„Präsentation einer Präsentation" **Gertrud Nolte**
Prof. Uwe Loesch, Prof. Dr. h.c. Bazon Brock
Kampagne für Zivilcourage **Eberhard Norden**
Prof. Uwe Loesch, Prof. Dr. h.c. Bazon Brock
Illustrationen zu satirischen Texten **Stefan Reimering**
Prof. Gerd Aretz, Privatdozent Prof. Dr. Heiner Mühlmann
Gesundheit – ein Kommunikationskonzept **Holger Schäfers**
Prof. Hans Günter Schmitz, Prof. Dr. Dr. h.c. Siegfried Maser
„Götterwörter", Illustrationen **Ellen Schulz**
Prof. Wil Sensen, Prof. Dr. Dr. h.c. Siegfried Maser
„Andalusien", Illustrationen für ein Buch **Tobias Schumann**
Prof. Gerd Aretz, Prof. Wil Sensen

Die Ausstellung ist
Bergische Universität Wuppertal
Fachrichtung Kommunikationsdesign **vom 1. bis 5. Juli 1997**
Haspeler Straße 27
links von der Friedrich-Engels-Allee **Dienstag bis Freitag**
zwischen Elberfeld und Barmen
an der Wupper **9 bis 19 Uhr geöffnet.**
Schwebebahnhaltestelle: Landgericht

Herzlich Willkommen.

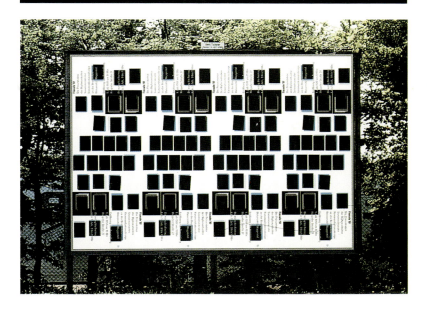

THE UNITED STATES OF
AMERICA
FEDERAL RESERVE NOTE

1

ONE

ONE

IN GOD WE TRUST

THE UNITED STATES OF AMERICA

THE UNITED STATES OF
AMERICA
FEDERAL RESERVE NOTE

5

FIVE

FIVE

IN GOD WE TRUST

THE UNITED STATES OF AMERICA

THE UNITED STATES OF
AMERICA
FEDERAL RESERVE NOTE

10

TEN

TEN

THE UNITED STATES OF AMERICA

Gifts: Indulging the Quirks

Ads Bound for Coffee Tables

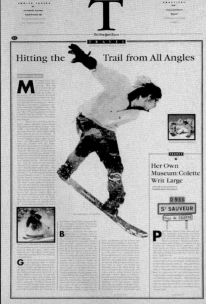

Hitting the Trail from All Angles

Her Own Museum: Colette Writ Large

Passion on the Field of Ice

Ready for the Big Game

A Brighter Home

Sit on the Future

BEST BETS

DECORATING WITH FRUITS

Lurid and Lethal

WHY THE TITANIC SANK

(opposite top)
Hye Won Chang
School of Visual Arts

(opposite middle)
Kai Leong Chu
School of Visual Arts

(opposite bottom)
Yim Cheng
School of Visual Arts

(this page)
Kai Leong Chu
School of Visual Arts

The New York Times

LIVING

The Ideal Stereo System for the Modern Home

BY KAI LEONG CHU

He sudden death of his mother forced Beethoven to return to Bonn to take responsibility for those children. In to met the most important residence of the time. Franz returned to Vienna as his student. His early works are filled with youthful enthusiasm. He maintains the best Classical traditions of form yet his use of melody, rhythm and harmony expands upon the musical vocabulary of other composers of the time. During this portion of his life (up to about the year 1802) he produced a string quartets, this middle period of Beethoven's life, another factor in the almost daemonic energy felt in his music. That factor was rage, the rage he felt at the loss of his hearing, her

continued page 111

Car from the 21st. Century

BY JOAN KLEIMAN

The sudden death of his mother forced Beethoven to return to Bonn to take responsibility for the children. In 1792, of the time, Franz Joseph Haydn in Vienna as his student. His early works are filled with youthful enthusiasm. He maintains the best Classical traditions of form yet his use of melody, rhythm and harmony expands upon the musical vocabulary of other composers of the time. During this portion of his life (up to about the year 1802) he produced 6 string quartets, 10 piano sonatas, and During this middle period of Beethoven's life, another factor in the almost daemonic energy felt in his music. That factor was rage, the rage he felt at the loss of his hearing. When Beethoven entered his thirtieth year, he began to suffer from an annoying ringing and buzzing in both ears, soon his hearing began to fail and, although for months at a time his hearing would return, his disabilities ended in complete deafness. Beethoven began to drink heavily causing severe inflammation of his digestive tract and liver damage. He wrote a will which has come to be known as the heigenstadt Testament, after the town in which he was staying. In it he gives us an

continued page 111

"The future is under your control"

Le baiser est le don sans retour de soi-même,
La première caresse et le geste suprême.

I love drama and outrageousness. I love crazy scenes. Always have. Getting started in New York meant going to nightclubs, galleries, and darkrooms. I spent a lot of my time on my own, printing, looking at pictures, reading Andy Warhol magazines. I always loved & movie stars & pop art, and fashion. That's what I come from. For me, taking photographs, planning them and working on them, is a big escape. I'm thankful to be able to do this really creative thing — to think of some wild fantasy and make it happen and get it published. I wanted to see color, and glamour — I want my pictures to be a break from reality, because I know that living in this difficult. think that anyone can be

beautiful in some way. A lot of people think it's all done on computer, but it's not. In fact, it's sort of important to me that these scenarios existed somewhere, for some period of time, even if it was only for an hour. It's more fun to photograph something real than to do it on a computer. I like to invent scenes. When someone comes in to be photographed, I'm not so interested in capturing their soul through their eyes. I'm more interested in what they are wearing, how they have their hair done. I think you can learn more about a person from the way they've pulled their outfit together than by looking at a black-and-white photograph of their eyeballs staring at the camera. There is a tradition of celebrity portraiture that attempts to uncover the "real person" behind the trappings of their celebrity; interested in those trappings.

drew
Barrymore
British
Premiere
19
95
New
York

I–1

(this spread)
Hye Won Chang
School of Visual Arts

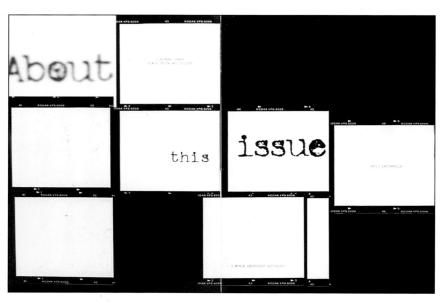

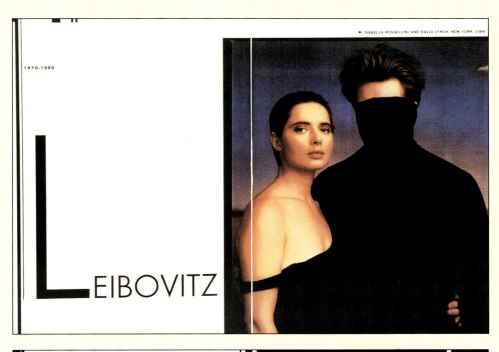

1970-1990

LEIBOVITZ

► ISABELLA ROSSELLINI AND DAVID LYNCH NEW YORK 1986

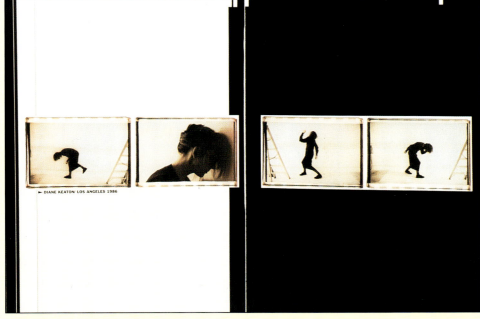

► DIANE KEATON LOS ANGELES 1986

LA
CHAPELLE

'Generally the music was undramatic, not just my own. It had an adverse effect on me, I think. I work best with a sense of competition. I really couldn't get it up for trying to compete with Kylie and Paula Abdul. The flabby state of music in the 80s just left me disinterested'.

by Ed Nimmervoll

David Bowie is the embodiment of change.

He changed his name. He changed the world he was born into, to one of his own invention. At one point he even hinted at having changed his sexual preference, but he said it with a smile, and we've never been absolutely sure.

David Bowie also changed music. There's no shortage of Bowie clones.

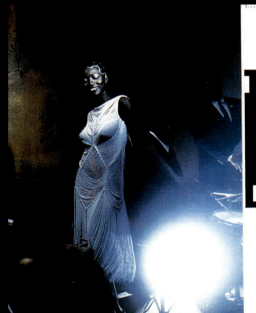
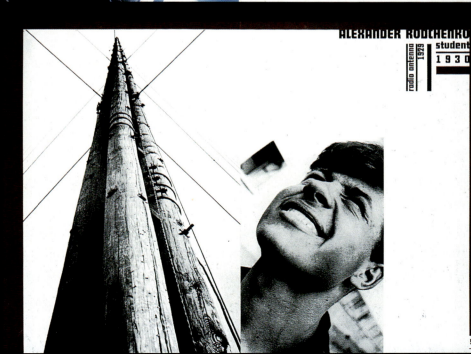

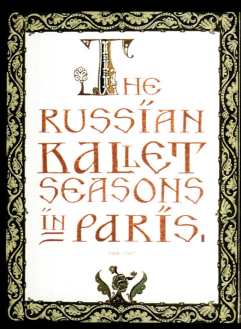

THE RUSSIAN BALLET SEASONS IN PARIS.

1908 - 1917

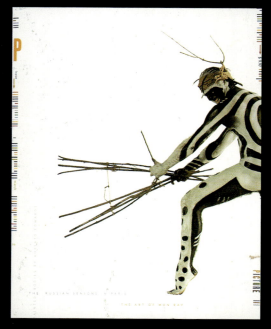

THE DE MEYERS HAD BECOME ESSENTIAL IN PHOTOGRAPHING THE LYRICAL AND EXCITING QUALITIES OF THE ENCHANTED WORLD OF RUSSIAN BALLET

DE MEYER FROM

L'APRES-MIDI D'UN FAUNE

(opposite)
Julia Michry
School of Visual Arts

(this page)
Paul Gobble
Penn State University

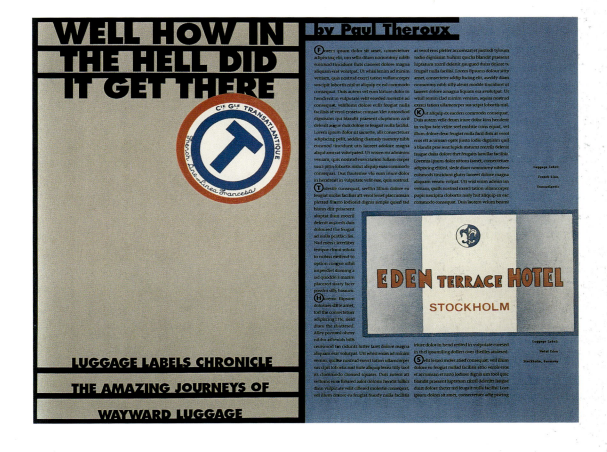

(this page)
Dave Gath
California State University
at Long Beach

(opposite)
Juan Cabrero
Penn State University

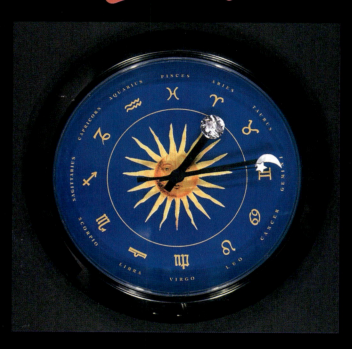

(opposite top)
Eric Shutte
School of Visual Arts

(opposite middle)
Julie Baron
School of Visual Arts

(opposite bottom)
L. Rodrigues
School of Visual Arts

(this page)
James Joseph Potsch
Illinois State University

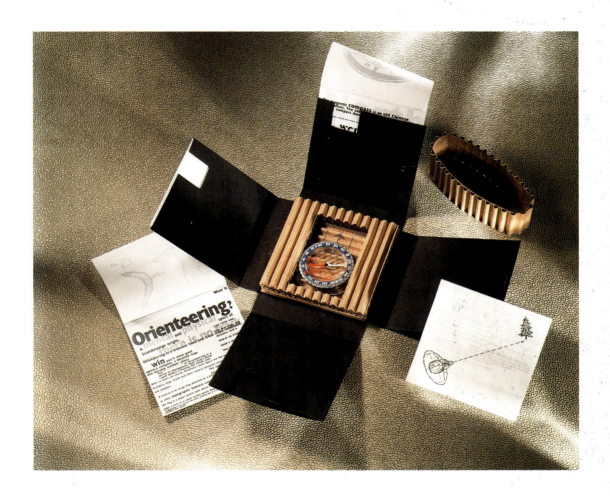

(top)
Jennifer Crute
School of Visual Arts

(bottom)
Renata Lauterback
School of Visual Arts

(middle)
Shawn Fields
School of Visual Arts

(top)
Jennifer Crute
School of Visual Arts

(middle)
Shawn Fields
School of Visual Arts

(top)
James Mandella
School of Visual Arts

(bottom)
Peter Franco
School of Visual Arts

(middle)
Lisa Neigenfind
Staatliche Akademie der
Bildenden Künste Stuttgart

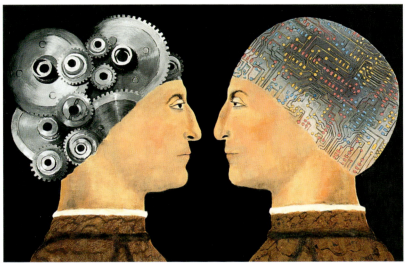

Masahito Tanaka
School of Visual Arts

Chris Torres
School of Visual Arts

(opposite, top)
Brian Donnelly
School of Visual Arts

(opposite, middle)
John Urso
School of Visual Arts

(opposite, bottom)
Vincent Ficarra
School of Visual Arts

(this page)
Edward Morges
School of Visual Arts

Beth Cloutier
School of Visual Arts

Brandon Cronk
Iowa State University

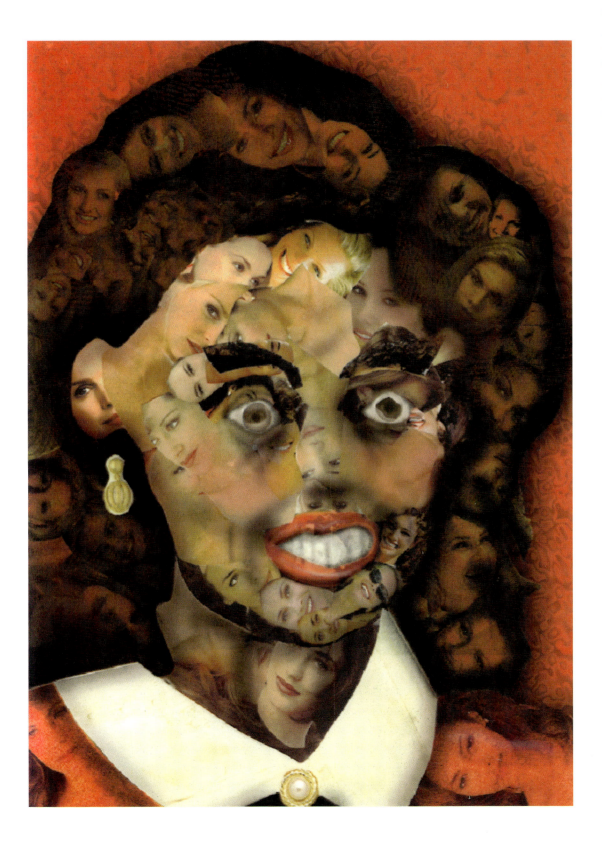

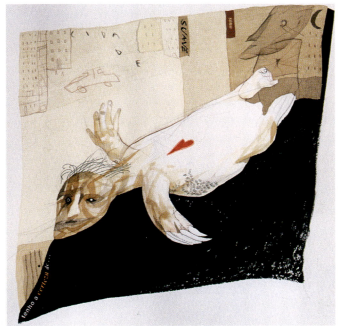

Chris Murphy
School of Visual Arts

S o n y

550 Madison Avenue

Corporation

33rd Floor New York

of America

NY 10022-3211

. P h o n e

212.833.6840

Facimilie

212.833.6938

S o n y

550 Madison Avenue

Corporation

33rd Floor New York

of America

NY 10022-3211

Timothy

Chief

John

Executive

Fisher

Officer

S o n y

550 Madison Avenue

Corporation

33rd Floor New York

of America

NY 10022-3211

Phone

212.833.6849

Facimilie

212.833.6938

Jin Chun
Academy of Art

(page130, top)
Wesley Cortes
Oregon State University

(page130, middle)
Aaron Lee
Oregon State University

(page130, bottom)
Duane Cordwell
Oregon State University

(page131, top)
Jason D. Guinn
Oregon State University

(page131, middle)
Natalie Becher
Oregon State University

(page131, bottom)
Ashley B. Carlson
Oregon State University

(opposite)
Trina H. Sultan
School of Visual Arts

(this page)
Christine Cucuzza
School of Visual Arts

CHAMPION

(top)
Isabel Wischermann
Universität GH Essen

(second from top)
Carrie Ferguson
Western Washington
University

(middle)
Group Project
Fachhochschule Mainz

(second from bottom)
Olga Mezhibovskaya
School of Visual Arts

(bottom)
Group Project
Fachhochschule Mainz

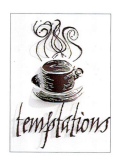

(top)
Chris Slivinsky
The Creative Circus

(second from top)
Sharon Slaughter
Portfolio Center

(middle, second from bottom)
Group Project
Fachhochschule Mainz

(bottom)
Pekka Piippo, Valterri Bade
University of Art and Design,
Helsinki

(this spread)
Felix Espermüller
Blocherer Schule

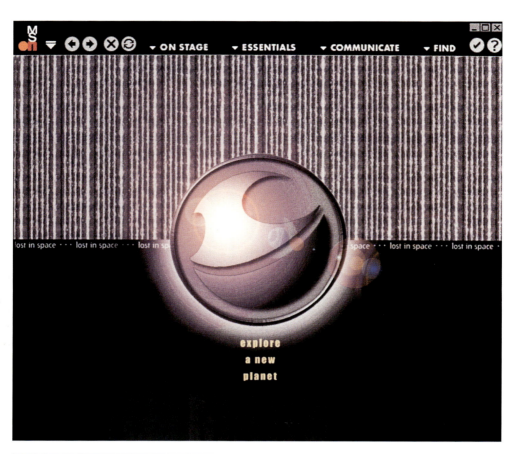

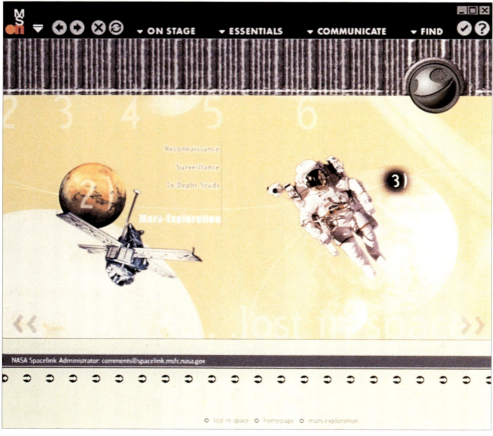

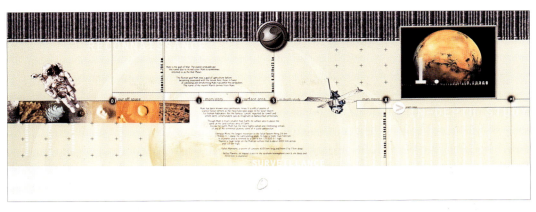

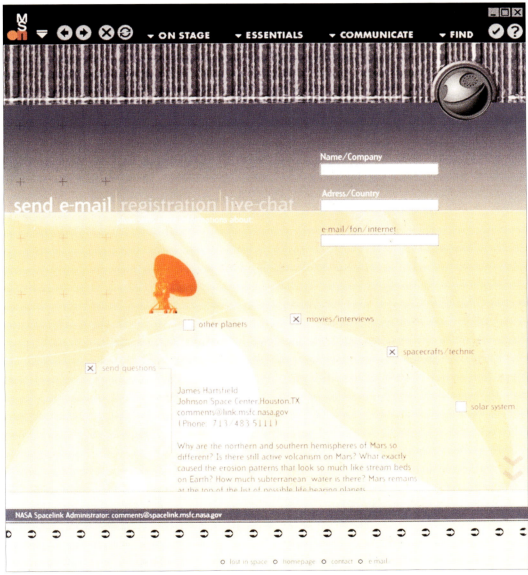

Fang Zhou
School of Visual Arts

Tracy Pamperin
School of Visual Arts

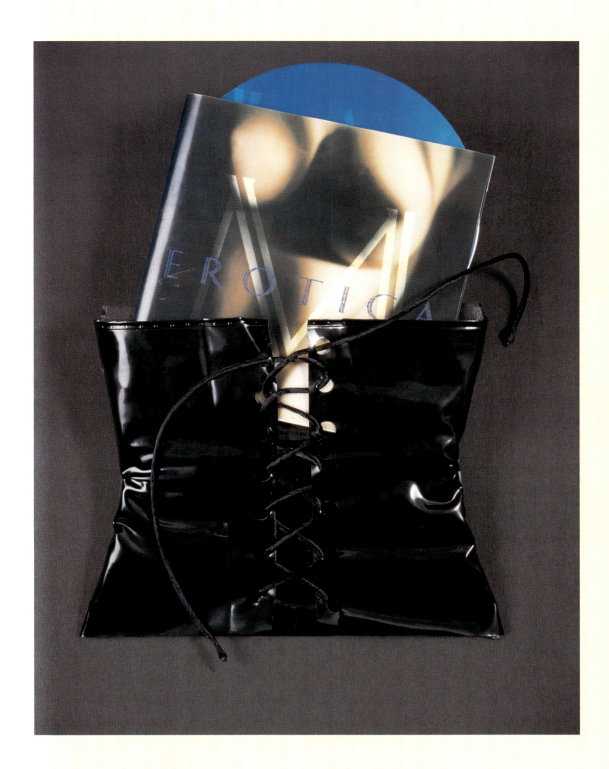

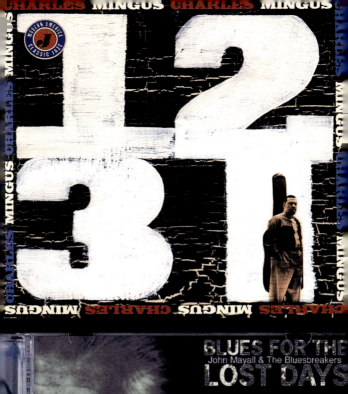

CHARLES MINGUS

1 2 3 1

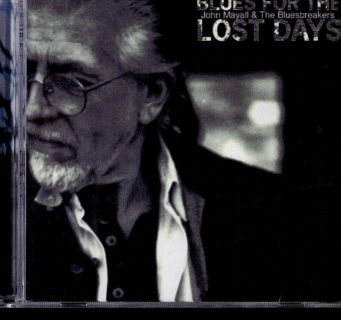

BLUES FOR THE
LOST DAYS
John Mayall & The Bluesbreakers

Dragonfly

makebelieve

(opposite top)
Xun–Lei Sheng
School of Visual Arts

(opposite middle)
Bong Lee
School of Visual Arts

(opposite bottom)
Celeste Rader
Texas Christian University

(this page, top)
Einat Lisa Day
School of Visual Arts

(this page, middle)
Bong Lee
School of Visual Arts

(this page, bottom)
Carrie E. Ferguson
Western Washington
University

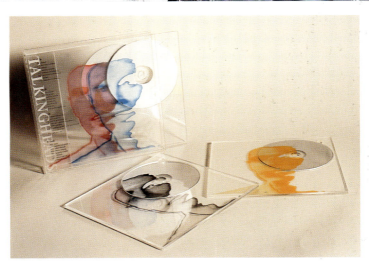

Karen Schmucker
Academy of Art

(opposite, top left)
Daren Clary
California State University
Long Beach

(opposite, top right)
Zhao Wen Li
School of Visual Arts

(opposite, middle left)
Minako So
University of Maryland

(opposite, middle right)
Lloyd Rodrigues
School of Visual Arts

(opposite, bottom left)
Einat Lisa Day
School of Visual Arts

(opposite, bottom right)
Nicole Lomonaco
California State University
Long Beach

(this page, top)
Christopher J. Klimasz
School of Visual Arts

(this page, bottom)
Minako So
University of Maryland

(top)
Kate Dickinson
Monash University

(bottom)
Julia Michry
School of Visual Arts

(opposite top, bottom)
Trina H. Sultan
School of Visual Arts

(opposite middle)
Karen Schmucker
Academy of Art

(opposite)
Dan Chau
Brigham Young University

(bottom)
Jason D. Guinn
Oregon State University

(this page, top)
Darcy Hockett
Oregon State University

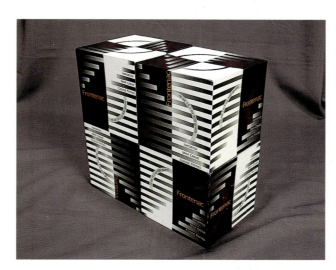

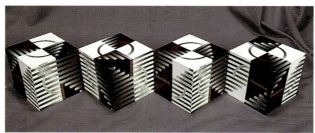

Karen Schmucker
Academy of Art

Reneé L. Yancey
Western Washington
University

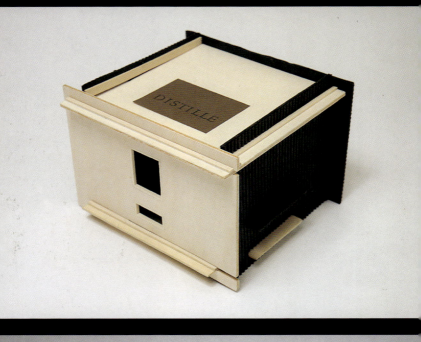

(opposite top, middle)
Margarita Encomienda
Rhode Island School
of Design

(opposite bottom)
Annie Sung
Rhode Island School
of Design

(this page)
Anne Brenden
Kent Institute of Art
and Design

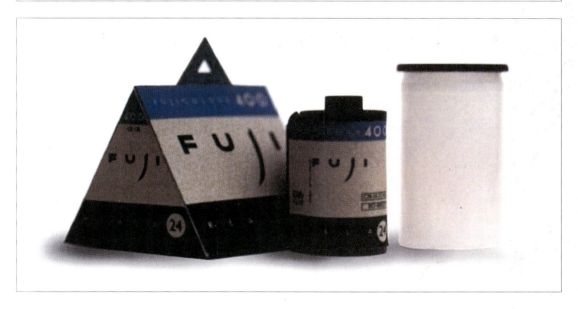

(this spread)
Chris Panagakis
School of Visual Arts

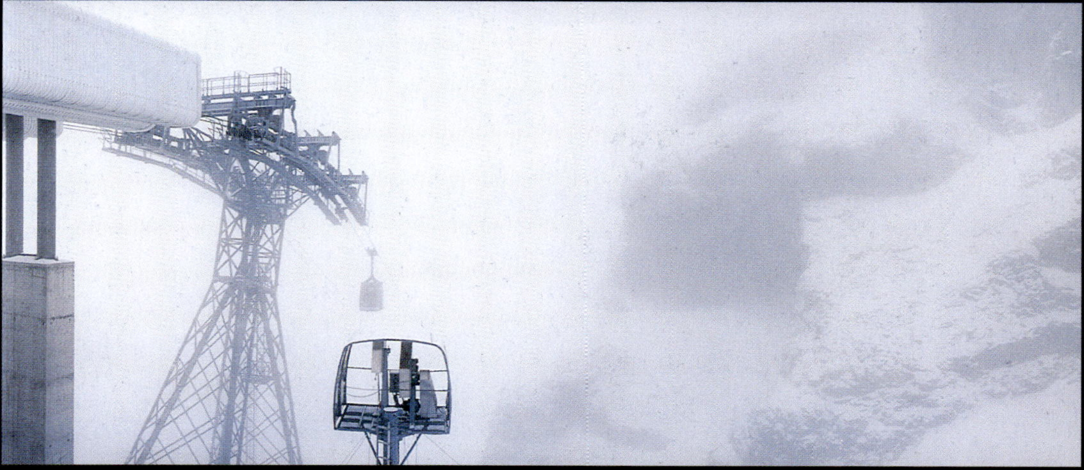

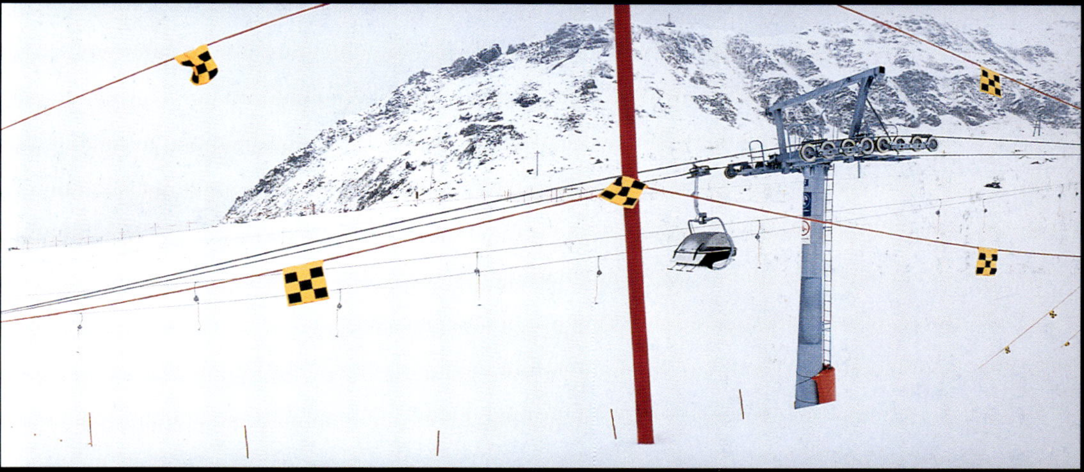

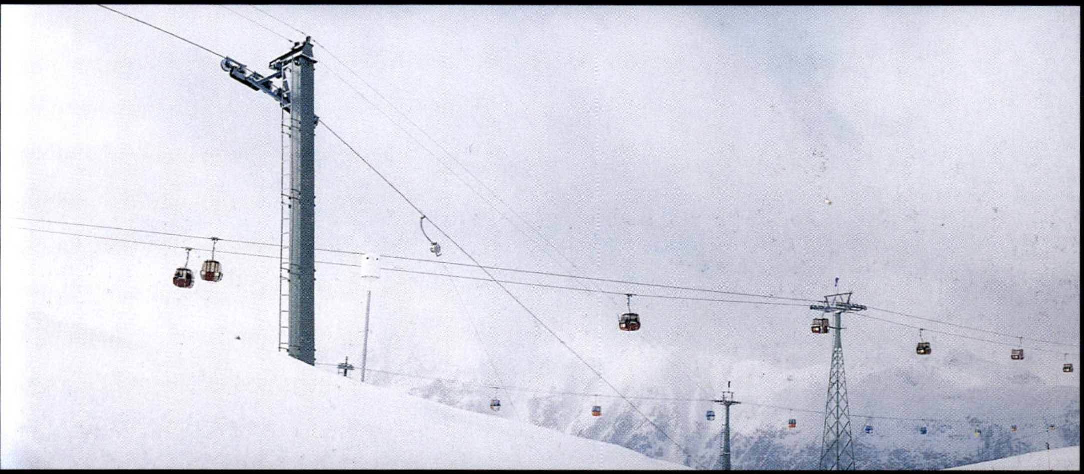

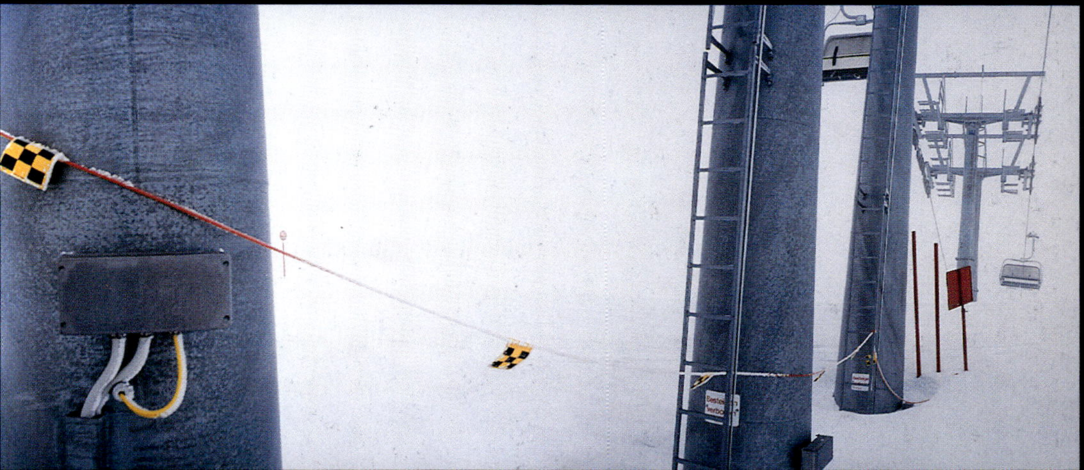

Christine Capps
Art Institute of Atlanta

Ryan Smith
Art Institute of Atlanta

Lori K. Sapio
Northern Illinois University

Geoffrey Wells
Portfolio Center

(this page)
Dominic Trautvetter
Fachhochschule Dortmund

(opposite)
Xun-Lei Sheng
School of Visual Arts

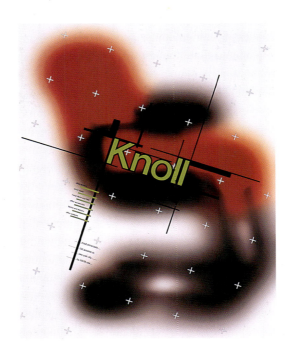

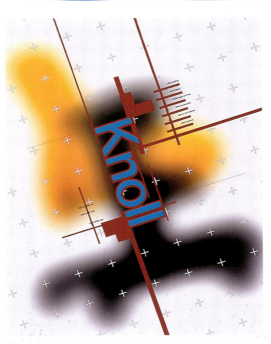

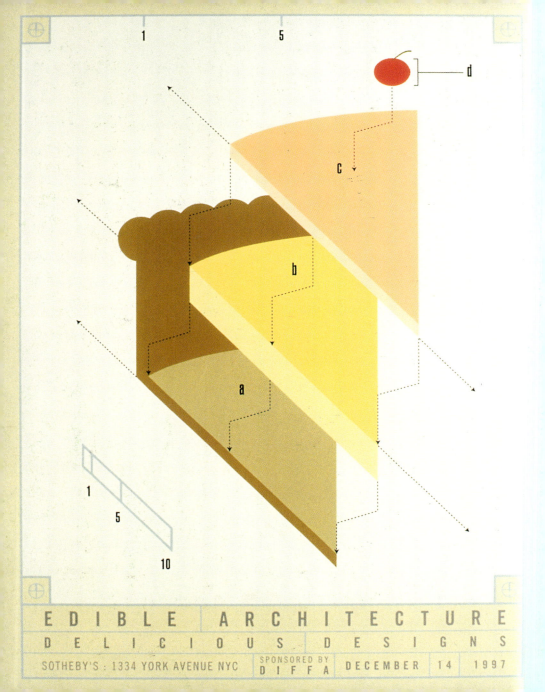

d

c

b

a

1   5

1
5
10

E D I B L E   A R C H I T E C T U R E
D E L I C I O U S   D E S I G N S
SOTHEBY'S : 1334 YORK AVENUE NYC   SPONSORED BY
D I F F A   DECEMBER   14   1997

The Object As **Invention**

Compact Discs are made from metal and are coated over with aluminum. They take up only 6.25 square inches. **Sony** and **Philips** brought the compact disc to the public.

Digital - The CD has digitized information that is read by a laser when it spins around. One main difference between conventional tapes and records compared to the CD is that the laser doesn't touch the CD's surface.

video

audio

Benefits of CD's are the increased quality of output for audio, and the amount of storage space (about $15,000$ pages of information.)

Reading sources for tapes and records touch the surface directly, causing damage over a long period of time, lessening the sound quality of the music.

Compact Discs

June 15- August 30

The Smithsonian Institute, Washington DC

James Tung
School of Visual Arts

(top)
Fons M. Hickmann
Bergische Universität GH Wuppertal

(bottom)
Claudia Oelert
Hochschule der Künste

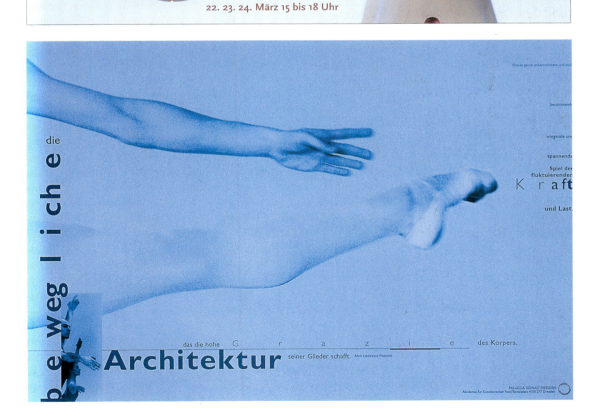

Benoit Jeay
ESAG

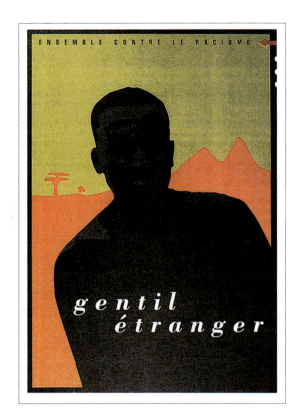

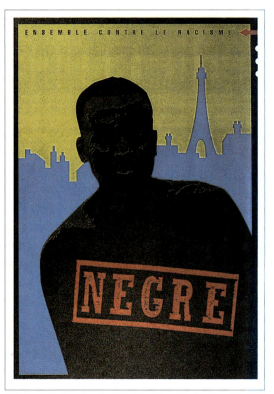

(left)
Amanda Barile
Penn State University

(right)
Triton Keugh
The Advertising Arts

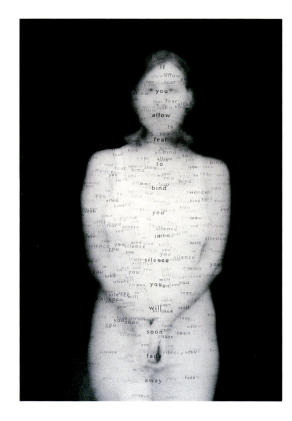

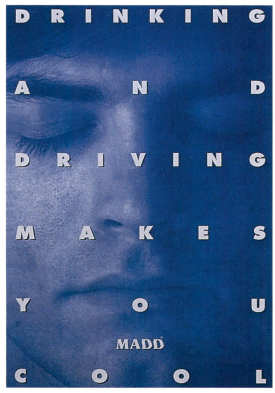

(opposite top)
Péter Vajda
Hungarian Academy
of Fine Arts

(opposite middle)
Nathan Savage
Southwest Texas State
University

(opposite bottom)
Hye Won Chang
School of Visual Arts

(this page)
Jon Sueda
California College of
Arts & Crafts

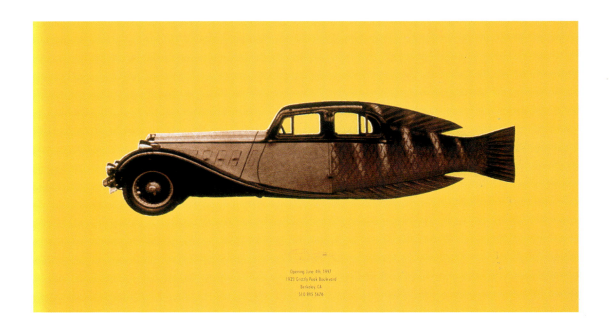

Opening June 4th 1997
1923 Grizzly Peak Boulevard
Berkeley, CA
510 835 5676

THE ALFRED HITCHCOCK FILM FESTIVAL.
Phipps Plaza proudly presents the best of Hitchcock
throughout the month of October.
For a listing of films and times, call 855-BIRD.

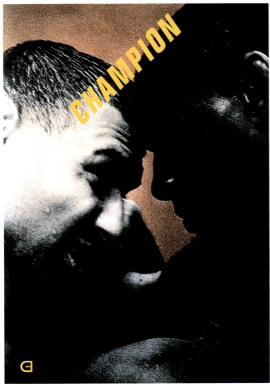

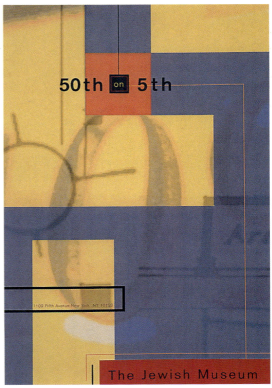

(top)
Arsenio García-Monsalve
Art Center College of Design

(middle)
Travis Rogers
Rhode Island School
of Design

(bottom)
Michelle Chong
Art Center College of Design

(opposite)
Peter Benarcilk
Art Center College of Design

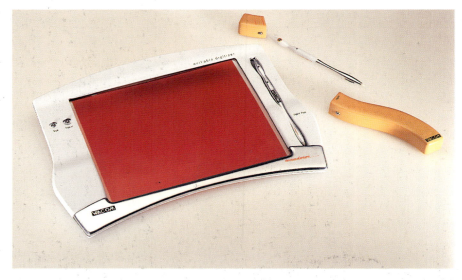

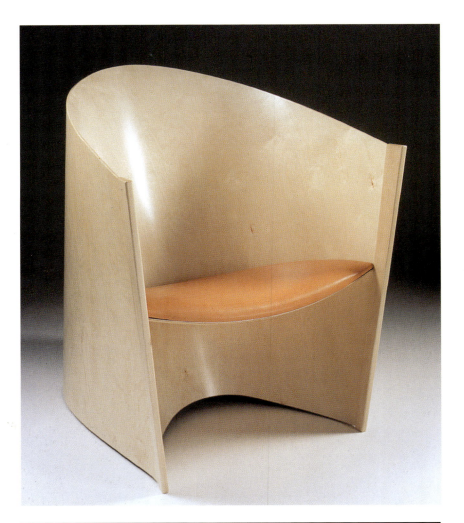

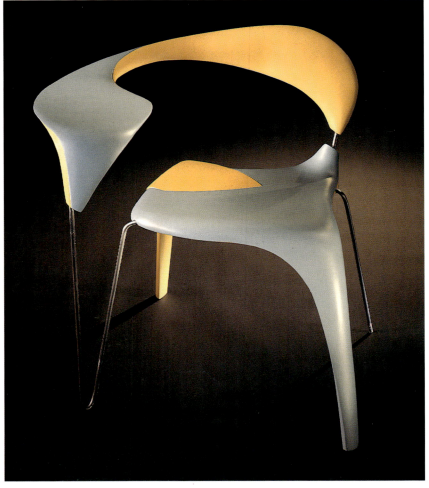

(opposite top)
Yuka Midorikawa Haelters
Rhode Island School
of Design

(opposite bottom)
Cecilia Vitas–Volcoff,
Arsenio García-Monsalve
Art Center College of Design

(this page)
Dario Antonioni
Art Center College of Design

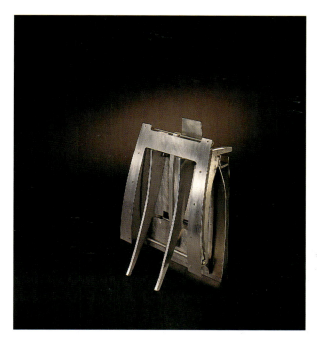

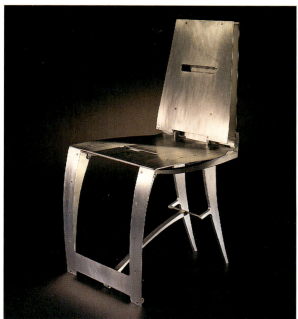

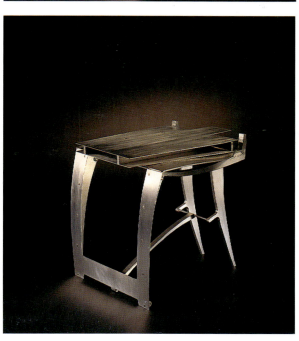

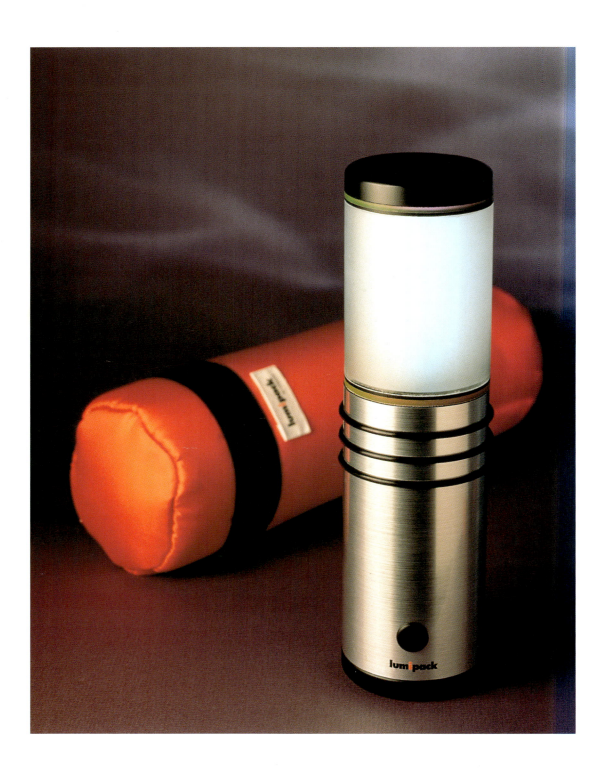

Bill Burns
California College
of Arts & Crafts

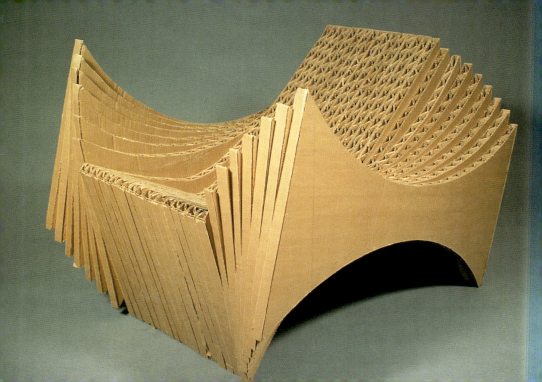

Elliott Hsu, Jim Doan,
Victor Fernandez
University of Illinois

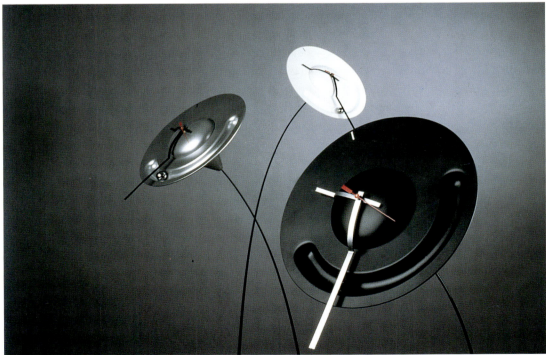

(this spread)
Rudy Widiaman
Art Center College of Design

(this page)
Brett Nystul
Art Center College of Design

(opposite)
Grant Delgatty
Art Center College of Design

Jeff Phillips, Scott Chandler
Virginia Tech

Richard Vasquez
California State University
Long Beach

(this spread)
Angela Pérez–Charneco
Penn State University

(this page top)
James Shum
School of Visual Arts

(this page bottom)
Yim Cheng
School of Visual Arts

(this page)
Llyod Rodriguez
School of Visual Arts

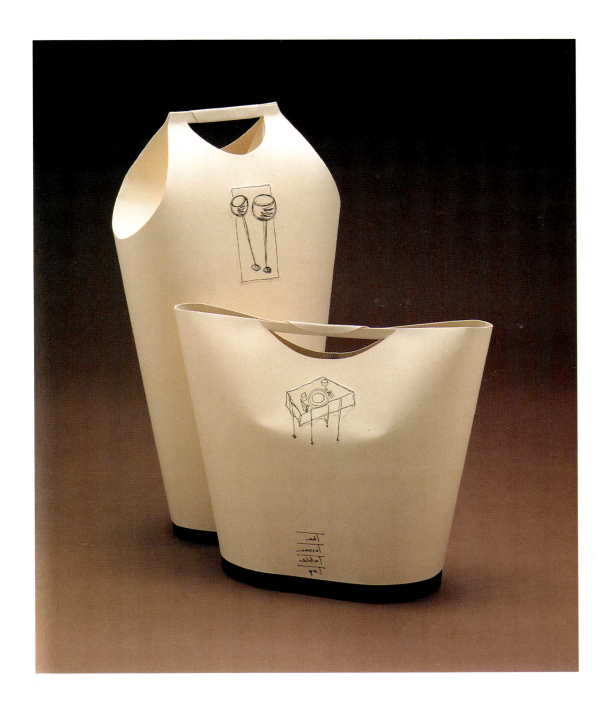

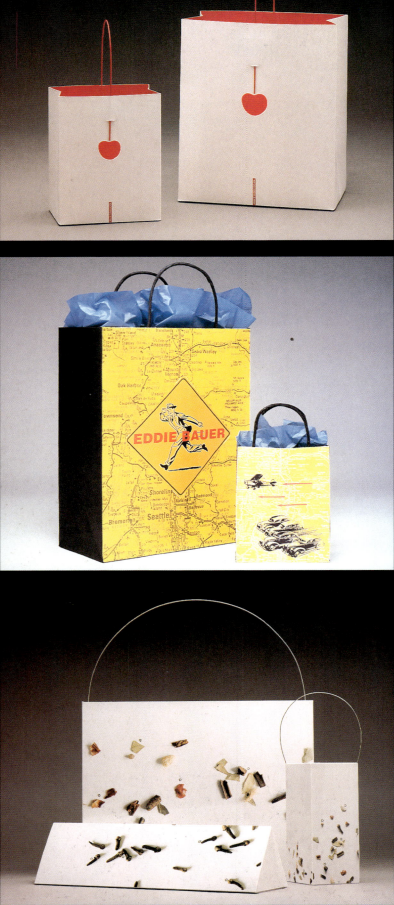

(opposite top)
Maureen Meyer
Penn State University

(opposite middle)
Mieko Kojima
School of Visual Arts

(opposite bottom)
Amanda Barile
Penn State University

(this page)
Hiro H. Westdorp
Pasadena City College

Matthew Smith
Monmouth University

utopia

lifestyle

45c

1930's
Australia

1997

Australia
1930's

future

aviation

$5

1997

1997

Australia
1930's

$1

innovation

speed

Australia
1930's

$10

architecture

bena

1997

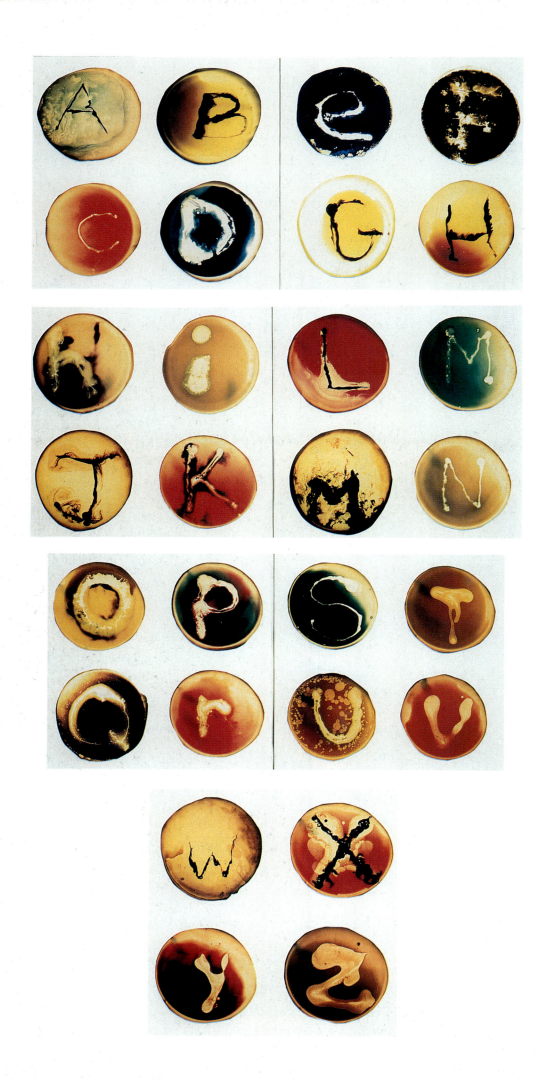

(opposite)
Mary Belibasakis
School of Visual Arts

(this page)
Blake Tannery
The Creative Circus

ABCDEFGHIJ

KLMNOPQRS

TUVWXYYZ

(this page)
Regina Krutoy
School of Visual Arts

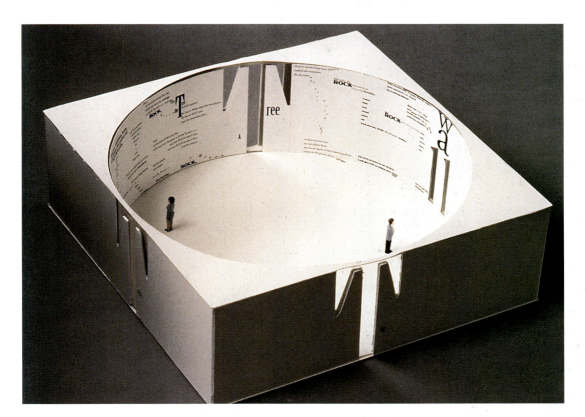

Frank Anselmo
School of Visual Arts

A B C D E
F G H I J
K L M N
O P Q R
S T U V
W X Y Z

Page 2
Student: Hilario Vilapouca / College: University of Ballarat Australia
Department: Graphic Design / Instructor: Helmut Stenzel
Project: Vodka bottle label and package design.
Projekt: Etikett und Verpackung für eine Wodka-Flasche.
Projet: Etiquette et packaging pour une bouteille de vodka.
Strategy: The aim was to keep the design reminiscent and meaningful to those associated with tragedies of war, and to reflect a personal feel of a place and time within history.
Strategie: Die Gestaltung sollte eine Verbindung zur Tragödie des Krieges haben und ein persönliches Gefühl für einen Ort und eine Zeit von geschichtlicher Bedeutung zum Ausdruck bringen.
Stratégie: Le design devait établir un lien avec les tragédies de la guerre et exprimer en même temps un sentiment personnel lié à un lieu et à un moment de l'histoire.
Medium, Materials: Material, paper, gold star

Page 4
Student: Manu Saluja / College: School of Visual Arts
Department: Illustration and Cartooning
Department Chair: Jack Endewelt / Instructor: M. Mattelson
Project: The assignment was to portray motion in picture.
Projekt: Die Aufgabe bestand im bildlichen Ausdruck von Bewegung.
Projet: L'objectif consistait à illustrer le mouvement par l'image.

Page 24 top, bottom
Student: Heather Plansker / College: School of Visual Arts
Department: Advertising and Graphic Design
Department Chair: Richard Wilde / Class: Advertising Portfolio
Instructor: Jeffrey Metzner
Caption: "A little more of what you need."
Bildlegende: «Ein bisschen mehr von dem, was man braucht.»
Légende: «Un peu plus que ce dont on a besoin.»

Page 24 middle
Student: Shane Neurman / College: School of Visual Arts
Department: Advertising and Graphic Design
Department Chair: Richard Wilde / Class: Advertising Portfolio
Instructor: Sal Devito
Caption: "At the end of the night, the ugly people will still be ugly."
Bildlegende: «Am Ende der Nacht werden die hässlichen Leute noch immer hässlich sein.»
Légende: «A la fin de la nuit, les gens laids sont toujours aussi laids.»

Page 25
Student: Sung Woo Hong / College: School of Visual Arts
Dean: David Rhodes / Department: Advertising
Department Chair: Richard Wilde
Class: Advertising Portfolio / Instructors: J. Claps, K. Krimstein
Strategy: Even though she is an old woman who is not healthy or strong enough to run, she is desperately chasing the coffee because it is her desire.
Strategie: Obgleich sie eigentlich nicht mehr gut laufen kann, versucht die gebrechliche alte Frau verzweifelt, an den von ihr so begehrten Kaffee heranzukommen.
Stratégie: Bien qu'elle n'ait plus assez de force pour courir, cette vieille femme en mauvaise santé essaie désespérément d'attraper ce café parce qu'elle en raffole.
Medium, Materials: Normal paper by Epson print

Page 26 top left
Student: Jeffrey Davila / College: School of Visual Arts
Department: Advertising, Graphic Design / Department Chair: Richard Wilde / Class: Portfolio / Instructor: Sal Devito
Project: O'Douls non-alcoholic brew
Caption: "Beer that goes great with liver."
Bildlegende: «Bier, das sich prima mit Leber verträgt.»
Légende: «Une bière qui s'entend à merveille avec votre foie.»
Strategy: Emphasize that the non-alcoholic beer is healthier for your liver, but still great tasting.
Strategie: Zeigen, dass alkoholfreies Bier bekömmlicher für die Leber ist und auch noch schmeckt.
Stratégie: Montrer qu'une bière sans alcool ménage le foie sans perdre pour autant de sa saveur.
Medium, Materials: Computer

Page 26 top right
Student: Kim Harley / College: The Creative Circus
Department Chairs: Norm Grey, Mike Jones-Kelley
Project: Sheriff Taylor's hot sauce.
Projekt: Sheriff Taylors scharfe Sauce.
Projet: Sauce piquante Sheriff Taylor.
Caption: "So hot it hurts to talk."
Bildlegende: «So scharf, dass es beim Sprechen wehtut.»
Légende: «Si piquante que cela fait mal d'en parler!»

Page 26 bottom left
Students: Amee Shah, Chris Surry / College: The Creative Circus
Departments: Art Direction, Copywriting / Department Chairs: Norm Grey, Mike Jones Kelley
Project: José Cuervo
Caption: "Married some 25 years and she still looks as pretty as the first day I saw her...A little goes a long way."
Bildlegende: «25 Jahre verheiratet, und sie ist noch immer so hübsch wie am ersten Tag ......Die kleinen Dinge halten lange.»
Légende: «25 ans de mariage et elle est toujours aussi jolie qu'au premier jour... Les petites choses durent longtemps.»

Page 26 bottom right
Student: Sung Woo Hong / College: School of Visual Arts
Dean: David Rhodes / Department: Advertising
Department Chair: Richard Wilde / Class: Advertising Portfolio
Instructors: J. Claps, K. Krimstein
Project: Red Devil hot oil.
Projekt: Red Devils scharf gewürztes Öl.
Projet: Huile piquante Red Devil.
Strategy: The student used an extreme picture so the target audience could imagine how hot the product is.
Strategie: Das extreme Bild soll dem Zielpublikum vermitteln, wie scharf das Produkt ist.
Stratégie: Cette image extrême doit montrer au public cible à quel point le produit est piquant.
Medium, Materials: Paper by Epson

Page 27 top
Student: Harold German / College: School of Visual Arts
Dean: David Rhodes / Department: Advertising, Graphic Design
Department Chair: Richard Wilde / Class: Advertising Portfolio
Instructor: Tom Gianfagna
Project: Smirnoff vodka
Projekt: Smirnoff-Wodka
Projet: La vodka Smirnoff
Caption: "There's a big difference between messengers in New York and messengers in Russia."
Bildlegende: «Zwischen Boten in New York und Boten in Russland gibt es einen grossen Unterschied.»
Légende: «Il y a une grande différence entre les messagers de New York et les messagers de Russie.»
Strategy: The student utilized a dull background, the bottle in full color, and Russian humor.
Strategie: Russischer Humor und eine farbige Flasche vor mattem Hintergrund sind hier die Ausdrucksmittel.
Stratégie: Verre coloré sur fond terne et humour russe constituent les moyens d'expression choisis par l'étudiant.
Medium, Materials: Adobe Photoshop, Quark Xpress

Page 27 bottom
Student: Jay Howard / College: California State Polytechnic University / Department: Art / Department Chair: M. Henderson
Class: Drawing for Illustration
Instructor: Babette Mayor
Project: Absolut LA shaker. The assignment was to create a new Absolut ad to be seen in an LA magazine.
Projekt: Absolut-Wodka ist bekannt durch die Anzeigen, die mit der Form der Flasche spielen und oft einen Bezug auf einen bestimmten Ort haben. Das Thema für die neue Anzeige, die im LA-Magazin erscheinen sollte, war Los Angeles.
Projet: Il s'agissait de créer une nouvelle publicité Absolut Vodka ayant trait à la ville de Los Angeles et devant paraître dans le magazine LA.
Strategy: The student created a seismographic readout of the bottle on architect's vellum and pasted it over two sheets of colored laser-printer paper.
Strategie: Die Lösung besteht in einer seismographischen Darstellung der Flasche auf Pergament, das auf zwei Blätter farbigen Laserdrucker-Papiers geklebt wurde.
Stratégie: L'étudiant a opté pour une représentation sismique de la bouteille sur du vélin collé sur deux feuilles de papier couleur pour imprimante laser.
Medium, Materials: Vellum and graphite, laser printer paper, illustration board

Page 28 top, bottom left
Student: Pichai Piyapongdacha / College: Center for Electronic Art
Dean: Harold Hedelman / Department: Multimedia Computer
Department Chair: Anthony Hall
Class: Quark Xpress
Instructor: Li Gardiner
Copywriters: Pichai Piyapongdacha, Wayne Corry
Project: Internet campaign created in Quark Xpress.
Projekt: Internet-Kampagne, mit Quark Xpress gestaltet.
Projet: Campagne Internet réalisée sur Quark Xpress.

Page 28 bottom right
Student: Kwasi Osei / College: School of Visual Arts
Department: Advertising and Graphic Design
Department Chair: Richard Wilde / Class: Advertising
Instructor: Jack Mariucci

Page 29 top
Student: Heather Plansker / College: School of Visual Arts
Department: Advertising and Graphic Design
Department Chair: Richard Wilde / Class: Advertising Portfolio
Instructor: Jack Mariucci
Caption: "Beg your mom to send you to your room."
Bildlegende: «Bitte deine Mutter, dich auf dein Zimmer zu schicken.»
Légende: «Dis donc à ta mère de t'envoyer dans ta chambre!»

Page 29 middle
Student: Jung Hwan Yoon / College: School of Visual Arts
Department: Advertising / Department Chair: Richard Wilde
Class: Ad Portfolio / Instructors: J. Clapps, K. Krimstein
Project: Netscape Navigator
Caption: "Helping millions of mice to find their homes."
Bildlegende: «Damit Millionen von Mäusen nach Hause finden können.»
Légende: «Pour que des millions de souris retrouvent leur chez soi.»
Strategy: The strategy was to emphasize the product as the most
widely used Web browser.
*Strategie: Das Produkt sollte als der beliebteste Web-Navigator
präsentiert werden.*
*Stratégie: Le produit devait être présenté comme l'instrument de navigation le
plus utilisé au monde pour surfer sur le Web.*

Page 29 bottom
Student: Sung Woo Hong / College: School of Visual Arts
Dean: David Rhodes / Department: Advertising
Department Chair: Richard Wilde / Class: Advertising Portfolio
Instructors: J. Clapps, K. Krimstein
Project: Netscape Navigator
Strategy: The student utilized space exploration to show how people
can easily explore miraculous worlds.
*Strategie: Die Erforschung des Weltraums diente als Metapher für die
Leichtigkeit, mit der geheimnisvolle Welten erkundet werden können.*
*Stratégie: La métaphore choisie par l'étudiant, à savoir l'exploration de l'e-
space, a pour but de montrer à quel point il est facile pour chacun d'entre nous
de découvrir des mondes mystérieux.*
Medium, Materials: Epson ink print, normal paper

Pages 30, 31
Student: Kerstin Hamburg / College: Bergische Universität Wuppertal
Department: Kommunikations Design
Department Chairs: Uwe Loesch, Marc Izikowitz
Project: Campaign for a new shampoo.
Projekt: Kampagne für ein neues Shampoo.
Projet: Campagne pour un nouveau shampoing.
Strategy: Extraordinary lifestyle photography was used with non-pro-
fessional models. The name of the product is the headline.
*Strategie: Aussergewöhnliche Lifestyle-Photographie mit Amateur-Modellen.
Die Headline ist der Name des Produktes.*
*Stratégie: Photographie lifestyle inhabituelle prise avec des modèles amateurs.
La headline est le nom du produit.*
Caption: "For all those who want it."
Bildlegende: «Für alle, die es haben wollen.»
Légende: «Pour tous ceux qui le veulent.»

Page 32 top
Student: Michael Czako / College: School of Visual Arts
Department: Advertising, Graphic Design
Department Chair: Richard Wilde / Class: Advertising Portfolio
Project: Nordic Track
Caption: "Recommended by your doctor with
over 12,000 second opinions."
*Bildlegende: «Von ihrem Arzt mit über 12000 zweiten Meinungen emp-
fohlen.» (Über 12000 weitere Ärzte empfehlen das Produkt ebenfalls.)*
Légende: «Recommandé par votre médecin et 12'000 de ses confrères.»

Page 32 bottom
Student: Salomon Sainvil Jr. / College: School of Visual Arts
Department: Advertising and Graphic Design
Department Chair: Richard Wilde / Instructor: Independent study
Project: Listermint mouthwash.
Projekt: Listermint-Mundwasser.
Projet: Eau dentifrice Listermint.
Medium, Materials: Mac, marker

Page 33 top, bottom
Student: Joseph Ferrazano / College: School of Visual Arts
Department: Advertising and Graphic Design / Department
Chair: Richard Wilde / Class: Advertising

Instructor: Jack Mariucci
Project: Weight Watchers
Caption: "The easiest way to get from point A to point B."
Bildlegende: «Die einfachste Art, um von A nach B zu gelangen.»
Légende: «Le moyen le plus simple d'aller de A à B.»

Page 33 middle
Student: Christine Baffa / College: School of Visual Arts
Department: Advertising and Graphic Design
Department Chair: Richard Wilde
Project: Weight Watchers

Page 34 top
Student: Mark Cook / College: Portfolio Center
Department: Advertising / Department Chair: Gus Pitsikovlis
Project: Iams

Page 34 bottom left
Student: Alexis Rodriguez / College: School of Visual Arts
Department: Advertising / Department Chair: Richard Wilde
Class: Advertising Portfolio / Instructor: Jack Mariucci
Project: American Standard

Page 34 bottom right
Student: Rafael Soberal / College: School of Visual Arts
Department: Advertising and Graphic Design / Department Chair:
Richard Wilde / Class: Advertising / Instructor: Sal Devito

Page 35
Student: Marco Morgella / College: School of Visual Arts
Department: Advertising, Graphic Design
Department Chair: Richard Wilde / Class: Ad Portfolio
Project: Create an ad for Toro snowblowers.
Projekt: Anzeige für Schneegebläse.
Projet: Publicité pour des chasse-neige.
Strategy: The ad emphasizes that you can seriously hurt your back
without the product.
*Strategie: Claim: Wenn man das Produkt nicht besitzt,
kann man sich den Rücken ruinieren.*
*Stratégie: La publicité souligne que, sans ce produit, on
risque de s'esquinter sérieusement le dos.*
Medium, Materials: Cactus print

Page 36
Student: Cora Haster / College: School of Visual Arts
Department: Advertising and Graphic Design / Department
Chair: Richard Wilde / Instructors: Jeffrey Metzner, Jack Mariucci

Page 37
Student: Yim Cheng / College: School of Visual Arts
Department: Advertising and Graphic Design
Department Chair: Richard Wilde / Class: Advertising
Instructors: Jack Mariucci, Jeffrey Metzner / Project: Advil
Caption: "Ouch! Take Advil."
Bildlegende: «Au! Nimm Advil.»
Légende: «Aïe! Prends Advil!»

Page 38 top, bottom
Student: Alice Butts / College: School of Visual Arts
Department: Advertising and Graphic Design
Department Chair: Richard Wilde / Class: Advertising Portfolio
Instructor: Jeffrey Metzner / Project: Advil
Caption: "As long as there are people, there will be headaches."
Bildlegende: «Solange es Menschen gibt, wird es Kopfschmerzen geben.»
Légende: «Tant qu'il y aura des hommes, il y aura des maux de tête.»

Page 38 middle
Student: Sung Woo Hong / College: School of Visual Arts
Dean: David Rhodes / Department: Advertising
Department Chair: Richard Wilde / Class: Advertising Portfolio
Instructor: Jeffrey Metzer / Project: Advil
Caption: "This is the right answer for your headache."
Bildlegende: «Das ist die richtige Lösung für Ihre Kopfschmerzen.»
Légende: «La réponse à vos maux de tête.»

Page 39
Student: James Helms / College: University of Delaware
Dean: Mart Richards / Department: College of Art
Department Chair: Martha Carothers / Class: Advertising Design
Instructors: Raymond Nichols, Martha Carothers
Art Director: James Helms
Project: Ikea furniture. Independent portfolio campaign.
Projekt: Ikea-Möbel.
Projet: Campagne Ikea.
Caption: "You can assemble our furniture even if you are øl tüms."
"How do we keep our prices down? We keep a couple of scrüz løøs."

Bildlegende: «Du kannst deine Möbel zusammenbauen, selbst wenn du zwei linke Hände hast.» «Wie wir unsere Preise so niedrig halten können? Wir haben ein paar Schrauben locker.» Im Originaltext sind schwedische Worte einge-streut, eine Anspielung auf das Heimatland des Herstellers.
Légende: «Même les plus maladroits arrivent à assembler nos meubles.» «Comment faisons-nous pour garder nos prix aussi bas? Nous devons être un peu marteaux!» (Dans la publicité originale, jeu de mots avec la langue du fabricant, le suédois.)
Medium, Materials: CLC fiery print

Page 40
Student: Lee Seidenberg / College: School of Visual Arts
Department: Advertising / Department Chair: Richard Wilde
Class: Advanced Advertising / Instructor: Sal Devito
Project: Sorell winter boots.
Projekt: Sorell-Winterstiefel.
Projet: Bottes d'hiver Sorell.
Caption: "Ever wonder how the guy who
drives the snowplow gets to his car?"
Bildlegende: «Haben Sie sich schon mal gefragt, wie der Mann, der den Scheepflug fährt, zu seinem Auto kommt.»
Légende: «Vous êtes-vous déjà demandé comment le gars qui conduit ce chasse-neige rejoint sa voiture?»
Strategy: Convince reader boots are designed for intense cold.
Strategie: Der Leser soll von der Eignung der Stiefel für extreme Kälte überzeugt werden.
Stratégie: Convaincre le consommateur que ces bottes sont spécialement conçues pour lutter contre le froid.

Page 41 top, bottom
Student: Yong Keh / College: School of Visual Arts
Department: Advertising / Department Chair: Richard Wilde
Class: Advertising Portfolio / Instructor: Tom Gianfagna
Project: Pirelli tire.
Projekt: Pirelli-Reifen.
Projet: Pneus Pirelli.

Page 41 middle
Student: Harold German / College: School of Visual Arts
Dean: David Rhodes / Department: Advertising and Graphic Design
Department Chair: Richard Wilde / Class: Advertising Portfolio
Instructor: Jack Mariucci
Project: Totes rubber galoshes.
Projekt: Totes-Gummischuhe.
Projet: Chaussures en caout-chouc Totes.
Strategy: The word rubber is used in a sexual yet humorous way to give life and excitement to a pretty dull product.
Strategie: Hier wird das Wort «Gummi» auf humorvolle Art mit Sex in Verbindung gebracht, um ein relativ langweiliges Produkt aufregender zu machen.
Stratégie: Le mot 'rubber' (caoutchouc) à connotation sexuelle est employé de façon humoristique afin de rendre un produit ennuyeux plus séduisant.
Medium, Materials: Adobe Photoshop, Quark Xpress

Page 42 top, bottom
Art Director: Sara Hochman / Photographer: Paul Ober
College: Portfolio Center / Department: Advertising
Department Chair: Gus Pitsikovlis / Class: Advertising Production
Instructor: Gemma Gatto
Project: Rawlings
Projekt: Baseball-Handschuh
Projet: Gants de baseball
Caption: "The sting you feel in the palm of your hand is nothing like the sting he's going to feel walking back to the bench."
Bildlegende: «Der Schmerz, den du in der Handfläche spürst, ist nichts gegen den Schmerz, den er empfindet, wenn er zur Bank zurückgeht.» claim: Dank des Rawling-Baseball-Handschuhs wird man den Ball fangen, und der Spieler wird beschämt zur Bank zurückgehen.
Légende: «La douleur que tu ressentiras dans la paume de ta main n'est rien comparé à celle qu'il ressentira lorsqu'il rejoindra le banc de son équipe.»

Page 42 middle
Student: Shayne Alexis Humphrey / College: School of Visual Arts
Department: Advertising and Graphic Design / Department Chair: Richard Wilde / Class: Advertising / Instructor: Jack Mariucci
Caption: "Another satisfied K2 snowboarder."
Bildlegende: «Noch ein zufriedener K2-Snowboarder.»
Légende: «Encore un snowboarder K2 satisfait.»

Page 43 bottom
Student: Jeremy Pippenger / College: School of Visual Arts
Department: Advertising / Department Chair: Richard Wilde
Instructor: Sal DeVito, Tom Gianfagna
Project: Merrell boots.
Projekt: Merrell-Stiefel.
Projet: Bottes Merrell.

Caption: "Putting on an extra 4 pounds could save the other 165"
Bildlegende: «Die zusätzlichen 2 Kilo könnten die anderen 75 Kilo retten.»
Claim: Das zusätzliche Gewicht der Stiefel zahlt sich beim Bergsteigen aus.
Légende: «Ces deux petits kilos supplémentaires pourraient bien sauver les 75 autres.»

Page 44 top
Student: Michael Czako / College: School of Visual Arts
Dean: David Rhodes / Department: Advertising and Graphic Design
Department Chair: Richard Wilde / Class: Advertising Portfolio
Instructor: Sal Devito
Project: Band Aid.
Projekt: Schnellverband / Pflaster.
Projet: Sparadrap.
Caption: "What you could be wearing instead of a bandaid."
Bildlegende «Was Sie statt eines Band-Aid-Schnellverbandes tragen könnten.»
Légende: «Voilà ce qui pourrait remplacer un sparadrap!»
Strategy: The strategy was to scare people by showing them what actually attacks a cut.
Strategie: Die Strategie bestand in der Darstellung der möglichen Verunreinigung einer Schnittwunde.
Stratégie: Faire peur aux gens en leur montrant les risques d'infection d'une plaie.
Medium, Materials: Power Macintosh, Quark Xpress, Adobe Photoshop

Page 44 middle
Student: Dana Betgilan / College: School of Visual Arts
Department: Advertising / Department Chair: Richard Wilde
Instructor: Sal Devito
Project: Pepto-Bismol
Caption "Just a reminder, it's tax season."
Bildlegende: «Nur zur Erinnerung: die Steuer-Saison hat begonnen.»
Légende: «Nota bene: c'est la saison des impôts.»

Page 44 bottom
Students: Cora Flaster, Heather Plansker / College: School of Visual Arts Department: Advertising and Graphic Design
Department Chair: Richard Wilde / Class: Advertising Portfolio
Instructor: Jack Mariucci

Page 45 top left
Student: Marco Morsella / College: School of Visual Arts
Department: Advertising and Graphic Design / Department Chair: Richard Wilde / Class: Advertising / Instructor : Jack Mariucci
Caption: "Everyday millions of people get infected because they don't use protection... Cover your cut or disgusting infecting little germs will."
Bildlegende: «Jeden Tag infizieren sich Millionen von Leuten, weil sie sich nicht schützen... Bedecken Sie ihre Schnittwunde, sonst übernehmen das abscheuliche kleine Bakterien.»
Légende: «Chaque jour, des millions de personnes contractent des maladies infectieuses parce qu'elles ne se protègent pas... Recouvrez votre plaie sinon d'horribles petites bactéries s'en chargeront à votre place!»

Page 45 top right
Copywriter: Grant Holland / Artistic Director: Jerry Underwood
College: The Creative Circus / Department: Art Direction and Copywriting / Department Chairs: Norm Grey, Mike Jones Kelley
Project: Tums

Page 45 bottom left
Student: Rafael Soberal / College: School of Visual Arts
Department: Advertising and Graphic Design
Department Chair: Richard Wilde / Class: Advertising Portfolio
Instructor: Jack Mariucci
Project: Dr. Scholl's foot powder.
Projekt: Dr. Scholls Fusspuder.
Projet: Talc pour les pieds Dr. Scholl.

Page 45 bottom right
Student: Emmanuel Santos / College: School of Visual Arts
Department: Advertising and Graphic Design / Department Chair: Richard Wilde / Class: Advertising / Instructor: Jack Mariucci
Project: Dr. Scholl's foot powder
Projekt: Dr. Scholls Fusspuder
Projet: Talc pour les pieds Dr. Scholl.

Page 46 top, bottom
Student: Eric Shutte / College: School of Visual Arts
Department: Advertising and Graphic Design / Department Chair: Richard Wilde / Class: Advertising Portfolio, Advanced Advertising
Instructor: Jack Mariucci
Caption: "We design our hair pieces to stay on in some intense environments."
Bildlegende: «Unsere Toupets bleiben auch unter extremen Bedingungen

an Ort und Stelle.»
Légende: «Nos toupets ne bougent pas, même dans les pires conditions.»
Caption: "The last time you had this problem, you were cute enough to get away with it."
Bildlegende: «Als Sie das letzte Mal mit diesem Problem zu tun hatten, waren Sie so niedlich, dass es nichts ausmachte.»
Légende: «La dernière fois que vous avez eu ce problème, vous étiez si mignon que ça ne se voyait pas.»

Page 46 middle
Student: Shayne-Alexis Humphrey / College: School of Visual Arts
Department: Advertising and Graphic Design / Department Chair:
Richard Wilde /Class: Advertising / Instructor: Jack Mariucci
Caption: "Fear of flying?"
Bildlegende: «Angst vorm Fliegen?»
Légende: «Peur de voler?»

Page 47
Student: Henry Belfor / College: School of Visual Arts
Department: Advertising and Graphic Design
Department Chair: Richard Wilde / Class: Advertising Portfolio
Instructor: Jeff Metzner
Project: American Spirit.
Projekt: Zigarettenmarke.
Projet: Marque de cigarettes.
Caption: "Other companies give you all you want in a cigarette and a lot more."
Bildlegende: «Andere Firmen geben Ihnen alles, was Sie von einer Zigarette verlangen und noch viel mehr.»
Légende: «Les autres fabricants vous donnent tout ce que l'on attend d'une cigarette et même un peu plus!»

Page 48
Student: Rafael Sobral / College: School of Visual Arts
Department: Advertising and Graphic Design / Department Chair:
Richard Wilde / Class: Advertising / Instructor: Sal Devito
Project: Rockport shoes.
Projekt: Rockport-Schuhe.
Projet: Chaussures Rockport.
Caption: "For that constant sore and pulling ache in your lower back, take two of these."
Bildlegende: «Gegen das Ziehen und den ständigen Schmerz im Kreuz nehmen Sie am besten ein Paar von diesen.»
Légende: «Prenez-en deux comme ça et dites adieu à votre mal de reins!»

Page 49
Students: Grant Holland, Jerry Underwood / College: The Creative Circus / Department: Art Direction and Copywriting
Department Chairs: Norm Grey, Mike Jones Kelley
Project: Atlanta Yellow Cab–alternative media.
Projekt: Taxis in Atlanta; Werbung in alternativen Medien.
Projet: Taxis d'Atlanta; publicité dans des médias alternatifs.
Caption: "If you're this far off the mark, call a cab."
Bildlegende: «Wenn Sie so schlecht zielen können, rufen Sie ein Taxi.»
Légende: «Si vous visez aussi mal que ça, appelez un taxi!»

Page 50 top
Student: Victoria Necea / College: School of Visual Arts
Department: Advertising and Graphic Design
Department Chair: Richard Wilde / Class: Advertising Portfolio
Instructor: Jeffrey Metzner

Page 50 bottom
Student: Dana Betgilan / College: School of Visual Arts
Department: Advertising and Graphic Design
Department Chair: Richard Wilde / Class: Advertising Portfolio
Instructor: Jeffrey Metzner
Caption: "No one had him in mind when they wrote the first amendment."
Bildlegende: «An ihn hat niemand ge-dacht, als sie das Recht auf freie Meinungs-äusserung in die Verfassung aufnahmen.»
Gezeigt ist Howard Stern, ein umstrittener Rundfunkmoderator in den USA.
Légende: «Personne n'a pensé à lui lorsque l'amendement pour la liberté d'expression a été adopté.» Image illustrant Howard Stern, un présentateur radio très controversé aux Etats-Unis.

Page 51 top
Student: Gabriel Medina / College: School of Visual Arts
Dean: David Rhodes / Department: Advertising and Graphic Design
Department Chair: Richard Wilde / Class: Advertising
Instructor: Jeffrey Metzner
Project: Visine
Caption: "Gets the red out....Don't ask how."
Bildlegende: «Kriegt das Rot raus...Frag' nicht wie.»
Légende: «Elimine le rouge... Mais ne me demandez pas comment!»

Page 51 middle
Student: Vincent Muratore / College: School of Visual Arts
Dean: David Rhodes / Department: Advertising
Department Chair: Richard Wilde / Class: Advertising Portfolio
Instructor: Jack Mariccui
Project: Mayflower Moving Co.
Projekt: Ein Umzugsunternehmen.
Projet: Entreprise de déménagement.
Strategy: The strategy was to emphasize why the public should use this company instead of another.
Strategie: Einen Grund liefern, warum das Publikum diese und keine andere Firma benutzen sollte.
Stratégie: Montrer pourquoi les gens devraient faire appel à cette entreprise plutôt qu'à une autre.

Page 51 bottom
Student: Dana Betgilan / College: School of Visual Arts
Department: Advertising / Department Chair: Richard Wilde
Instructor: Sal Devito
Project: New York waterway.
Projekt: New Yorker Wasserwege.
Projet: Canalisations de New York
Caption: "Rush hour."
Bildlegende: «Stosszeit.»
Légende: Heure d'affluence.

Page 52 top, bottom
Student: Yong Keh / College: School of Visual Arts
Department: Advertising / Department Chair: Richard Wilde
Class: Advanced Advertising / Instructor: Sal Devito
Project: Amtrak

Page 52 middle
Student: Shawn Brown / College: Portfolio Center
Department: Advertising / Department Chair: Gus Pitsikoulis
Project: H&R Block

Page 53 left
Student: Jaydee Jana / College: School of Visual Arts
Department: Advertising and Graphic Design / Department Chair:
Richard Wilde / Class: Advertising / Instructor: Jack Mariucci
Caption: "Don't settle for front row seats."
Bildlegende: «Geben Sie sich nicht mit den ersten Reihen zufrieden.» Werbung für einen Telephondienst, der Auskunft über das Kinoprogramm gibt. Die ersten Reihen sind im Kino bekanntlich nicht die besten.
Légende: «Ne vous contentez pas des premiers rangs!» Publicité pour le service téléphonique 777 qui donne des informations sur les films, les salles de cinéma où ils passent, etc. Allusion aux premières rangées de sièges dans les salles de cinéma.

Page 53 right
Student: Wendell Woodford / College: The Creative Circus
Department: Art Direction and Copywriting / Department Chairs:
Norm Grey, Mike Jones Kelley
Project: H&R Block

Page 54 top left
Student: Dana Betgilan / College: School of Visual Arts
Department: Advertising / Department Chair: Richard Wilde
Instructor: Sal Devito
Project: Planned Parenthood poster.
Projekt: Plakat für Familienplanung.
Projet: Affiche pour la planification familiale.
Caption: "And you thought homework kept you up late."
Bildlegende: «Und man dachte, man kam wegen der Hausaufgaben spät ins Bett.»
Légende: «Et toi qui croyais que les devoirs du petit t'empêcheraient d'aller au lit!»

Page 54 top right
Student: Jennie Lee / College: School of Visual Arts
Department: Advertising and Graphic Design / Department Chair:
Richard Wilde / Class: Advertising / Instructor: Jack Mariucci
Project: American Society for the Prevention of Cruelty to Animals, Adopt-a-Pet campaign.
Projekt: Kampagne für eine Tierschutz-organisation, die zur Anschaffung eines Haustiers ermuntert.
Projet: Campagne d'une société pour la protection des animaux visant à encourager les gens à adopter un animal domestique.
Caption: "Now that your kids are grown, it'll be nice to hear the pit-ter-patter of little feet again."
Bildlegende: «Nachdem die Kinder jetzt gross sind, wäre es schön, wieder das Trippeln kleiner Füsse zu hören.»
Légende: «Main-tenant que les enfants sont grands, ne serait-ce pas agréable d'entendre des petits pas dans la maison?»

Page 54 bottom left
Student: Michael Czako / College: School of Visual Arts
Dean: David Rhodes / Department: Advertising and Graphic Design
Department Chair: Richard Wilde / Class: Advertising Concepts
Instructors: Abi Aron, Leslie Sweet
Project: Encourage people to vote.
Projekt: Appell an die Stimmbürger, zur Wahl zu gehen.
Projet: Encourager les citoyens à aller voter.
Caption: "Just a reminder, some
politicians actually do keep their word."
*Bildlegende: «Nur zur Erinnerung: einige Politiker halten
tatsächlich Wort.»*
*Légende: «Incroyable mais vrai: certains hommes politiques
tiennent parole.»*
Medium, Materials: Power Macintosh, Quark Xpress,
Adobe Photoshop

Page 54 bottom right
Student: Sung Woo Hong / College: School of Visual Arts
Dean: David Rhodes / Department: Advertising
Department Chair: Richard Wilde / Class: Advanced Advertising
Instructor: Sal Devito
Project: Anti-smoking campaign.
Projekt: Kampagne gegen das Rauchen.
Projet: Campagne anti-tabac.
Strategy: The camel which is normally alive on the cigarette pack
is dead due to heavy smoking.
*Strategie: Statt eines lebendigen Kamels auf der Zigarettenpackung ein
Kamel, das sich zu Tode geraucht hat.*
Stratégie: A force de fumer, le célèbre chameau y a laissé sa peau!
Medium, Materials: Paper by Epson Print

Page 55 top
Student: Eric Shutte / College: School of Visual Arts
Dean: David Rhodes / Department: Advertising, Graphic Design
Department Chair: Richard Wilde / Class: Advanced Advertising
Instructors: Abby Aron, Leslie Sweat
Project: Encourage people to vote.
Projekt: Appell an die Stimmbürger, zur Wahl zu gehen.
Projet: Encourager les citoyens à aller voter.
Caption: "Once every four years, people have the power to
overthrow the government."
*Bildlegende: «Alle vier Jahre hat das Volk die Möglichkeit, die Regierung
zu stürzen.»*
*Légende: «Tous les quatre ans, le peuple a l'occasion de renverser le
gouvernement.»*
Medium, Materials: Computer, imagination.

Page 55 bottom
Student: Shayne-Alexis Humphrey / College: School of Visual Arts
Department: Advertising and Graphic Design / Department Chair:
Richard Wilde / Class: Advertising / Instructor: Jack Mariucci
Project: Sierra Club
Caption: "Keep fashion alive."
Bildlegende: «Mode soll lebendig sein.»
Légende: «Laissons vivre la mode!»

Pages 56, 57
Student: Ingeburg Bölitz / College: Fachhochschule Mainz
Department: Communication and Design / Department Chair:
Roland Sigrist / Class: graduate project / Instructor: Jörg Osterspey
Project: A special sports shoe with gel in its sole, which reacts to
pressure, warms up and warms the feet.
*Projekt: Ein besonderer Sportschuh mit Gel in der Sohle, der sich bei
Druck erwärmt und so die Füsse warm hält.*
*Projet: Chaussure de sport spéciale avec du gel dans la semelle qui se
réchauffe à chaque pression et tient ainsi les pieds au chaud.*
Strategy: Heat is the central theme of the campaign, which included
print ads, a trade promotion, point-of-sale promotion, leaflets and
Internet pages.
*Strategie: Hitze ist das zentrale Thema der Kampagne, zu der Presse-
Anzeigen, Fachhandelwerbung, Heftchen, Laden-Promotionen und
Internet-Seiten gehören.*
Stratégie: Campagne multimédia ayant la chaleur pour thème principal.

Page 58
Student: Sung-Yoon Lee / College: School of Visual Arts
Department: Advertising / Department Chair: Richard Wilde
Class: Advanced Advertising / Instructor: Sal Devito
Project: Bell helmets.
Projekt: Bell-Helme.
Projet: Casques Bell.
Caption: "Who said nothing lasts forever?"
Bildlegende: «Wer hat behauptet, dass nichts ewig hält?»
Légende: «Qui a dit que rien n'était éternel?»

Page 59 top
Student: Jeffrey Davila / College: School of Visual Arts
Department: Advertising, Graphic Design
Department Chair: Richard Wilde / Class: Advanced Advertising
Instructor: Sal Devito
Project: Bell Helmets.
Projekt: Bell-Helme.
Projet: Casques Bell.
Caption: "We suggest you use the left side to save the right."
"If you think it looks ugly on paper, you should see it on concrete."
*Bildlegende: «Wir schlagen vor, dass Sie die linke Hälfte benutzen, um
die rechte zu retten.» «Wenn Sie finden, dass es auf Papier hässlich
aussieht, sollten Sie es mal auf Beton sehen.»*
*Légende: «Nous vous suggérons d'utiliser la partie gauche pour sauver la
droite.» «Si vous trouvez que c'est moche sur du papier, attendez de voir
ce que ça donne sur du béton!»*

Page 59 bottom
Student: Eric Shutte / College: School of Visual Arts
Department: Advertising, Graphic Design / Department Chair:
Richard Wilde / Class: Advertising / Instructor: Jack Mariucci
Project: Bell Helmets.
Projekt: Bell-Helme.
Projet: Casques Bell.
Caption: "Just a reminder, the road of life is lined with
telephone poles."
*Bildlegende: «Nur zur Erinnerung: der Lebensweg ist von
Telephonmasten gesäumt.»*
*Légende: «Mettez-vous bien ça dans la tête: la vie est un long chemin
semé de poteaux téléphoniques!»*

Page 60
Student: Beverly Kasman / College: Austin Community College
Department: Commercial Art / Department Chair: Daniel Traverso
Class: Graphic Design II / Instructor: Linda Smarzik
Project: Harley-Davidson annual report 1997.
Projekt: Jahresbericht 1997 für Harley Davidson.
Projet: Rapport annuel 1997 Harley Davidson.
Strategy: Type was used to redesign the annual report.
*Strategie: Mit Hilfe der Typographie wurde der Jahresbericht optisch
aufgefrischt.*
Stratégie: Rapport annuel revisité sur la base d'une nouvelle typographie.
Medium, Materials: Bolts, Harley Davidson patch.
All copy from 1997 Harley-Davidson annual report.

Page 61
Student: Paul Neely / College: Monash University
Dean: John Redmond / Department: Graphic Design
Department Chair: Jenny Allen
Project: Volkswagen annual report.
Projekt: Jahresbericht für Volkswagen.
Projet: Rapport annuel de Volkswagen.
Strategy: The grid structure for this annual report uses the classic
shapes of the Volkswagen for its main emphasis. Bold illustrations are
juxtaposed with technical drawings for balance and excitement.
*Strategie. Die klassischen Formen des Volkswagens bilden die Grundlage
der Rasterstruktur des Berichtes. Auffällige Illustrationen werden technischen
Zeichnungen gegenüber-gestellt, was für Spannung und
Ausgewogenheit sorgt.*
*Stratégie: Les lignes classiques de Volkswagen forment la trame de base du
rapport. Les illustrations audacieuses contrastent avec les dessins techniques
et créent ainsi tension et équilibre.*
Medium, Materials: Quark Xpress, Illustrator, Photoshop

Page 62
Student: Cliff Jew / College: California College of Arts and Crafts
Dean: Michael Vanderbyl / Department: Graphic Design
Department Chair: Leslie Becker
Class: Typography 3 / Instructor: Martin Venezky
Project: "Ode to my socks" by Pablo Neruda. The assignment
was to design a poem in a way that reflects its meaning and feel.
*Projekt: ‹Ode an meine Socken› von Pablo Neruda. Die Aufgabe bestand
in der visuellen Interpretation eines Gedichtes.*
*Projet: «Ode à mes chaussettes» de Pablo Neruda. Objectif: interpréter
visuellement un poème.*
Medium, Materials: Board, paper, photoprints. End sheets:
Photoillustrations by Matt Kirschenbau.

Page 63
Student: James Tung / College: School of Visual Arts
Dean: David Rhodes / Department: Graphic Design
Department Chair: Richard Wilde / Class: Typography and Design
Instructor: Richard Povun
Project: Typographic identification describing all parts of type.
Projekt: Beschreibung aller Teile der Schrift.

Projet: Identification typographique de tous les éléments d'un caractère.
Strategy: Using poster-size spreads, the aim was to relate typography
with architecture. Letterforms show structural elements with
miniature people interacting with them.
*Strategie: Mit Hilfe von Seiten in Plakatgrösse wird eine Verbindung
zwischen Typographie und Architektur hergestellt.*
*Stratégie: Etablir un lien entre la typographie et l'architecture en utilisant
des feuilles présentant le format d'une affiche.*
Medium, Materials: Quark Xpress, Photoshop

Page 64
Student: Sabine Kobel / College: Staatliche Akademie der Bildenden
Künste Dean: Prof. Lehmann / Department: Graphic Design
Department Chair: M. Kroplein / Class: Ilustration, Advertising and
Design / Instructor: Heinz Edelmann
Strategy: The theme was reflection about different manners
of seeing things.
Strategie: Das Thema waren die verschiedenen Arten, Dinge zu sehen.
Stratégie: Thème choisi: les différentes façons de considérer quelque chose.

Page 65 top left
Student: Fred Pesce / College: School of Visual Arts
Department Chair: Richard Wilde / Department: Advertising and
Graphic Design / Instructor: Skip Sorvino

Page 65 top right
Student: Sung-Hee Ham / College: School of Visual Arts
Department Chair: Richard Wilde / Department: Advertising and
Graphic Design / Instructor: Skip Sorvino

Page 65 middle left
Student: Eddie Larios / College: School of Visual Arts
Department Chair: Richard Wilde / Department: Advertising and
Graphic Design / Instructor: Skip Sorvino

Page 65 middle right
Student: David Morrow / College: School of Visual Arts
Department Chair: Richard Wilde / Department: Advertising and
Graphic Design / Instructor: Skip Sorvino

Page 65 bottom left
Student: Jeff Wainer / College: School of Visual Arts
Department Chair: Richard Wilde / Department: Advertising and
Graphic Design / Instructor: Skip Sorvino

Page 65 bottom right
Student: Kwasi Osei / College: School of Visual Arts
Department Chair: Richard Wilde / Department: Advertising and
Graphic Design / Instructor: Skip Sorvino

Pages 66, 67
Student: Rafael Soberal / College: School of Visual Arts
Department: Graphic Design / Department Chair: Richard Wilde
Instructor: Carin Goldberg
Project: The objective was to create a children's dictionary that
does not resemble a children's book.
*Projekt: Es ging um die Schaffung eines Lexikons für Kinder, das nicht
wie ein Kinderbuch aussehen sollte.*
Projet: Conception d'un dictionnaire pour enfants original.
Strategy: Russian constructivism, strong colors, and visually
captivating layouts were used to lure children into what could
have been a boring book.
*Strategie: Russischer Konstruktivismus, starke Farb-en und optisch
ansprechende Layouts wurden eingesetzt, um Kindern Lust auf etwas zu
machen, das sonst wahrscheinlich ein langweiliges Buch wäre.*
*Stratégie: Constructivisme russe, couleurs franches et layouts accrocheurs
ont été utilisés pour attirer l'attention des enfants sur un ouvrage considéré
comme ennuyeux en temps normal.*
Medium, Materials: Scanner, Power Mac 7100, printed on Cyclone

Page 68
Student: James Winagle / College: School of Visual Arts
Department: Graphic Design / Department Chair: Richard Wilde
Class: Senior Portfolio / Instructor: Chris Austopchuk
Project: Book design for book on American national parks.
Projekt: Gestaltung eines Buches über amerikanische Nationalparks.
Projet: Conception d'un livre sur les parcs nationaux américains.

Page 69
Student: Claudia Oelert / College: Academy of Fine Arts Berlin
Dean: Olaf Schwencke / Department: Graphics
Instructor: Holger Matthies
Project: Presentation of the Palucca School Dance Academy
in Dresden.
Projekt: Darstellung der Tanzakademie der Palucca-Schule in Dresden.

Projet: Présentation de l'Académie de danse de l'Ecole Palucca de Dresde.
Strategy: The intention was to show what it takes to become a
dancer, from training to performance. The three-fold book allows
the images to change in a manner simulating dance.
*Strategie: Hier ging es darum zu zeigen, was eine Tanzausbildung
beinhaltet, vom Training bis zur Aufführung. Die ausklappbaren Seiten des
Buches werden zu einer Art Bühne, so dass eine grosse Fläche entsteht
umd beim Blättern Bewegung und Rhythmus ausgedrückt werden.*
*Stratégie: Il s'agissait de montrer les diverses étapes qui mènent à une
carrière de danseur, des longues heures d'entraînement à la scène. Le livre
présente deux volets dépliants, ce qui permet de former de nouvelles
constellations d'images de sorte à simuler une danse.*

Pages 70, 71
Student: Jan Federmann / College: Bergische Universität Wuppertal
Department: Kommunikationsdesign
Instructors: Uwe Loesch, Bason Brock
Project: Concept, copy, photography and research of a book about
the relationship between two lives in 20th-century Germany.
*Projekt: Buchkonzept, Text, Photographie und Unter-suchung des
Zusammenhangs zwischen zwei Leben im Deutschland des 20.
Jahrhunderts.*
*Projet: Concept de livre, texte, photographie et recherche sur la relation
existant entre deux personnes vivant en Allemagne au 20e siècle.*
Strategy: Stories about the lives of the author and the author's uncle,
a German soldier who died in WWII, are portrayed side by side.
Both life stories meet at the point of the soldier's death.
*Strategie: Die Lebensgeschichten des Autors und seines Onkels, eines
deutschen Soldaten, der im 2. Weltkrieg fiel, werden nebeneinander
dargestellt. Die beiden Geschichten treffen sich beim Tod des Soldaten.*
*Stratégie: L'histoire de l'auteur et celle de son oncle, un soldat allemand
tombé durant la Seconde Guerre mondiale, sont présentées côte à côte.
Les deux histoires se rejoignent à la mort du soldat.*

Page 72 top
Student: Yim Cheng / College: School of Visual Arts / Department:
Advertising and Graphic Design / Department Chair: Richard Wilde
Class: Portfolio/Graphic Design / Instructor: Carin Goldberg
Project: Hemingway book-cover series.
Projekt: Eine Reihe von Hemingway-Buchumschlägen.
Projet: Série de couvertures de livre destinées aux œuvres d'Hemingway.
Strategy: Since the titles are so well known, there was no need
to place them entirely on the cover. The student chose instead to
wrap them around the books for visual interest. The colors match
the themes of the books.
*Strategie: Angesichts der Bekanntheit der Titel war es nicht notwendig,
sie vollständig auf dem Umschlag zu zeigen. Stattdessen liess der
Student sie aus optischen Gründen um den gesamten Umschlag laufen.
Die Farben sind auf die Themen der Bücher abgestimmt.*
*Stratégie: Les titres des ouvrages étant très connus, il n'était pas nécessaire
de les présenter intégralement sur la couverture. En lieu et place, l'étudiant
a préféré, pour des raisons visuelles, les faire courir tout autour du livre.
Les couleurs reprennent les thèmes de chaque ouvrage.*

Page 72 bottom
Student: Marc Stephens / College: The Creative Circus
Department: Design / Department Chair: Rob Lawton
Class: Design III (Books) / Instructor: Rob Lawton
Project: Gulliver's Travels book jacket.
Projekt: Umschlag für Gullivers Reisen.
Projet: Jaquette des Voyages de Gulliver.
Medium, Materials: Cut paper, 3D letters

Page 73
Student: Sae Won Kim / College: School of Visual Arts
Department: Graphic Design / Department Chair: Richard Wilde
Class: Portfolio / Instructor: Carin Goldberg
Project: Book-cover series.
Projekt: Eine Reihe von Buchumschlägen.
Projet: Série de couvertures de livre.

Page 74
Student: Cliff Jew / College: California College of Arts and Crafts
Dean: Michael Vanderbyl / Department: Graphic Design
Department Chair: Leslie Becker / Class: Typography III
Instructor: Martin Venezky
Project: "At the Buffalo Bill Museum" by Jane Tompkins.
The assignment was to interpret this 20-page essay in a way that
reinforces its content and meaning.
*Projekt: Die Aufgabe bestand in der Interpretation dieses zwanzigseitigen
Essays von Jane Tompkins.*
*Projet: Donner une interprétation de "At the Buffalo Bill Museum,"
un essai de 20 pages signé Jane Tompkins, qui en renforce le contenu
et la signification.*
Medium, Materials: Board, card, paper, wood

Page 75
Student: Nancy Smith / College: School of Visual Arts
Department: Graphic Design / Department Chair: Richard Wilde
Class: Portfolio / Instructor: Carin Goldberg
Photographer: Richard Bachmann
Project: Create a 20- to 30-page book using three photographers.
*Projekt: Schaffung eines 20- bis 30-seitigen Buches mit Hilfe von drei
Photographen.*
*Projet: Créer un livre de 20 à 30 pages en recourant au travail de trois
photographes.*
Strategy: The design was based on clean, classic spreads.
Strategie: Die Lösung: ein klares, klassisches Layout.
Stratégie: La solution consiste en un layout épuré et classique.

Page 76
Student: Susanne Lerha / College: School of Visual Arts
Department: Graphic Design / Department Chair: Richard Wilde
Class: Type and Design / Instructor: Carin Goldberg
Project: Illustrate the voice of an author by designing three books,
either a series or individual books.
*Projekt: Die Aufgabe bestand in der Gestaltung von drei Büchern eines
Autors, entweder als Reihe oder als einzelne Bücher.*
*Projet: Conception de trois livres d'un même auteur, en tant que série ou
livre individuel.*
Strategy: The story takes place in the time of prehistoric man. Three
symbols of significant importance were drawn with pigment and then
scanned. Although the author's name is important, it was placed on the
back so it is not missed and does not interfere with the symbolic beauty.
*Strategie: Die Handlung spielt in der Vorgeschichte. Drei Symbole von grosser
Bedeutung wurden mit Pigment gezeichnet und dann eingescannt. Obwohl
der Name des Autors wichtig ist, wurde er auf die Rückseite verbannt, um die
symbolische Schönheit der Vorderseite nicht zu stören.*
*Stratégie: L'intrigue a lieu au temps de la préhistoire. Trois symboles
d'une importance capitale ont été dessinés au pigment puis scannés.
Bien que le nom de l'auteur revête son importance, il apparaît sur le dos
de la couverture pour ne pas interférer avec la beauté symbolique du
design.*
Medium, Materials: Acetone transfers on handmade paper

Page 77
Student: Barbara Vasquez / College: School of Visual Arts
Department: Advertising and Graphic Design
Department Chair: Richard Wilde / Instructor: Gail Anderson

Page 78
Student: Jesse Wan / College: Academy of Art
Department: Graphic Design /Department Chair: Howard York
Class: Graphic Design III / Instructor: Kathryn Morgan
Photographer: Richard Jeung
Project: Sky Eyes Museum
Strategy: Create museum concept and develop a promotional
and informational brochure.
*Strategie: Die Schaffung eines Museum-Konzepts und Entwicklung einer
Broschüre, die gleichzeitig informiert und für das Museum wirbt.*
*Stratégie: Concept de musée et développement d'une brochure à la fois promo-
tionnelle et informative.*

Page 79
Student: Louise Karlssen / College: Academy of Art
Department: Graphic Design / Department Chair: Howard York
Class: Graphic Design III / Instructor: Kathryn Morgan
Photographer: Richard Jeung
Project: Book about Imogen Cunningham.
Projekt: Ein Buch über die Photographin Imogen Cunningham.
Projet: Un ouvrage consacré à la photographe Imogen Cunningham.
Strategy: The design was created to be appropriate to the photos,
classic and elegant.
*Strategie: Die Lösung bestand in einem klassischen, eleganten
Layout im Einklang mit den Photos.*
*Stratégie: La solution proposée consiste en un layout classique et élégant
en harmonie avec les photographies.*

Page 80
Student: Pei-Chun Hsu / College: Academy of Art
Department: Graphic Design / Department Chair: Howard York
Class: Graphic Design III / Instructor: Tia Stoller
Photographer: Richard Jeung
Project: Promotional materials for Paris 2000 event.
Projekt: Promotionsmaterial für die Veranstaltung Paris 2000.
Projet: Matériel promotionnel pour la manifestation Paris 2000.
Strategy: The design was meant to be unique, distinctive,
appropriate for Paris, and appealing.
*Strategie: Die Lösung bestand in einem einzigartigen, ansprechenden
Design, das ganz auf Paris ausgerichtet ist.*
Stratégie: Le design est à l'image de Paris: unique, séduisant, accrocheur.

Page 81
Student: Sung Fong / College: Academy of Art
Department: Graphic Design / Department Chair: Howard York
Class: Print II / Instructor: Russell Baker
Photographer: Richard Jeung
Project: Harley Davidson young adult clothing line.
Projekt: Eine Harley-Davidson-Kleiderlinie für junge Leute.
Projet: Ligne de vêtements Harley Davidson destinée aux jeunes.
Strategy: This design was meant to portray the clothing line as
young, yet high-quality and unique.
*Strategie: Ein Design für junge Mode, die ganz speziell und dabei von
erstklassiger Qualität ist.*
*Stratégie: Cette marque de vêtements doit donner l'impression de
s'adresser aux jeunes, d'être unique et de première qualité.*

Page 82
Student: Nicholas Angel / College: Academy of Art
Department: Graphic Design / Department Chair: Howard York
Class: Print II / Instructor: Russell Baker
Photographer: Richard Jeung
Project: Harley Davidson clothing brochure
Projekt: Broschüre für Kleidung von Harley Davidson.
Projet: Brochure pour des vêtements Harley Davidson.
Strategy: The design was meant to be contemporary, distinctive,
visually strong and appropriate for customers.
*Strategie: Ein zeitgemässes, unverwechselbares und prägnantes Design -
ausgerichtet auf die spezielle Kundschaft.*
Stratégie: Design contemporain, unique et marquant s'adressant au public cible.

Page 83
Student: Natasha Schroter / College: The Swinburne School
of Design / Dean: Helmut Lueckenhausen / Department: Graphic
Design / Department Chair, Instructor: John Bassani
Class: Graphic Design / Photographer: Isamu Sawa
Project: Door furniture products brochure.
The furniture hardware from the retailer has a jewelry-like
quality. The designer digitally enhanced the photography to
create strong visuals that demand a tactile consideration.
Simple color use and product change were considered in the
design solution.
Medium, Materials: Digital output

Page 84
Designers: Annett Göhlich, Michael Kempf / Photographer: Thomas
Hartmann / Copywriters: Olaf Leu, Jörg Osterspey,
Eberhard W. Abele / School: Fachhochschule Mainz with
Fachbereich Design and Deutsches Weininstitut
Paper: Beckett R.S.V.P., Beckett Expression / Printer: Fewa-Druck

Page 86
Student: Ines Oehlmam / College: School of Visual Arts
Department: Graphic Design / Department Chair: Richard Wilde
Instructor: Mike Kaye
Medium, Materials: Computer, Freehand

Page 87
Student: Effie Tsu / College: School of Visual Arts
Dean: David Rhodes / Department: Graphic Design
Department Chair: Richard Wilde / Instructor: Christine Heun
Project: 11 x 17 calendar.
Projekt: Kalender.
Projet: Calendrier.
Strategy Different faces and colors set the mood for each month
in this typographic calendar.
*Strategie: Verschiedene Schriften und Farben kennzeichnen die
verschiedenen Monate in diesem typographischen Kalender.*
*Stratégie: Les différents caractères et couleurs utilisés pour ce calendrier
typographique reflètent chaque mois de l'année.*
Medium, Materials: Illustrator

Pages 88, 89
Student: Marcel Teine / College: Fachhochschule Mainz
Department: Corporate Design / Class: Thesis / Instructor: Olaf Leu

Page 90
Student: Joey Fong / College: Academy of Art
Department: Graphic Design / Department Chair: Howard York
Class: Identity II / Instructor: Howard York
Photographer: Richard Jeung
Project: Union 76 Unocal identity program.
Projekt: Firmenerscheinungsbild.
Projet: Programme d'identité institutionnelle.
Strategy: Update image, create retail image for outlets,
strengthen image against competition, and create a
comprehensive system / manual.

Strategie: Auffrischung des Firmenimages und ein neuer Auftritt für die Verkaufsstellen, einschliesslich eines umfassenden Handbuchs.
Stratégie: Toilettage de l'identité de la société, de l'image des points de vente et conception d'un manuel volumineux.

Page 91
Student: Teresa Shenberger / College: School of Visual Arts
Department Chair: Richard Wilde / Department: Graphic Design
Class: Portfolio / Instructor: C. Austopchuk
Project: Company identity.
Projekt: Firmenerscheinungsbild.
Projet: Identité institutionnelle.
Strategy: The redesign for a hat shop portrays the sophistication and quality of the hats sold.
Strategie: Auffrischung des Erscheinungsbildes eines Hutladens, wobei das Thema die hervorragende Qualität der Hüte ist.
Stratégie: Rafraîchir l'image d'un magasin de chapeaux en mettant l'accent sur la qualité des articles proposés.
Medium, Materials: Illustrator, Photoshop, Quark Xpress, hat box, hat, hat pins

Pages 92, 93
Student: Oliver Wagner / College: Fachhochschule Mainz
Department: Corporate Design / Class: Thesis / Instructor: Olaf Leu

Page 94
Student: Roger Siu / College: Academy of Art
Department: Graphic Design / Department Chair, Instructor: Howard York / Class: Corporate Systems
Photographer: Richard Jeung
Project: DHL identity program.
Projekt: C.I.-Programm für DHL.
Projet: Programme d'identité institutionnelle pour DHL.
Strategy: Create a stronger graphic identity with greater impact and recognition while updating the old image.
Strategie: Auffrischung des alten Images und Schaffung eines stärkeren, eindrucksvolleren graphischen Auftritts.
Stratégie: Création d'une identité graphique plus marquante.

Page 95
Student: Stephanie Fernandez / College: Academy of Art
Department: Graphic Design / Department Chair and Instructor: Howard York / Class: Corporate Systems
Photographer: Richard Jeung
Project: Wahaka identity program.
Projekt: Erscheinungsbild für Wahaka.
Projet: Programme d'identité visuelle pour Wahaka.
Strategy: Update and modernize; emphasize higher-quality and less trendy position as unique against competition.
Strategie: Auffrischung des Erscheinungsbildes, wobei das Schwer-gewicht auf Qualität statt wie zuvor auf 'modisch' liegt.
Stratégie: Création d'une nouvelle image graphique axée désormais sur la qualité plutôt que le côté «tendance».

Pages 96, 97
Student: Group Project / College: Fachhochschule Mainz
Department: Corporate Design / Class: Graduate
Instructor: Olaf Leu
Project: Trademark and application for an insurance company.
Projekt: Markenzeichen und dessen Anwendung für eine Versicherungsgesellschaft.
Projet: Création et application d'une marque de fabrique pour une compagnie d'assurances.

Page 98 top
Student: Nancy Smith / College: School of Visual Arts
Department: Graphic Design / Department Chair: Richard Wilde
Class: Portfolio / Instructor: Carin Goldberg
Photographer: Richard Bachmann
Project: Design a hangtag, catalog, shopping bag, and shipping carton for a company of choice.
Projekt: Entwurf eines Anhänge-Etiketts, eines Katalogs, einer Tragtasche und eines Versandkartons für eine beliebige Firma.
Projet: Design d'une étiquette, d'un catalogue, d'un sac et d'un carton pour une société à choix.
Strategy: Using the Vermont Teddy Bear Company, the student played off the fact that Teddy Roosevelt originated the teddy bear name and used fur to make Roosevelt's seriousness more humorous.
Strategie: Gewählt wurde ein Hersteller von Teddy-Bären. Die Tatsache, dass die Bezeichnung Teddy-Bär auf Teddy Roosevelt zurückgeht, lieferte die Idee, wobei das Fell für eine humorvolle Note sorgt.
Stratégie: L'étudiant a porté son choix sur un fabricant d'ours en peluche. Le fait que le terme «teddy bear» remonte à Teddy Roosevelt a fourni l'idée de base. La fourrure devait conférer une touche humoristique au personnage historique.
Medium, Materials: Fur, metal, paper

Page 98 bottom
Student: Mark Wong / College: Academy of Art
Department: Graphic Design / Department Chair: Howard York
Class: Identity II / Photographer: Richard Jeung
Project: Identity for Sonoma Mission Inn.
Projekt: Erscheinungsbild für das Sonoma-Missions-Hospiz.
Projet: Identité visuelle pour l'hospice de la mission Sonoma.
Strategy: Strengthen unique history, upgrade high-end appeal.
Strategie: Betonung der einzigartigen Geschichte und des gehobenen Niveaus.
Stratégie: L'accent est mis sur l'histoire unique de la mission et son niveau élevé.

Page 99
Student: Gertrud Nolte / College: Bergische Universität Wuppertal
Department: Kommunikations-design
Department Chairs: Uwe Loesch, Bazon Brock
Project: Campaign and corporate design for the exhibition and public presentation of the works of the communication design department at the Universität Wuppertal.
Projekt: Kampagne und C.I. Design für die öffentliche Ausstellung der Arbeiten des Studienganges Kommunikationsdesign der Univers-ität Wuppertal.
Projet: Campagne et identité institutionnelle réalisées pour une exposition publique des travaux des étudiants en design de communication de l'Université de Wuppertal.
Medium, Materials: Campaign in different media: posters, invitation card, Web page.

Page 100
Student: Julie Baron / College: School of Visual Arts
Department: Advertising and Graphic Design
Department Chair: Richard Wilde / Instructor: Henrietta Condak

Page 101
Student: Lisa Vega / College: School of Visual Arts
Department: Graphic Design / Department Chair: Richard Wilde
Class: Communication Graphic Design
Instructor: Henrietta Condak
Project: New design for U.S. currency
Strategy: The currency uses American writers on the front and where they lived on the reverse.
Strategie: Auf der Vorderseite sind amerikanische Autoren porträtiert, auf der Rückseite ihre Wohnorte.
Stratégie: Le recto présente des auteurs américains et le verso, l'endroit où ils ont vécu.
Medium, Materials: Pastels

Page 102 top
Student: Hye Won Chang / College: School of Visual Arts
Department Chair: Richard Wilde / Department: Graphic Design
Class: Senior Portfolio / Instructor: Carin Goldberg
Project: Redesign of The New York Times.
Projekt: Neugestaltung der New York Times.
Projet: Nouveau graphisme du New York Times.
Medium, Materials: Quark Xpress

Page 102 middle
Student: Kai Leong Chu / College: School of Visual Arts
Department: Graphic Design / Department Chair: Richard Wilde
Instructor: Carin Goldberg
Project: Redesign of the home and sport sections of The New York Times
Projekt: Neugestaltung des Sportsektors der New York Times.
Projet: Nouveau graphisme de la rubrique «Sports» du New York Times.
Strategy: Different scales were used to create contrast, tone, and balance.
Strategie: Verschiedene Bildgrössen sorgen für Kontraste, Farbe und Ausgewogenheit.
Stratégie: Les différents formats des images ont été utilisés à la fois pour créer un effet de contraste et d'équilibre.

Page 102 bottom
Student: Yim Cheng / College: School of Visual Arts
Department: Advertising and Graphic Design / Department Chair: Richard Wilde Class: Portfolio Graphic Design
Instructor: Carin Goldberg
Project: Using different typography, give a new look to the The New York Times.
Projekt: Ein neues Gesicht für die New York Times, mit Hilfe von verschiedenen Schriften.
Projet: Le New York Times sous un nouveau jour grâce à l'utilisation de différentes polices de caractères.

Page 103
Student: Kai Leong Chu / College: School of Visual Arts
Department: Graphic Design / Department Chair: Richard Wilde
Instructor: Carin Goldberg

Project: Redesign the living section of The New York Times.
Projekt: Neugestaltung der Rubrik «Leben» in der New York Times.
Nouvelle mise en pages de la rubrique «Vivre» du New York Times.

Pages 104, 105
Student: Zhao Wen Li / College: School of Visual Arts
Department: Graphic Design / Department Chair: Richard Wilde
Class: Senior Portfolio / Instructor: Carin Goldberg
Project: For a book/magazine entitled Picture, feature the work of three known photographers and show a layout that will work for three covers.
Projekt: Gestaltung einer Broschüre/Zeitschrift mit dem Titel Picture, in der die Arbeiten von drei bekannten Photographen vorgestellt werden. Ausserdem ein Layout, das sich für drei Umschläge eignen würde.
Projet: Conception d'un livre ou d'un magazine intitulé Picture dans lequel sont présentés les travaux de trois photographes célèbres et création d'un layout adapté aux trois couvertures.
Medium, Materials: Digital output

Pages 106, 107
Student: Hye Won Chang / College: School of Visual Arts
Department Chair: Richard Wilde / Department: Graphic Design
Class: Senior Portfolio / Instructor: Carin Goldberg
Project: For a book/magazine entitled Picture, feature the work of three known photographers and show a layout that will work for three covers.
Projekt: Gestaltung einer Broschüre/Zeitschrift mit dem Titel Picture, in der die Arbeiten von drei bekannten Photographen vorgestellt werden. Ausserdem ein Layout, das sich für drei Umschläge eignen würde.
Projet: Conception d'un livre ou d'un magazine intitulé Picture dans lequel sont présentés les travaux de trois photographes célèbres et création d'un layout adapté aux trois couvertures.
Medium, Materials: Photoshop Quark XPress

Page 108
Students: Jason Campbell, Leigh Jenner / College: Monash University
Dean: John Redmond / Department: Graphic Design
Department Chair: Jenny Allen / Class: Graphic Design
Instructors: Russell Kennedy, Neil Barnett
Cover Design: Russell Simm / Editor: Anne Sinatore
Photographer: Verushka
Project: Sin magazine, a theme-based quarterly exploring psychology, pop culture and fashion.
Projekt: Eine vierteljährlich erscheinende Zeitschrift, die sich mit Psychologie, der Pop-Kultur und Mode befasst.
Projet: Conception d'un magazine trimestriel consacré à la psychologie, à la culture pop et à la mode.
Medium, Materials: Power Mac, Quark XPress, Illustrator, Photoshop, photocopier, scanner

Page 109 top
Student: Julia Michry / College: School of Visual Arts
Department: Graphic Design / Department Chair: Richard Wilde
Class: Portfolio / Instructor: Carin Goldberg
Project: Design a photography magazine entitled Picture including cover, logo, table of contents, an about-this-issue page and three articles about three photographers.
Projekt: Gestaltung des Photo-Magazins Picture: Umschlag, Logo, Inhaltsverzeichnis, Editorial-Seite und drei Artikel über drei Photographen.
Projet: Conception du magazine Picture, consacré à la photographie: couverture, logo, sommaire, page de l'éditorial et trois articles sur des photographes.
Strategy: The student brought elements of photography to the design through the use of lines like those on the edge of film and color from color charts.
Strategie: Elemente der Photographie – Ränder von Filmstreifen und Farbskalas – wurden ins Design integriert.
Stratégie: L'étudiante a intégré des éléments propres à la photographie: les bords d'une pellicule de film et des échelles de couleurs.

Page 109 middle
Student: Mary Belibasakis / College: School of Visual Arts
Dean: David Rhodes / Department: Graphic Design
Department Chair: Richard Wilde / Class: Portfolio
Instructor: Carin Goldberg
Project: Feature from Picture magazine displaying the work of a photographer of the student's choice.
Projekt: Gestaltung eines Beitrags aus dem Photomagazin Picture über einen beliebigen Photographen.
Projet: Layout d'un article sur un photographe à choix pour le magazine Picture.

Page 109 bottom
Student: Christine Cucuzza / College: School of Visual Arts
Dean: David Rhodes / Department: Graphic Design
Department Chair: Richard Wilde / Class: Portfolio 97
Instructor: Carin Goldberg / Photographer: Alexander Rodchenko

Project: Picture magazine displaying the work of three photographers.
Projekt: Gestaltung des Photomagazins Picture, in dem die Arbeiten von drei Photographen vorgestellt werden.
Projet: Conception du magazine Picture présentant les travaux de trois photographes.
Strategy: The student focused on the period in which the images were created.
Strategie: Die Studentin befasste sich mit der Zeit, in der die Bilder gemacht wurden.
Stratégie: L'étudiante s'est intéressée à la période durant laquelle les photographies ont été prises.

Page 110
Student: Julia Michry / College: School of Visual Arts
Department: Graphic Design / Department Chair: Richard Wilde
Class: Portfolio / Instructor: Carin Goldberg
Project: Design a photography magazine entitled Picture including cover, logo, table of contents, an about-this-issue page, and three articles about three photographers.
Projekt: Gestaltung eines Photo-Magazins, Picture: Umschlag, Logo, Inhaltsverzeichnis, Editorial-Seite und drei Artikel über drei Photographen.
Projet: Conception du magazine Picture, consacré à la photographie: couverture, logo, sommaire, page de l'éditorial et trois articles sur des photographes.
Strategy: The student brought elements of photography to the design through the use of lines like those on the edge of film and color from color charts.
Strategie: Elemente der Photographie – Ränder von Filmstreifen und Farbskalas – wurden als Linien und Farben im Design aufgenommen.
Stratégie: L'étudiante a intégré des éléments propres à la photographie: les bords d'une pellicule de film et des échelles de couleurs.
Medium, Materials: Computer

Page 111
Student: Paul Gobble / College: Pennsylvania State University
Dean: Neil Porterfield / Department: Graphic Design
Department Chair: Jim Stephenson / Class: Magazine Design
Instructor, Art Director: Lanny Sommese
Medium/Materials: Black-and-white photography, pen and ink, watercolor.

Page 112
Student: Dave Gath / College: California State University Long Beach Dean: Wade Hobgood / Department: Graphic Design
Department Chair: Jay Kvopil / Class: Senior Year
Instructor: Jim Van Eimeren / Photography: Dave Gath
Project: Insect photo essay. Students were asked to create a layout featuring their own photography.
Projekt: Photo-Essay über Insekten. Die Studenten sollten die Seiten für ihre Photos selbst gestalten.
Projet: Essai photographique sur les insectes. Les étudiants ont dû créer un layout intégrant leurs photographies.
Strategy: The unclean edges and background were meant to give that "dirty feeling most people get when thinking of insects."
Strategie: Die unsauberen Kanten und der Hintergrund sollen das «Gefühl von Schmutz» ausdrücken, das der Gedanke an Insekten bei den meisten Leuten hervorruft.
Stratégie: Les bords «bâclés» et le fond devaient refléter l'impression qu'éprouvent la plupart des gens à la vue d'un insecte, à savoir le dégoût.

Page 113
Student: Juan Cabrero (design, photography, illustration)
College: Pennsylvania State University / Dean: Neil Porterfield
Department: Graphic Design / Department Chair: Jim Stephenson
Class: Senior Problem/Magazine Design
Instructor and Art Director: Lanny Sommese
Project: Write a proposal for a hypothetical magazine which outlines the editorial policy, intended audience and relevant functional parameters for the proposed periodical. Design a magazine that replies to the criteria outlined in the written proposal.
Projekt: Schriftliche Formulierung eines Vorschlags für ein hypothetisches Magazin. Er musste das redaktionelle Konzept, das Zielpublikum und den Anspruch der Zeitschrift beinhalten.
Projet: Rédiger une proposition pour un magazine en présentant le concept rédactionnel, le public cible et les paramètres fonctionnels.
Strategy: Pandemonium was designed to target a young audience that enjoys an "alternative" lifestyle. The magazine's oversized format (10.5" x 16.5") mirrors its audience's need to stand out and be different. Its name implies chaos and disorder.
Strategie: Pandemonium richtet sich an eine junge Leserschaft mit einem 'alternativen' Lebensstil. Das Überformat (ca. 25x35cm) der Zeitschrift entspricht dem Wunsch seiner Leserschaft, sich abzuheben, anders zu sein. Der Name impliziert Chaos und Unordnung.
Stratégie: Le magazine Pandemonium s'adresse à un lectorat jeune au style de vie non conventionnel. Son format surdimensionné (env. 25x35cm) reflète les aspirations du public cible: être différent, se distinguer de la masse. Le titre du magazine évoque la corruption et le désordre.

Page 114 top
Student: Eric Shutte / College: School of Visual Arts
Department: Advertising and Graphic Design
Department Chair: Richard Wilde / Instructor: Henrietta Condak

Page 114 middle
Student: Julie Baron / College: School of Visual Arts
Department: Advertising and Graphic Design
Department Chair: Richard Wilde / Instructor: Henrietta Condak

Page 114 bottom
Student: L. Rodrigues / College: School of Visual Arts
Department: Advertising and Graphic Design
Department Chair: Richard Wilde / Instructor: Henrietta Condak

Page 115
Student: James Joseph Potsch / College: Illinois State University
Dean: Alan Godfarb / Department: Art / Department Chair:
John Walker / Class: Graphic Design IV / Instructor: Pam Tannura
Photographers: Brian Sapp, John Susmaras
Project: Produce a minimum of four informative panels and an
enclosure for them.
*Projekt: Es ging um die Herstellung von mindestens 4 Informationstafeln
einschliesslich einer Verpackung.*
Projet: Réalisation de quatre panneaux informatifs et de leur emballage.
Strategy: The student chose a compass for the top of the
enclosure. The "package" holds four panels in connected envelopes
so that it opens in a north, south, east and west pattern to reveal
a compass in the middle. The type is laid out in a complex fashion,
symbolizing the ability of the compass to help one find one's way.
*Strategie: Der Student setzte einen Kompass oben auf die Verpackung.
Darin enthalten sind vier Tafeln in Umschlägen, die mit einander
verbunden sind und beim Öffnen in alle vier Himmelsrichtungen zeigen,
wobei in der Mitte der Kompass freigelegt wird. Die typographische
Gestaltung ist sehr komplex – ein Hinweis auf die Fähigkeit des
Kompasses, den Weg zu weisen.*
*Stratégie: L'étudiant a placé un compas sur le dessus de l'«emballage»,
qui contient les quatre panneaux placés dans des enveloppes reliées entre elles.
Ces dernières, une fois décachetées, pointent respectivement vers le nord,
le sud, l'est et l'ouest et présentent un compas en leur milieu.
La typographie se distingue par sa complexité, et le compas sert en
quelque sorte à retrouver son chemin.*
Medium, Materials: Canson paper, corrugated cardboard, packing
material, vellum, cyclone prints.

Page 116 top
Student: Jennifer Crute / College: School of Visual Arts
Department: Illustration and Cartooning
Department Chair: Jack Endewelt / Instructor: S. Martine
Project: Motion in picture.
Projekt: Bewegung im Bild.
Projet: Le mouvement par l'image.

Page 116 middle
Student: Shawn Fields / College: School of Visual Arts
Department: Illustration and Cartooning
Department Chair: Jack Endewelt / Instructor: Ginsburg
Project: Motion in picture.
Projekt: Bewegung im Bild.
Projet: Le mouvement par l'image.

Page 116 bottom
Student: Renata Lauterback / College: School of Visual Arts
Department: Illustration and Cartooning
Department Chair: Jack Endewelt

Page 117 top
Student: James Mandella / College: School of Visual Arts
Department: Illustration and Cartooning / Department Chair:
Jack Endewelt / Instructor: T. Woodruff
Project: Motion in picture.
Projekt: Bewegung im Bild.
Projet: Le mouvement par l'image.

Page 117 middle
Student: Lisa Neigenfind / College: ABK Stuttgart
Dean: Prof. Lehmann / Department: Graphic Design
Department Chair: Manfred Kröplien
Instructor: Manfred Kröplien
Project: Illustration for an article about the past and the future
of humanity.
*Projekt: Illustration für einen Artikel über Geschichte und Zukunft
der Menschheit.*
*Projet: Illustration pour un article consacré à l'histoire et à l'avenir de
l'Humanité.*
Medium, Materials: Gouache on paper.

Page 117 bottom
Student: Peter Franco / College: School of Visual Arts
Department: Illustration and Cartooning
Department Chair: Jack Endewelt / Instructor: S. Martine
Project: Motion in picture.
Projekt: Bewegung im Bild.
Projet: Le mouvement par l'image.

Page 118
Student: Masahito Tanaka / College: School of Visual Arts
Department: Illustration and Cartooning
Department Chair: Jack Endewelt

Page 119
Student: Chris Torres / College: School of Visual Arts
Department: Illustration and Cartooning
Department Chair: Jack Endewelt / Instructor: S. Martucci
Project: Motion in picture.
Projekt: Bewegung im Bild.
Projet: Le mouvement par l'image.

Page 120 top
Student: Brian Donnelly / College: School of Visual Arts
Department: Illustration and Cartooning
Department Chair: Jack Endewelt

Page 120 middle
Student: John Urso / College: School of Visual Arts
Department: Illustration and Cartooning
Department Chair: Jack Endewelt / Instructor: Teresa Fasolino
Project: To express motion in picture.
Projekt: Bewegung im Bild.
Projet: Le mouvement par l'image.

Page 120 bottom
Student: Vincent Ficarra / College: School of Visual Arts
Department: Illustration and Cartooning
Department Chair: Jack Endewelt

Page 121
Student: Edward Morges / College: School of Visual Arts
Department: Illustration and Cartooning
Department Chair: Jack Endewelt / Instructor: A. Torres
Project: Motion in picture.
Projekt: Bewegung im Bild.
Projet: Le mouvement par l'image.

Page 122
Student: Beth Cloutier / College: School of Visual Arts
Department: Illustration and Cartooning
Department Chair: Jack Endewelt / Instructor: Teresa Fasolino
Project: To express motion in picture.
Projekt: Bewegung im Bild.
Projet: Le mouvement par l'image.

Page 123
Student: Brandon Cronk / College: Iowa State University
Dean: M. Engelbrecht / Department: Art and Design
Department Chair: Nancy Polster / Class: Corporate Identity
Instructor: John Gruber
Project: The new Betty Crocker.
*Projekt: Eine neue Ausgabe des Betty-Crocker-Kochbuchs, das in den
USA sehr populär ist.*
*Projet: Une nouvelle édition du Betty Crocker, un livre de cuisine très
populaire aux Etats-Unis.*
Strategy: This assignment began as a collage, was digitally
manipulated, and tested at various sizes.
*Strategie: Das Projekt begann als Collage, die digital bearbeitet und in
verschiedenen Grössen ausprobiert wurde.*
*Stratégie: Au début, le projet se présentait sous la forme d'un collage qui a
été retravaillé numériquement par la suite dans divers formats.*
Medium, Materials: Collage, Photoshop

Page 124
Student: Tara Cheesman / College: School of Visual Arts
Department: Illustration and Cartooning
Department Chair: Jack Endewelt

Page 125
Student: José Manuel Saraiva / College: Faculdade de Belas Artes da
Universidade do Porto / Department: Graphic Design
Instructor: Jorge Afonso
Project: To produce personal and original work for a text.
Projekt: Eine persönliche, originelle Arbeit für einen Text.
Projet: Assortir un texte d'une image personnelle originale.
Strategy: The first illustration was based on Milan Kundera's

The Unbearable Lightness of Being. The second portrays the similarities between creatures described by Kafka and people who choose to isolate themselves from society. The last illustration is an allegory based on Hemingway's The Sun Also Rises, in which the main character looks to the things he likes most in life.
Strategie: Die Illustration basiert auf Milan Kunderas Die unerträgliche Leichtigkeit des Seins.
Stratégie: L'illustration se réfère au roman de Milan Kundera, L'Insoutenable Légèreté de l'être.
Medium, Materials: Watercolors, colored pencil, collage, gouache.

Page 126 left
Student: Richard Chonezynski / College: School of Visual Arts
Department: Illustration and Cartooning
Department Chair: Jack Endewelt

Page 126 right
Student: Kevin Schneider / College: School of Visual Arts
Department: Illustration and Cartooning
Department Chair: Jack Endewelt / Instructor: T. Woodruff

Page 127
Student: Chris Murphy / College: School of Visual Arts
Department: Illustration and Cartooning
Department Chair: Jack Endewelt / Instructor: A. Torres
Project: To express motion in picture
Projekt: Ausdruck von Bewegung im Bild.
Projet: Exprimer le mouvement par l'image.

Page 128
Student: Tim Fisher / College: Bowling Green State University
Department: Design Division / Department Chair, Instructor:
Ron Jacomini / Class: Corporate Identity
Project: Letterhead business system.
Projekt: Briefpapier für ein Unternehmen.
Projet: Papier à lettres à en-têtes pour une entreprise.
Strategy: A new logo was incorporated into a business system for Sony Corporation.
Strategie: Ein neues Logo wird in das Briefpapier der Sony Corporation integriert.
Stratégie: Un nouveau logo a été intégré au papier à lettres de Sony Corporation.
Medium, Materials: Power Mac, Freehand, Photoshop

Page 129 Student: Jin Chun / College: Academy of Art
Department: Graphic Design / Department Chair: Howard York
Class: Identity II / Instructor: Howard York
Photographer: Richard Jeung
Project: Shogun Japanese restaurant identity.
Projekt: Erscheinungsbild für das japanische Restaurant Shogun.
Projet: Identité visuelle du restaurant japonais Shogun.
Strategy: The identity needed to portray a strong Japanese image, be appetizing, appealing, impactful and unified.
Strategie: Ein starker, typisch japanischer Auftritt, der appetitlich, ansprechend, eindrucksvoll und homogen wirkt.
Stratégie: Créer une image japonaise forte, séduisante, homogène et «appétissante».

Page 130 top
Student: Wesley Cortes / College: Oregon State University
Dean: Kay Schaffer / Department: Art / Department Chair: David Hardesty / Class: Graphic Design 3 / Instructor: David Hardesty
Project: Letterhead system.
Projekt: Briefschaften.
Projet: Papier à lettres à en-têtes.
Strategy: This identity defines the essence and formal qualities appropriate to the organization.
Strategie: Dieses Erscheinungsbild reflektiert das Wesen und die formalen Eigenschaften der Organisation.
Stratégie: Cette identité reflète l'essence et les qualités formelles de l'organisation.

Page 130 middle
Student: Aaron Lee / College: Oregon State University
Dean: Kay Schaffer / Department: Art / Department Chair,
Instructor: David Hardesty / Class: Graphic Design III
Project: Letterhead system.
Projekt: Briefpapier.
Projet: Papier à lettres à en-têtes
Strategy: This identity defines the essence and formal qualities appropriate to the organization.
Strategie: Dieses Erscheinungsbild reflektiert das Wesen und die formalen Eigenschaften der Organisation.
Stratégie: Cette identité reflète l'essence et les qualités formelles de l'organisation.
Medium, Materials: Computer output

Page 130 bottom
Student: Duane Cordwell / College: Oregon State University

Dean: Kay Schaffer / Department: Art / Department Chair,
Instructor: David Hardesty / Class: Graphic Design III
Project: Letterhead system.
Projekt: Briefschaften.
Projet: Papier à lettres à en-têtes.
Strategy: This identity defines the essence and formal qualities appropriate to the organization.
Strategie: Dieses Erschein-ungsbild reflektiert das Wesen und die formalen Eigenschaften der Organisation.
Stratégie: Cette identité reflète l'essence et les qualités formelles de l'organisation.

Page 131 top
Student: Jason D. Guinn / College: Oregon State University
Dean: Kay Schaffer / Department: Art / Department Chair,
Instructor: David Hardesty / Class: Graphic Design III
Project: Letterhead system.
Projekt: Briefschaften.
Projet: Papier à lettres à en-têtes.
Strategy: This identity defines the essence and formal qualities appropriate to the organization.
Strategie: Dieses Erscheinungsbild reflektiert das Wesen und die formalen Eigenschaften der Organisation.
Stratégie: Cette identité reflète l'essence et les qualités formelles de l'organisation.

Page 131 middle
Student: Natalie Becher / College: Oregon State University
Dean: Kay Schaffer / Department: Art / Department Chair,
Instructor: David Hardesty / Class: Graphic Design III
Project: Letterhead system.
Projekt: Briefschaften.
Projet: Papier à lettres à en-têtes.
Strategy: This identity defines the essence and formal qualities appropriate to the organization.
Strategie: Dieser Auftritt reflektiert das Wesen und die formalen Eigenschaften der Organisation.
Stratégie: Cette identité reflète l'essence et les qualités formelles de l'organisation.

Page 131 bottom
Student: Ashley Carlson / College: Oregon State University
Dean: Kay Schaffer / Department: Art / Department Chair,
Instructor: David Hardesty / Class: Graphic Design III
Project: Letterhead system.
Projekt: Briefschaften.
Projet: Papier à lettres à en-têtes.
Strategy: This identity defines the essence and formal qualities appropriate to the organization.
Strategie: Dieser Auftritt reflektiert das Wesen und die formalen Eigenschaften der Organisation.
Stratégie: Cette identité reflète l'essence et les qualités formelles de l'organisation.

Page 132
Student: Trina H. Sultan / College: School of Visual Arts
Department: Graphic Design / Department Chair: Richard Wilde
Class: Portfolio / Instructor: Paula Scher
Project: Design a graphics campaign for Knoll Designs, using its existing logo but altering it.
Projekt: Entwurf einer graphischen Kampagne für Knoll-Möbel, wobei das vorhandene Logo in veränderter Form eingesetzt werden sollte.
Projet: Créer une campagne graphique pour les meubles Knoll en intégrant le logo modifié de la société.
Strategy The furniture was integrated into the logo.
Strategie: Die Möbel wurden in das Logo integriert.
Stratégie: Les meubles ont été intégrés au logo.
Medium, Materials: Photos, Photoshop, Quark Xpress

Page 133
Student: Christine Cucuzza / College: School of Visual Arts
Dean: David Rhodes / Department: Graphic Design
Department Chair: Richard Wilde / Class: Portfolio 97
Instructor: Carin Goldberg
Project: Minskoff theater stationery.
Projekt: Briefpapier für ein Theater.
Projet: Papier à lettres pour le théâtre Minskoff.
Strategy: The format of an old ticket was used for the logo and then reconstructed for the stationery.
Strategie: Das Logo, das auch die Basis des Briefpapiers ist, ähnelt einer alten Eintrittskarte.
Stratégie: Le logo présente le format d'un ancien billet d'entrée, qui a été retravaillé par la suite pour figurer sur le papier à lettres.

Page 134 top
Student Matthew Staab / College: The Creative Circus
Department: Design / Department Chair, Instructor:
Rob Lawton / Class: Logos and Logotypes
Project: Logo for Ellis Construction, Inc.
Projekt: Logo für die Baufirma Ellis Construction.

Projet: Logo pour l'entreprise de construction Ellis Construction.
Strategy: The strategy was to create an identifiable image for a construction company that incorporates the first letter of its name.
Strategie: Ein aussagekräftiges Symbol für eine Baufirma, in das der erste Buchstabe des Namens integriert ist.
Stratégie: Symbole accrocheur pour une entreprise de construction, qui intègre la première lettre du nom.

Page 134 second from top
Student: Slade Scaholm / College: Southwest Texas StateI University
Dean: Richard Cheatham / Department: Art
Department Chair: Brian Row / Class: Corporate Identity
Instructor: Roger Christian
Project: Texas Culinary Institute logo.
Projekt: Logo für das Texas Culinary Institute.
Projet: Logo pour le Texas Culinary Institute.

Page 134 middle
Student: Regina Krutoy / College: School of Visual Arts
Dean: David Rhodes / Department: Graphic Design
Department Chair: Richard Wilde / Class: Portfolio
Instructor: Paula Scher
Project: Redesign logotype for champion sports.
Projekt: Überarbeitung des Logos von Champion Sports.
Projet: Nouveau logo pour Champion Sports.
Strategy: Geometric shapes are used to create the letter "C" representing the departments of the retail store. The type was set in folio oblique with kerning of 20, to represent motion and action.
Strategie: Geometrische Formen wurden eingesetzt, um den Buchstaben «C» zu bilden. Sie stehen für die verschiedenen Abteilungen des Einzelhandelgeschäftes. Die Schrift Folio Oblique wurde unterschnitten, um Bewegung und Aktion auszudrücken.
Stratégie: Des formes géométriques ont été utilisées pour créer la lettre «C». Elles représentent les différents rayons de ce magasin de détail. Le caractère Folio Oblique a été choisi pour transmettre une impression de mouvement et d'action.
Medium, Materials: Adobe Illustrator

Page 134 second from bottom
Student: Chad Huff / College: Southwest Texas State University
Dean: Richard Cheatham / Department: Art Department
Department Chair: Brian Row / Class: Corporate Identity
Instructor: Roger Christian
Project: Wimberley Painting Company.

Page 134 bottom
Student: Chris Slivinsky / College: The Creative Circus
Department: Design / Department Chair, Instructor:
Rob Lawton / Class: Logos and Logotypes
Project: Industrial logo for United Parking.
Projekt: Logo für United Parking.
Projet: Logo pour United Parking.
Strategy: The "U" was used to represent the parking lot.
Strategie: Das «U» wurde als Symbol für einen Parkplatz eingesetzt.
Stratégie: Le «U» sert de symbole pour un parking.
Medium, Materials: Hand-rendered, stat

Page 135
Student: Tim Fisher / College: Bowling Green State University
Department: Design Division / Department Chair, Instructor:
Ron Jacomini / Class: Corporate Identity
Project: Logomark for Sony.
Projekt: Logo für Sony.
Projet: Logo Sony.
Medium, Materials: Power Mac, Photoshop, Illustrator

Page 136 top
Student: Isabel Wischermann / College: Universität Essen
Dean: Dr. Rohe / Department: Kommunikations Design
Instructor: Volker Küster
Project: Logo for a restaurant. The student could decide on the type of restaurant.
Projekt: Logo für ein Restaurant. Die Art war frei wählbar.
Projet: Logo pour un restaurant à choix.
Strategy: A Japanese restaurant, symbolised by a combination of Japanese chopsticks and bowls with the Japanese flag.
Strategie: Japanisches Restaurant: Kombination von japanischen Ess-stäbchen und Schälchen mit der japanischen Flagge.
Stratégie: Le choix de l'étudiante s'est porté sur un restaurant japonais, symbolisé par les baguettes et les bols présentant le drapeau japonais.

Page 136 second from top
Student: Carrie Ferguson / College: Western Washington University
Dean: Bertil Van Boer / Department: Art / Department Chair: Elsi Vassdal-Ellis / Class: 3D Graphic Design / Instructor: Kent Smith
Project: 3D signage translation of 2D logo.
Projekt: Übersetzung eines Logos in eine dreidimensionale Form.

Projet: Transposition tridimensionnelle d'un logo.
Strategy: The 3D signage emphasizes the richness and subtleties of the coffee/dessert business. Calligraphy underlines the shop's individuality.
Strategie: Die Schilder unterstreichen die Reichhaltigkeit und Feinheit des Kaffee/Dessert-Angebots. Der Einsatz von Kalligraphie unterstreicht die persönliche Atmosphäre.
Stratégie: La signalétique met l'accent sur la richesse et le raffinement du café et des desserts proposés dans l'assortiment. L'emploi de la calligraphie souligne l'atmosphère personnelle.

Page 136 middle
Student: Group Project / College: Fachhochschule Mainz
Department: Corporate Design / Class: Graduate
Instructor: Olaf Leu
Project: Trademark and applications for an insurance company.
Projekt: Entwicklung eines Logos und dessen Anwendung für eine Projet: Versicherungs-gesellschaft.
Projet: Développement d'un logo et de ses applications pour une compagnie d'assurances.

Page 136 second from bottom
Student: Olga Mezhibovskaya / College: School of Visual Arts
Dean: David Rhodes / Department: Graphic Design
Department Chair: Richard Wilde / Class: Portfolio
Instructor: Carin Goldberg
Project: Logo for an existing play at one of the New York theaters.
Projekt: Logo für ein Stück, das von einem New Yorker Theater aufgeführt wird.
Projet: Logo pour une pièce de théâtre jouée à New York.
Strategy: In working with the scale and repetition of the letterforms and with the negative/positive effect in the logo, the student wished to express the experimental character of La Mama Theatre.
Strategie: Durch das Spiel mit den Grössen und Wiederholungen der Buch-stabenformen und den Negativ-Positiv-Effekt des Logos soll der experimentelle Charakter des La Mama Theatre zum Ausdruck kommen.
Stratégie: Les différents corps de caractère, leur répétition et l'effet positif/négatif du logo reflètent le caractère expérimental du théâtre La Mama.
Medium, Materials: Paper, computer output

Page 136 bottom
Student: Group Project / College: Fachhochschule Mainz
Department: Corporate / Design Class: Graduate
Instructor: Olaf Leu
Project: Trademark and applications for an insurance company.
Projet: Entwicklung eines Logos und dessen Anwendung für eine Versicherungsgesell-schaft.
Projet: Développement d'un logo et de ses applications pour une compagnie d'assurances.

Page 137 top
Student: Chris Slivinsky / College: The Creative Circus
Department: Design / Department Chair, Instructor: Rob Lawton
Class: Logos and Logotypes
Project: Logo for Zucco Highway Contractors, a construction company.
Projekt: Logo für Zucco Highway Contractors, eine Baufirma.
Projet: Logo pour Zucco Highway Contractors, une entreprise de construction.
Strategy: The logo is designed as the hazard symbol, incorporating the letter "Z."
Strategie: Die Basis des Logos ist das Symbol für Gefahr, unter Einbezug des Buchstaben «Z».
Stratégie: Le logo reprend le symbole du danger en intégrant la lettre «Z».
Medium, Materials: Hand-rendered, Mac

Page 137 second from top
Student: Sharon Slaughter / College: Portfolio Center
Department: Design / Department Chair: Hank Richardson
Class: Logo Design / Instructor: Ted Fabella
Project: Logo for Hashiguchi Sushi.
Projekt: Logo für Hashiguchi Sushi.
Projet: Logo pour Hashiguchi Sushi.

Page 137 middle and second from bottom
Student: Group Project / College: Fachhochschule Mainz
Department: Corporate Design / Class: Graduate / Instructor: Olaf Leu
Project: Trademark and applications for an insurance company.
Projekt: Entwicklung eines Logos und dessen Anwendung für eine Versicherungsgesellschaft.
Projet: Développement d'un logo et de ses applications pour une compagnie d'assurances.

Page 137 bottom
Students: Pekka Piippo, Valtteri Bade / College: University of Art and Design Helsinki / Dean: Yrjö Sotamaa / Department: Graphic Design / Department Chair: Tapani Aartomaa
Instructor: Kari Piippo

Project: Logo for Finland's 80-year anniversary
Projekt: Logo für die 80-Jahresfeier Finnlands.
Projet: Logo commémorant les 80 ans de la Finlande.
Strategy: The logo reflects Finland's seasons, lakes, forests, fields, and urban areas.
Strategie: Ein Logo, das die Jahreszeiten in Finnland, seine Seen, Wälder, Felder und Städte widerspiegelt.
Stratégie: Ce logo reflète les saisons de la Finlande, ses lacs, ses forêts, ses champs et ses villes.

Pages 138, 139
Student: Felix Espermüller / College: Blocherer Schule
Department: Graphic Design / Department Chair:
Annemarie Loeffelholz / Class: 8 Semester / Instructor: Klaus Müller
Project: The vision of a travel agency: "Mars."
Projekt: Vision eines Reiseunternehmens: «Mars».
Projet: La vision d'une agence de voyages: «Mars».

Page 140
Student: Fang Zhou / College: School of Visual Arts
Department Chair: Richard Wilde / Department: Graphic Design
Class: Portfolio / Instructor: Paula Scher
Project: A series of three cds and poster in a jazz collection
Projekt: Eine Reihe von 3 Jazz-CDs und ein Plakat.
Projet: Collection de trois CD de jazz et affiche.
Strategy: The design is based on the music, and attempts to reflect the character of Monk's jazz.
Strategie: Die Ausgangsbasis des Designs ist Musik, wobei es speziell um eine Interpretation von Monks Jazz geht.
Stratégie: Le design est basé sur la musique, plus précisément sur le jazz de Monk.
Medium, Materials: Photoshop

Page 141
Student: Tracy Pamperin / College: School of Visual Arts
Department: Graphic Design / Department Chair: Richard Wilde
Project: CD redesign without using a jewel case.
Projekt: Gestaltung einer CD ohne die übliche Hülle.
Projet: Packaging de CD sans le traditionnel boîtier.
Strategy: The corset represents Madonna's erotica. The act of untying the laces encourages the viewer to pick up the piece and look at it.
Strategie: Das Korsett steht für Madonnas Erotika. Durch die Spitzen wird der Betrachter angeregt, zur CD zu greifen und sie anzuschauen.
Stratégie: Le corset évoque l'érotisme de Madonna. La dentelle doit inciter le consommateur à saisir le CD pour découvrir ce qui se cache à l'intérieur.
Medium, Materials: Mat board, shower curtain, silk cord, computer

Page 142
Student: Haejung Noh / College: School of Visual Arts
Department: Graphic Design / Department Chair: Richard Wilde
Class: Portfolio / Instructor: Alex Nowlton
Project: CD packaging.
Projekt: Verpackung für eine CD.
Projet: Packaging de CD.
Strategy: The design was based on a manhole cover.
Strategie: Grundlage des Designs ist ein Kanalisationsdeckel.
Stratégie: Design s'inspirant d'une bouche d'égout.
Medium, Materials: Modeling paste, paper, paint

Page 143 top
Student: Nancy Smith / College: School of Visual Arts
Department: Graphic Design / Department Chair: Richard Wilde
Class: Portfolio / Instructor: Carin Goldberg
Photographer: Richard Bachmann
Project: Design a four-CD box set.
Projekt: Gestaltung einer Box für 4 CDs.
Projet: Boîtier pour 4 CD.
Strategy: The design was based on the way the student thought Bob Marley would want it. The pack of rolling papers serves as the booklet for the box set.
Strategie: Die Studentin liess sich von seiner Vorstellung von Bob Marleys Wünschen leiten. Die Packung mit den Papierröllchen dient als Broschüre für das Set.
Stratégie: L'étudiante s'est inspirée du «style de vie» de Bob Marley en choisissant du papier à rouler pour le livret.
Medium, Materials: Wood, yarn, plastic, metal

Page 143 middle, bottom
Student: Mary Belibasakis / College: School of Visual Arts
Dean: David Rhodes / Department: Graphic Design
Department Chair: Richard Wilde / Class: Portfolio
Instructor: Carin Goldberg
Project: Series of movie soundtracks with western, romance, and sci-fi categories.
Projekt: Gestaltung von Musik-CDs mit Filmmusik für Western, Liebesfilme und Science-Fiction-Filme.
Projet: Série de CD de musiques de film: western, film d'amour et science fiction.

Page 144 top
Student: Xun-Lei Sheng / College: School of Visual Arts
Department: Graphic Design / Department Chair: Richard Wilde
Class: Senior Portfolio / Instructor: Paula Scher
Project: Charles Mingus three-CD jazz set
Projekt: Gestaltung einer Box für 3 Charles-Mingus-CDs.
Projet: Boîtier pour 3 CD de Charles Mingus.
Strategy: The design was meant to be modern and classic.
Strategie: Die Lösung: ein modernes, klassisches Design.
Stratégie: La solution consiste en un design à la fois classique et moderne.
Medium, Materials: Computer printout, hand-painted lettering

Page 144 middle
Student: Bong Lee / College: School of Visual Arts
Department: Graphic Design / Department Chair: Richard Wilde
Class: CD Package Design / Instructor: Jackie Murphy
Photographer: Byun Sun Chuel
Project: CD package design for John Mayall and the Bluesbreakers.
Projekt: Verpackung einer CD von John Mayall and the Bluesbreakers.
Projet: Packaging d'un CD de John Mayall and the Bluesbreakers.
Strategy: Inkjet print creates very soft tone.
Strategie: Der Tintenstrahldruck sorgt für einen sehr weichen Farbton.
Stratégie: L'impression au jet d'encre confère un ton très doux aux couleurs.

Page 144 bottom
Student: Celeste Rader / College: Texas Christian University
Dean: Garwell / Department: Art / Department Chair: Ron Watson
Class: Computer Applications to Graphic Design
Instructor: Roby McEven
Project: Dragonfly CD package.
Projekt: Verpackung für eine Dragonfly-CD.
Projet: Packaging pour un CD de Dragonfly.
Strategy: The design integrates the name of the band and its love for the beauty of nature.
Strategie: Der Name der Band und ihre Liebe zur Natur stehen im Mittelpunkt des Designs.
Stratégie: Le design se réfère au nom du groupe et à leur amour de la nature.
Medium, Materials: Electronic output

Page 145 top
Student: Einat Lisa Day / College: School of Visual Arts
Department: Graphic Design and Advertising / Department Chair:
Richard Wilde / Class: Portfolio / Instructor: Carin Goldberg
Project: Billie Holiday CD packaging.
Projekt: Verpackung einer CD von Billie Holiday.
Projet: Packaging pour un CD de Billie Holiday.
Strategy: The patterns and colors were used to represent the moods of Billie Holiday's work.
Strategie: Die Muster und Farben reflektieren die Stimmungen von Billie Holidays Musik.
Stratégie: Les motifs et les couleurs sont une interprétation de la musique de Billie Holiday.

Page 145 middle
Student: Bong Lee / College: School of Visual Arts
Department: Graphic Design / Department Chair:
Richard Wilde / Class: CD Package Design
Instructor: Jackie Murphy
Photographer: Byun Sun Chuel
Project: CD package design for John Mayall and the Bluesbreakers.
Projekt: Verpackung einer CD von John Mayall and the Bluesbreakers.
Projet: Packaging d'un CD de John Mayall and the Bluesbreakers.
Strategy: Inkjet print creates very soft tone.
Strategie: Der Tintenstrahldruck sorgt für einen sehr weichen Farbton.
Stratégie: L'impression au jet d'encre confère un ton très doux aux couleurs.

Page 145 bottom
Student: Carrie Ferguson / College: Western Washington University
Dean: Bertil Van Boer / Department: Art
Department Chair: Elsi Vassdal-Ellis / Class: Three Dimensional
Graphic Design
Instructor: Kent Smith
Project: CD box set.
Projekt: Gestaltung einer CD-Box.
Projet: Boîtier CD.
Strategy: This CD packaging aimed to reflect the visual aspect of the Talking Heads. The transparent quality along with color separations allude to the digital feel and movement.
Strategie: Diese Verpackung ist eine visuelle Interpretation der Talking Heads. Die Transparenz der Hülle und die Plastikstücke in den vier Farben von Farboffsetfilmen sind eine Anspielung auf die digitale Qualität und eine Interpretation von Bewegung.
Stratégie: Ce packaging est une interprétation visuelle des Talking Heads. La transparence et les couleurs font allusion à la musique du groupe et doivent refléter l'idée de mouvement.
Medium, Materials: Plexiglass

Student: Amy Zuckerman / College: Pennsylvania State University
Dean: Neil Porterfield / Department: Graphic Design
Department Chair: Jim Stephenson / Class: Packaging
Instructor: Kristin Breslin Sommese / Photographer: Dave Shelly
Art Director: Kristin Sommese
Project: Design a wine bottle that would be sent to clients on
Valentine's day promoting our design firm, Art 376.
*Projekt: Gestaltung einer Weinflasche, die als Werbung der Designfirma
Art 376 zum Valentinstag an Kunden verschickt wird.*
*Projet: Design d'une bouteille de vin autopromotionnelle offerte à la
clientèle de l'agence de design Art 376 à l'occasion de la Saint-Valentin.*
Strategy: Instead of the typical Valentine day "mushiness," the student
created an "anti-Valentines day" promotion for those who have
fallen out of love. The container is an antique keepsake box framing
a picture of a couple, the man's face seemingly poked out in anger.
The inside, opposite the heart-shaped wine bottle, is filled with
revenge-stricken tintypes and "dead" rose petals. The bottle rests on
a bed of black satin and a tear-stained handkerchief.
*Strategie: Die Studentin entschied sich für eine Anti-Valentinstag-Variante,
für all jene, die nicht mehr verliebt sind. Die Verpackung besteht aus einer
alten Schachtel für Erinnerungsstücke mit dem Photo eines Paars, auf dem
der Kopf des Mannes fehlt – offenbar in einem Wutanfall abgerissen.
Das Innere ist mit alten Ferrotypien und vertrockneten Rosenblättern
gefüllt, wobei die herzförmige Flasche auf schwarzem Satin und einem
tränendurchnässten Taschentuch ruht.*
*Stratégie: L'étudiante a décidé de créer un design «anti-Saint-Valentin»
pour tous ceux qui ne sont plus amoureux. Le packaging comprend une
vieille boîte à souvenirs où figure un couple. La tête de l'homme semble
avoir été arrachée dans un accès de colère. La boîte renferme des ferrotypies
vengeresses, des pétales de rose séchés, une bouteille en forme de cœur sur
du satin noir et un mouchoir détrempé par les larmes.*
Medium, Materials: Antique tin types, dried rose petals, gold lock

Page 147 top
Student: Susanne Cerha / College: School of Visual Arts
Department: Graphic Design / Department Chair: Richard Wilde
Class: Type and Design / Instructor: Carin Goldberg
Project: Redefine what a wine label is and integrate it with the
bottle. The name of the wine is "stem," so all type was given a
vertical solution.
*Projekt: Neudefinierung des Weinetiketts und seine Anbringung auf der
Flasche. Der Name des Weins ist «stem» (Stamm), weswegen sämtliche
Schriften eine vertikale Ausrichtung haben.*
*Projet: Réinventer l'étiquette de vin et son emplacement sur la bouteille.
Le nom du vin est «stem» (tige), d'où l'orientation verticale des caractères.*
Medium, Materials: Acetone transfer on fabric, glued onto a
wine bottle.

Page 147 middle left
Student: Hye Won Chang / College: School of Visual Arts
Department Chair: Richard Wilde / Department: Graphic Design
Class: Senior Design Portfolio / Instructor: Carin Goldberg
Project: Wine label for "Soleo," white and red wine.
Projekt: Etikett für «Soleo», einen Weiss- und einen Rotwein.
Projet: Etiquette pour «Soleo», un vin blanc et un vin rouge.
Strategy: The simple and bold design embodying New York
style is meant to give the product a distinguishing look on
liquor store shelves.
Strategie: Ein schlichtes, ausdrucksstarkes Design im Stil New Yorks.
Stratégie: Design épuré et accrocheur, à l'image de New York.
Medium, Materials: Quark Xpress

Page 147 middle right
Student: Daron Clary / College: California State University-Long
Beach / Department: Art / Department Chair: Jay Kuvapil
Class: Visual Communication Design / Instructor: Archie Boston
Project: Identity and collateral for a Greek restaurant—Mykonos
restaurant. Wine bottle label.
*Projekt: Erscheinungsbild einschliesslich sämtlicher Drucksachen für ein
griechisches Restaurant, das «Mykonos» heisst. Ausserdem ein Flaschenetikett.*
Projet: Identité visuelle et imprimés pour le restaurant grec «Mykonos».
Medium, Materials: Created and illustrated in Illustrator

Page 147 bottom left
Student: Susan Burroughs / College: Pennsylvania State University
Dean: Neil Porterfield / Department: Graphic Design
Department Chair: Jim Stephenson / Class: Art 376 Packaging
Instructor: Kristin Breslin Sommese / Photographer: Dave Ackley
Art Director: Kristin Sommese
Project: Design a wine bottle promoting the design studio to be sent
to clients on Halloween.
*Projekt: Entwurf einer Weinflasche, die als Werbung eines Design-Studios
an Halloween an die Kunden versandt wird.*
*Projet: Design d'une bouteille de vin autopromotionnelle envoyée aux clients
à l'occasion de Halloween.*

Strategy: The yellow color of the wine suggests the color of the
moon. The witch, moon and type are clear and the rest of the bottle
is frosted by sandblasting. The square-shaped typeface mimics a
cityscape below the flying witch.
*Strategie: Die gelbe Farbe des Weins erinnert an die Farbe des Mondes.
Die Hexe, der Mond und die Schrift sind scharf, der Rest der Flasche ist
durch Sandstrahlung mattiert. Die eckige Schrift simuliert die Silhouette
einer Stadt, über die die Hexe hinwegfliegt.*
*Stratégie: La couleur jaune du vin rappelle celle de la lune. La sorcière,
la lune et la typographie ressortent nettement sur le fond mat dépoli à la
sableuse. Les caractères angulaires évoquent une ville, survolée par la sorcière.*
Medium, Materials: Sand-blasted wine bottle, Adobe Illustrator

Page 147 bottom right
Student: Christine Cucuzza / College: School of Visual Arts
Dean: David Rhodes / Department: Graphic Design
Department Chair: Richard Wilde / Class: Portfolio 97
Instructor: Carin Goldberg
Project: Create wine labels for Estrella wine.
Projekt: Etiketten für einen Wein mit dem Namen «Estrella».
Projet: Etiquettes pour un vin nommé «Estrella».
Strategy: Since "estrella" means "star," the student used the star
as the main design element.
*Strategie: «Estrella» bedeutet Stern, und dieser wurde zum wichtigsten
Gestalt-ungselement.*
Stratégie: Ce design s'inspire du mot «Estrella» (étoile).
Medium, Materials: Wine bottles, metallic star stickers.

Page 148
Student: Karen Schmucker / College: Academy of Art
Department: Graphic Design / Department Chair: Howard York
Class: Package Design IV / Instructor: Jesse McAnulty
Product Photographer: Richard Jeung
Project: Glenmorangie scotch.
Projekt: Überarbeitung der Flasche von Glenmorangie-Scotch.
Projet: Nouveau concept de la bouteille de scotch Glenmorangie.
Strategy: The student wished to emphasize quality and heritage, make
the design more modern but classic, and create better name recognition.
*Strategie: Betonung von Qualität und Tradition durch ein moderneres, aber
klassisches Design und bessere Herausstellung des Names.*
*Stratégie: Mise en évidence de la qualité et de la tradition par le biais d'un design
à la fois moderne et classique pour une meilleure identification de la marque.*

Page 149
Student: Kristin Konz / College: The Creative Circus
Department: Design / Department Chair and Instructor:
Rob Lawton / Class: Packaging
Project: Wine bottle for Domaine St. George.
Projekt: Weinflasche für Domaine St. George.
Projet: Bouteille de vin Domaine St. George.
Strategy: The calligraphy was designed to look like the knight's chain
mail armour cross.
Strategie: Eine Kalligraphie, die wie das Kreuz auf St. Georgs Rüstung aussieht.
Stratégie: Calligraphie rappelant la croix sur l'armure de St. Georges.
Medium, Materials: Hand lettering, Mac

Page 150 top left
Student: Daren Clary / College: California State University-Long
Beach / Department: Art / Department Chair: Jay Kuvapil
Class: Visual Communication Design / Instructor: Archie Boston
Project: Create a label for a liquor beverage.
Projekt: Etikett für eine Schnapsflasche.
Projet: Etiquette pour une eau-de-vie.
Medium, Materials: Illustrator

Page 150 top right
Student: Zhao Wen Li / College: School of Visual Arts
Department: Graphic Design / Department Chair: Richard Wilde
Class: Senior Portfolio / Instructor: Carin Goldberg
Project: Design a wine label.
Projekt: Gestaltung eines Weinetiketts.
Projet: Design d'une étiquette de vin.
Strategy: The student invented the wine name Sonata and represent-
ed it in the simplest form possible to give it an essence of elegance.
*Strategie: Der selbstgewählte Name Sonata wurde auf ganz schlichte, elegante
Art dargestellt.*
*Stratégie: Le design du vin «Sonata», nom choisi par l'étudiant, allie simplic-
ité et élégance.*

Page 150 middle left
Student: Minako So / College: University of Maryland-Baltimore
County Dean: G. Welsch / Department: Visual Arts
Department Chair: David Yager / Class: Advanced Graphic Design
Instructor: Ferris Crane
Strategy: The student created a series of three package designs for a
beverage targeting urbanites on the go. The package suggests the bev-

erage is energizing in the morning, refreshing in the afternoon and relaxing in the evening.

Strategie: Entwicklung einer Serie von drei Verpackungen für ein Getränk, das vor allem junge, aktive Städter ansprechen sollte. Die Verpackungen versprechen Energie am Morgen, Erfrischung am Nachmittag und Entspannung am Abend.

Stratégie: Développement d'une série de trois emballages pour une boisson destinée avant tout aux citadins jeunes et dynamiques. Energie le matin, rafraîchissement l'après-midi et détente le soir, telles sont les promesses de ces emballages.

Medium, Materials: Glass bottles, spray paint, tempera paint, printed on adhesive acetate.

Page 150 middle right

Student: Lloyd Rodrigues / College: School of Visual Arts
Department: Graphic Design / Department Chair: Richard Wilde
Class: Typography / Instructor: Henrietta Condak
Project: Apply a designed typeface to a subject choice.
Projekt: Anwendung einer Schrift für einen beliebigen Gegenstand.
Projet: Création d'une famille de caractères pour un objet à choix.
Strategy: The student created a label for a black beer lager.
Strategie: Etikett für ein dunkles Bier.
Stratégie: Etiquette pour une bière.

Page 150 bottom left

Student: Einat Lisa Day / College: School of Visual Arts
Department: Graphic Design and Advertising / Department Chair: Richard Wilde / Class: Portfolio / Instructor: Carin Goldberg
Project: Label for a wine from Vienna.
Projekt: Etikett für einen Wiener Wein.
Projet: Etiquette pour un vin viennois.

Page 150 bottom right

Student: Nicole Lomonaco / College: California State University-Long Beach / Department: Art / Department Chair: Archie Boston
Class: Special Studies in Visual Communication
Instructor: Archie Boston
Project: Design a label for a lemon liquor inspired by a fictitious "female" lemon (Limon Cela Lomonaco).
Projekt: Gestaltung eines Etiketts für einen Zitronenschnaps, inspiriert von einer fiktiven «weiblichen» Zitrone (Limon Cela Lomonaco).
Projet: Création d'une étiquette pour une eau-de-vie citronnée, inspirée d'un citron fictif présentant les formes d'une femme.
Medium, Materials: Illustrator

Page 151 top

Student: Christopher Klimasz / College: School of Visual Arts
Department: Graphic Design and Advertising
Department Chair: Richard Wilde
Class: Graphic Design Portfolio / Instructor: Stacey Drummond
Project: Design bottle for Nike sports drink called "Quench."
Projekt: Gestaltung einer Flasche für ein Sportgetränk mit dem Namen Quench (Durstlöscher).
Projet: Design de bouteille pour une boisson énergisante appelée «Quench» (qui signifie «désaltérer»).
Strategy: The student wanted to design bottles that fit the consumer's hand.
Strategie: Der menschlichen Hand angepasste Flaschen.
Stratégie: Bouteille ergonomique adaptée à la forme de la main.
Medium, Materials: Vivac plastic, vacuum form, spray paint

Page 151 bottom

Student: Minako So / College: University of Maryland-Baltimore County / Dean: G. Welsch / Department: Visual Arts
Department Chair: David Yager / Class: Advanced Graphic Design
Instructor: Ferris Crane
Strategy: The student created a series of three package designs for a beverage targeting urbanites on the go. The package suggests the beverage is energizing in the morning, refreshing in the afternoon and relaxing in the evening.
Strategie: Entwicklung einer Serie von drei Verpackungen für ein Getränk, das vor allem junge, aktive Städter ansprechen sollte. Die Verpackungen versprechen Energie am Morgen, Erfrischung am Nachmittag und Entspannung am Abend.
Stratégie: Développement d'une série de trois emballages pour une boisson destinée avant tout aux citadins jeunes et dynamiques. Energie le matin, rafraîchissement l'après-midi et détente le soir, telles sont les promesses de ces emballages.
Medium, Materials: Glass bottles, spray paint, tempera paint, printed on adhesive acetate.

Page 152

Student: Joelle Garofalo / College: Pennsylvania State University
Dean: Neil Porterfield / Department: Graphic Design
Department Chair: Jim Stephenson / Class: Packaging
Instructor: Kristin Sommese / Photographer: Dave Shelley
Art Director: Kristin Breslin Sommese

Project: Design a line of bath and body products for men.
Title: "Mondo dei Sogni" or "World of Dreams."
Projekt: Entwurf einer Linie von Körperpflegeprodukten für Männer unter dem Namen «Mondo dei sogni» (Welt der Träume).
Projet: Création d'une ligne de produits de soins corporels pour hommes intitulée «Mondo dei sogni» (Monde de Rêves).
Strategy: Use texture, type, and color.
Strategie: Die gewünschte Wirkung wird durch die Ober-flächenbeschaffenheit des Materials, die Typographie und Farbe erzielt.
Stratégie: Texture, typographie et couleur créent l'effet désiré.
Medium, Materials: Acetate, cardstock, color prints, glycerin soap, Adobe Illustrator

Page 153

Student: Nicholas Angel / College: Academy of Art
Department: Graphic Design / Department Chair: Howard York
Product Photographer: Richard Jeung / Project: Euphoric perfume.
Projet: Gestaltung einer Parfumflasche.
Projet: Flacon de parfum.
Strategy: The student wanted to design an elegant and distinctive container for a new product. He also designed the typeface for the logo.
Strategie: Entwurf einer neuen Schrift für einen eleganten, aussergewöhnlichen Flakon.
Stratégie: Création d'un nouveau caractère pour un flacon élégant.

Page 154 top

Student: Paul D. Gobble / College: Pennsylvania State University
Dean: Neil Porterfield / Department: Graphic Design
Department Chair: Jim Stephenson / Class: Packaging
Instructor: Kristin Breslin Sommese / Photographer: Dick Ackley
Art Director: Kristin Breslin Sommese
Project: Design the packaging for a line of utility hand soaps to be sold in fine stores.
Projekt: Gestaltung einer Verpackung für Handseife, die in Spezialgeschäften angeboten wird.
Projet: Packaging pour un savon vendu dans des magasins spécialisés.
Strategy: The utilitarian personality of the product is reinforced by the student's choice to package it in an ordinary aluminum can. The can itself is the label—minimal in design, bold in application.
Strategie: Der Aspekt des täglichen Ge-brauchs bestimmte die Art der Verpackung: eine gewöhnliche Aluminium-Dose, sandgestrahlt, mit ausgespartem Logo.
Stratégie: L'usage quotidien du produit a influencé le design: une boîte en alu au design simple.
Medium, Materials: Sandblasted aluminum with the logo masked out.

Page 154 middle

Student: Amy Zuckerman / College: Pennsylvania State University
Dean: Neil Porterfield / Department: Graphic Design
Department Chair: Jim Stephenson / Class: Packaging
Instructor: Kristin Breslin Sommese / Photographer: Dave Shelly
Art Director: Kristin Sommese
Project: The assignment was to design a line of bath and body products for both men and women.
Projekt: Entwurf einer Körper-pflegelinie für Männer und Frauen.
Projet: Ligne unisexe de produits pour les soins corporels.
Strategy: The student entitled the line of body products "From Dusk 'Til Dawn." The student believes people use too many products with too many scents at one time. This line is meant to be used at any time. The black top of the bottle represents night falling on the colorful sky of dusk or dawn.
Strategie: Der selbstgewählte Name der Linie: «Von Sonnenaufgang bis Sonnenuntergang.» Die Idee ist, dass man statt vieler verschieden parfümierter Produkte von morgens bis abends nur diese Linie benutzen soll. Die schwarze Kappe der Flasche symbolisiert die Nacht.
Stratégie: L'étudiante a intitulé sa ligne de produits «De l'aube au crépuscule», suggérant ainsi que ces produits peuvent être utilisés du matin au soir. Le bouchon noir de la bouteille symbolise la nuit.

Page 154 bottom

Student: Angela Perez-Charneco / College: Pennsylvania State University / Dean: Neil Porterfield / Department: Graphic Design
Department Chair: Jim Stephenson / Class: Packaging
Instructor and Art Director: Kristin Breslin Sommese
Photographer: Dwain Harbst
Illustrator: Angela Perez Charneco
Project: Design a line of body and bath products for men.
Projekt: Entwurf einer Körperpflegelinie für Männer.
Projet: Ligne de produits pour les soins corporels, destinée aux hommes.
Strategy The design is meant to be humorous and elegant at once. The illustration is of an aristocrat enjoying the product while bathing in luxury. The black bottles create a solid, neutral background and make the labels more prominent.
Strategie: Das Design soll humorvoll und doch elegant wirken. Die

Illustration zeigt einen Aristokraten, der das Produkt geniesst. Die schwarzen Flaschen bilden einen soliden, neutralen Hintergrund, der die Wirkung der Etiketten verstärkt.
Stratégie: Le design est sensé être à la fois humoristique et élégant. L'illustration présente un aristocrate en train de prendre un bain dans une débauche de luxe. La couleur noire des flacons vise à faire ressortir les étiquettes.
Medium, Materials: Xerox copies, cardboard stock paper, wire

Page 155
Student: Fridolin T. Beisert / College: Art Center
Department: Product Design / Department Chair: Marty Smith
Class: Packaging / Instructor: Tom Schorer
Photographer: Fiel Valdez
Project: Luxurious hotel shampoo set for a fictious hotel.
Projekt: Ein Satz luxuriöser Shampoos für ein fiktives Hotel.
Projet: Ligne de shampoings raffinée pour un hôtel fictif.
Strategy: The Eclypse Hotel shampoo set comprises five bottles, each with different contents. The inside of each bottle is shaped like the moon in a given phase, giving each bottle a different volume.
Strategie: Das Shampoo-Set für das Hotel Eclypse umfasst Flaschen mit unterschiedlichem Inhalt. Innen sind die Flaschen wie der Mond in verschiedenen Phasen geformt, so dass jede Flasche ein anderes Volumen hat.
Stratégie: A l'intérieur, les cinq shampoings créés pour l'hôtel Edypse se présentent sous la forme d'une lune dont la contenance varie en fonction des phases de lune.
Medium, Materials: Glass with aluminum caps

Page 156 top
Student: Kate Dickinson / College: Monash University
Dean: John Redmond / Department: Graphic Design
Department Chair: Jenny Allen / Class: Graphic Design
Instructors: Russell Kennedy, Neil Barnett
Project: Colorado Adventurewear shoebox
Projekt: Entwurf einer Schuhschachtel für Bergstiefel der Marke «Colorado Adventurewear».
Projet: Boîte à chaussures destinée aux bottes de montagne «Colorado Adventurewear».
Strategy: The unusual trapezoid-shaped shoebox is suggestive of the rugged mountain regions from which it is named. The boxes can be easily stacked on top of each other, or creatively placed for display.
Strategie: Die ungewöhnliche Trapezform der Schuhschachtel ist eine Anspielung auf die rauhen Bergregionen Colorados. Die Boxen lassen sich problemlos stapeln und effektvoll im Laden präsentieren.
Stratégie: La forme trapézoïdale de la boîte est une allusion aux contours déchiquetés des montagnes du Colorado. Les boîtes se laissent facilement empiler et permettent de réaliser des agencements créatifs en magasin.
Medium, Materials: Corrugated board, screen print

Page 156 bottom
Student: Julia Michry / College: School of Visual Arts
Dean: Richard Wilde / Department: Graphic Design
Department Chair: Richard Wilde / Class: Portfolio
Instructor: Carin Goldberg
Project: Logo, packaging and stationery for Osh Kosh, a baby clothing and overalls company.
Projekt: Logo, Verpackung und Briefpapier für Osh Kosh, Hersteller von Baby-Textilien.
Projet: Logo, packaging et papier à lettres pour Osh Kosh, un fabricant de vêtements pour bébés.
Medium, Materials: Computer, pen and ink for logo

Page 157 top
Student: Trina Sultan / College: School of Visual Arts
Department: Graphic Design / Department Chair: Richard Wilde
Class: Typography and Design / Instructor: Carin Goldberg
Project: Store design, logo and packaging for a retail store.
Projekt: Gestaltung eines Ladens, einschliesslich Logo und Verpackungen.
Projet: Concept de magasin avec logo et packaging.
Strategy: Design for Blue Systems, a store in Hong Kong. Actual items serve as packaging: shopping bags are jeans, shirt box is a shirt, underwear box is unzipped fly, etc.
Strategie: Es handelt sich um Blue Systems, einen Laden in Hongkong. Als Verpackung dient richtige Ware: die Tragtaschen sind Jeans, die Hemdenschachtel besteht aus einem Hemd, der Karton für Unterwäsche ist ein offener Hosenschlitz, etc.
Stratégie: Design pour Blue Systems, un magasin de Hong-kong. Les articles du magasin ont servi de packaging: les sacs sont faits à partir de jeans, la boîte à chemise est une chemise et le carton à sous-vêtements, une braguette ouverte.
Medium/Materials: Scans on computer in Photoshop

Page 157 middle
Student: Karen Schmucker / College: Academy of Art
Department: Graphic Design / Department Chair: Howard York
Class: Package Design III / Instructor: Dan Andrist
Photographer: Richard Jeung
Project: Martex sheets.

Projekt: Verpackung für Bettlaken der Marke Martex.
Projet: Packaging pour les draps de lit Martex.
Strategy: This design unifies brand labeling and upgrades image appeal to feminine customers.
Strategie: Ein Design, das die Marke betont und speziell Frauen anspricht.
Stratégie: Un design qui met l'accent sur le nom de la marque et s'adresse à un public cible féminin.

Page 157 bottom
Student: Trina Sultan / College: School of Visual Arts
Department: Graphic Design / Department Chair: Richard Wilde
Class: Portfolio / Instructor: Paula Scher
Project: Packaging and promotion for Champion sportswear retail store.
Projekt: Verpackungen und Werbematerial für ein Sportgeschäft, das «Champion» heisst.
Projet: Packaging et matériel promotionnel pour le magasin de sports «Champion».
Strategy: "Just do it" and other sports promotions are boiled down to an exclamation point, so the student used the same idea with the name, dividing it into champ and on!
Strategie: Die in der Sportbranche heute übliche Art, einen Slogan auf ein Minimum zu reduzieren, wie z.B. das Nike-Häkchen, inspirierte zu einer Lösung, die aus der Trennung des Namens besteht: Champ - on.
Stratégie: La tendance actuelle qui veut que l'on réduise à sa plus simple expression un slogan publicitaire ou un logo (Nike) a inspiré l'étudiant qui a divisé le nom de la marque en: Champ et on!
Medium, Materials: Photos, computer, Photoshop, Quark, Illustrator

Page 158 Student: Dan Chau / College: Brigham Young University
Department: Graphic Design and Visual Arts / Department Chair: Robert Barrett / Class: Special Problems in Graphic Design II
Instructor: Linda Sullivan / Photographer: Marjorie Stevenson
Project: Packaging for Levi's store
Projekt: Verpackungen für einen Levi's Laden.
Projet: Packaging pour des points de vente Levi's.
Strategy: This design keeps the strong identity of Levi's: mainstream, clean, comtemporary. A strong identity was used for the underwear packaging by using tubes; the size of the underwear is easily readable.
Strategie: Grundsätzlich wurde Levi's starkes Image unterstrichen: unkompliziert, sauber, zeitgemäss. Für die Unterwäsche wurde eine aussergewöhnliche Verpackung in Form von Rollen benutzt, wobei die Grössenangaben deutlich lesbar sind.
Stratégie: Le design souligne la forte image inhérente à la marque Levi's: propre, contemporaine, dans le ton. Un packaging inhabituel sous forme de tube a été choisi pour les sous-vêtements dont la taille est clairement indiquée.
Medium, Materials: Mailing tubes

Page 159 top
Student: Darcy Hockett / College: Oregon State University
Dean: Kay Shaffer / Department: Art
Department Chair: David Hardesty / Class: Graphic Design III
Instructor: David Hardesty
Project: Packaging for cookies; define essence of product and assign visual qualities appropriate to the product.
Projekt: Verpackung für Kekse, wobei das Wesentliche des Produktes zum Ausdruck kommen soll.
Projet: Créer un packaging pour des biscuits en faisant ressortir les principales caractéristiques du produit.
Strategy: Each side of the package is different and can serve as the front panel when placed randomly on store shelves.
Strategie: Alle Seiten einer Verpackung sind verschieden, und jede kann als Vorderseite dienen.
Stratégie: Chaque côté du packaging est différent et peut être présenté de face.
Medium, Materials: Computer printout

Page 159 bottom
Student: Jason Guinn / College: Oregon State University
Dean: Schaffer / Department: Art / Department Chair: David Hardesty / Class: Graphic Design III / Instructor: David Hardesty
Project: Packaging for tea; define essence of product and assign visual qualities appropriate to the product.
Projekt: Eine Verpackung für Tee, die das Wesentliche des Produktes zum Ausdruck bringen soll.
Projet: Créer un packaging pour un thé en faisant ressortir les principales caractéristiques du produit.
Strategy: These packages were designed to create gestalt when assembled on store shelves. Each side of the package is different and can serve as the front panel when placed randomly on store shelves.
Strategie: Im Ladengestell ergeben die Verpackungen zusammen ein spezielles Bild, wobei alle Seiten einer Verpackung verschieden sind und jede als Vorderseite dienen kann.
Stratégie: Ces emballages ont été créés pour former un ensemble original une fois présentés dans les rayonnages d'un magasin. Chaque côté du packaging est différent et peut être présenté de face.
Medium, Materials: Computer printout

Page 160
Student: Karen Schmucker / College: Academy of Art
Department: Graphic Design / Department Chair: Howard York
Class: Package Design IV / Instructor: Jesse McAnulty
Photographer: Richard Jeung
Project: Redesign of Colombo bread packaging.
Projekt: Überarbeitung der Verpackung für Colombo-Brot.
Projet: Nouvel emballage pour le pain Colombo.

Page 161
Student: Reneé Yancey / College: Western Washington University
Dean: Bertil Van Boer / Department: Art
Department Chair: Elsi Vassdal Ellis / Class: 3D Graphic Design
Instructor: Kent Smith
Project: Packaging for organic bird seed.
Projekt: Verpackung für biologische Vogelkörner.
Projet: Packaging pour des graines d'oiseau bio.
Strategy: The product targets serious bird lovers. The pattern was
created from bird silhouettes from a field guide. A simple two-color
run was done on kraft paper.
*Strategie: Das Produkt richtet sich an ernsthafte Vogelliebhaber. Das Muster
besteht aus Vogelsilhouetten, die einem Vogelführer entnomen wurden.
Einfacher Zweifarbendruck auf Packpapier.*
*Stratégie: Le produit s'adresse aux «ornith-ophiles». Le motif se présente sous
la forme de silhouettes d'oiseaux extraites d'un guide sur les oiseaux.
Impression bicolore sur du papier kraft.*
Medium, Materials: Silkscreen, transfer letters.

Page 162 top
Student: Mike Hirsch / College: The Creative Circus
Department: Design / Department Chair: Rob Lawton
Class: Packaging / Instructor: Rob Lawton
Project: Self-dispensing container for Ronzoni spaghetti.
Projekt: Verpackung mit Dosierverschluss für Ronzoni-Spaghetti.
Projet: Packaging avec doseur pour les spaghetti Ronzoni.
Strategy: The packaging is see-through, so you can almost touch the
product. The end turns to dispense the desired number of servings.
*Strategie: Die transparente Verpackung schafft Nähe zum Produkt. Der Verschluss
lässt sich drehen, sodass der Verbraucher die Menge genau dosieren kann.*
*Stratégie: L'emballage transparent donne l'impression de pouvoir en toucher
le contenu. Le doseur peut être tourné afin de déterminer la quantité exacte
de spaghetti.*
Medium, Materials: Hand-lettered acetate.

Page 162 middle
Student: Naomi Herskovic / College: Monash University
Department: Graphic Design / Department Chair: John Seddon
Class: Design Practice / Instructor: Russell Kennedy
Project: Southern Cross packaging awards. Range of chocolates
wrapped in foil and retailing for less than $10.
Projekt: In Folie verpackte Schokolade, die weniger als $10 kostet.
Projet: Chocolat conditionné dans une feuille.
Strategy: The Manhattan Club is reminiscent of New York and
skyscrapers. The art deco feeling relates to the design of bars and
clubs in the 1930s. The chocolates are also flavored with alcohol.
*Strategie: Der Manhattan Club erinnert an New York und seine
Wolkenkratzer. Der Art-deco-Stil bezieht sich auf die Bars und Clubs der
30er Jahre. Die Schokolade enthält Alkohol.*
*Stratégie: Le Manhattan Club rappelle New York et ses gratte-ciel. Le
style art déco évoque les bars et les clubs des années 30. Ce chocolat
contient de l'alcool.*
Medium, Materials: Cardboard, acetate, aluminum foil, chocolates

Page 162 bottom
Student: Annemarit Brenden / College: Kent Institute of Art and
Design / Dean: Peter Sanger / Department: Communication Media
and Graphic Design / Department Chair: Jackie Cobb
Class: Third-Year Graphic Design
Instructors: Ned West Sherring, Ian Vickers
Project: Egg packaging for six eggs targeting upscale consumers who
shop at Harvey Nicols, London.
*Projekt: Gestaltung einer Verpackung für 6 Eier. Zielpublikum sind
anspruchsvolle Verbraucher, die bei Harvey Nicols in London einkaufen.*
*Projet: Carton d'œufs. Public cible: des consommateurs exigeants qui font leurs
achats chez Harvey Nichols à Londres.*
Strategy: The student designed a wave-shaped packet measuring
37cm x 10cm x 6cm. Each egg has its own "room" and lies in a bed
of shredded paper. The lid is made of clear vacuumed plastic, so it is
light weight and easy to stack.
*Strategie: Die Lösung besteht in einer wellenförmigen Verpackung von
37x10x6cm. Jedes Ei hat seinen eigenen «Raum» und liegt in einem Bett
von Papierschnipseln. Der Deckel besteht aus transparentem Schaumstoff,
wodurch ein geringes Gewicht und leichte Lagerung gewährleistet sind.*
*Stratégie: La solution consiste en un carton ondulé de 37x10x6cm. Chaque
œuf dispose de son propre «espace» et repose sur un lit de morceaux de papier.
Le couvercle se compose de plastique alvéolaire transparent afin de rendre l'em-*

ballage léger et facile à conserver.
Medium, Materials: Corrugated paper, vacuumed plastic,
shredded paper.

Page 163 top
Student: Karen Schmucker / College: Academy of Art
Department: Graphic Design / Department Chair: Howard York
Class: Package Design III / Instructor: Dan Andrist
Package Photographer: Richard Jeung
Project: Lipton tea.
Projekt: Verpackung für Lipton-Tee.
Projet: Packaging pour le thé Lipton.
Strategy: The student wanted to update the product's image while
maintaining its brand equity, strengthen its shelf impact, and unify all
packages.
*Strategie: Auffrischung des Images unter Beibehaltung der Marke, Verbesserung
der Wirkung im Gestell und ein homogener Auftritt für die verschiedenen Sorten.*
*Stratégie: Rafraîchir l'image en conservant les caractéristiques de la marque,
obtenir un plus grand impact dans les rayonnages de magasin et créer une
présentation homogène pour les différents produits.*

Page 163 middle
Student: Maureen Meyer / College: Pennsylvania State University
Dean: Neil Porterfield / Department: Graphic Design
Department Chair: Jim Stephenson / Class: Packaging
Instructor: Kristin Breslin Sommese / Art Director: Kristin Sommese
Photographer: Dave Shelley
Project: The assignment was to design a series of four sauces to be
used with seafood and Caribbean cuisine.
*Projekt: Verpackung für eine Linie von vier Saucen, die für Meeresfrüchte
und die karibische Küche geeignet sind.*
*Projet: Packaging pour un assortiment de quatre sauces destinées à
accompagner des fruits de mer et des plats typiques des Caraïbes.*
Strategy: The bright colors of the sauces and the bottles resemble
waves and give the product a tropical look. The student created
photograms and used them on each bottle to create underwater
scenes of the food (fish) the sauce is used for, the utensils (forks)
used to eat it, and the ingredients within the sauce.
*Strategie: Die leuchtenden Farben der Saucen und die Flaschen erinnern
an Wellen und geben dem Produkt ein tropisches Aussehen. Die Studentin
machte Photogramme, die er auf jeder Flasche verwendete, um Unterwas-ser-
szenen mit den Nahrungsmitteln (Fische), den Ess-Utensilien (Gabeln)
und den Ingredienzen der Saucen zu erzeugen.*
*Stratégie: Les couleurs lumineuses des sauces et les bouteilles rappellent des
vagues et confèrent une touche tropicale au produit. L'étudiante a réalisé des
photogrammes et les a utilisés sur chaque bouteille pour créer des scènes sub-
aquatiques montrant de la nourriture (les poissons), des ustensiles (fourchettes)
et les ingrédients des sauces.*
Medium, Materials: Photographic paper, forks, lemons, oranges, limes,
jalapeño peppers, glass bottles, onions.

Page 163 bottom
Student: Colleen MacDermott / College: School of Visual Arts
Department: Graphic Design / Department Chair: Richard Wilde
Class: Portfolio / Instructor: S. Drummond
Project: Redesign an existing food package, keeping in mind both
visual and practical considerations.
*Projekt: Überarbeitung einer vorhandenen Verpackung nach optischen und
praktischen Gesichtspunkten.*
Projet: Rafraîchir le packaging en considérant les aspects visuels et pratiques.
Strategy: The student chose to redesign the package for bagel chips.
She used a can to prevent the chips from breaking.
*Strategie: Die Studentin entschied sich für die Verpackung von Bagel-Chips
und wählte eine Dose, um die Chips gut zu schützen.*
*Stratégie: L'étudiante a choisi de créer un emballage pour des chips baguel.
La conserve vise à conserver les chips intacts.*

Page 164 top, middle
Student: Margarita Encomienda / College: Rhode Island School
of Design / Department: Graphic Design / Department Chair:
Hans Van Dijk / Class: Package Design / Instructor: Aki Nurosi
Project: Design a package for a chosen product that minimizes the
use of wasted material by incorporating corrugated board.
*Projekt: Verpackung für ein beliebiges Produkt, wobei dank Wellkarton
möglichst wenig Abfall erzeugt werden sollte.*
*Projet: Créer un packaging d'un produit à choix en réduisant au minimum le
matériel employé, dont du carton ondulé.*
Strategy: The package design instills a sense of permanence through
the design and materials. The package consists of panels that can be
easily taken apart and reassembled.
*Strategie: Gestaltung und Material vermitteln ein Gefühl von
Dauerhaftigkeit. Die Verpackung besteht aus einzelnen Teilen, die sich leicht
auseinandernehmen und wieder zusammensetzen lassen.*
*Stratégie: Le design et le matériel donnent une impression de durabilité. Le packaging
se compose de plusieurs éléments qui peuvent être facilement séparés et réassemblés.*
Medium, Materials: Bass wood, corrugated board

Page 164 bottom
Student: Annie Sung / College: Rhode Island School of Design
Dean: Roger Mandle / Department: Graphic Design
Department Chair: Hans Van Dijk / Class: Package Graphics
Instructor: Akefeh Nurosi / Photographer: Michael J. Kilpatrick
Project: Create a name, logo and packaging for a fragile item, incorporating the use of corrugated board.
Projekt: Schaffung eines Namens, eines Logos und einer Verpackung für ein zerbrechliches Produkt unter Verwendung von Wellkarton.
Projet: Trouver un nom pour un article fragile, créer un logo et un packaging et utiliser du carton ondulé.
Strategy: Taking its shape from the glass holiday ornaments it contains, the packaging is star-shaped and protected by corrugated board. The lid is die cut to show the product name.
Strategie: Die Sternform der Verpackung ist ihrem Inhalt angepasst: Weihnachtssterne aus Glas, die durch Wellkarton geschützt sind. Eine Ausstanzung im Deckel lässt den Produktnamen erkennen.
Stratégie: La forme stellaire du packaging est adaptée au contenu: des étoiles de Noël protégées par du carton ondulé. Le nom du produit est estampé sur le couvercle.
Medium, Materials: Corrugated board, glue

Page 165
Student: Anne Brenden / College: Kent Institute of Art and Design
Dean: Peter Snager / Department: Communication Media and Graphic Design / Department Chair: Jackie Cobb / Class: Third-Year Graphic Design / Instructors: Ned West Sherring, Ian Wickers
Project: Create new packaging and logo for Fuji film.
Projekt: Eine neue Verpackung und ein neues Logo für Fuji-Film.
Projet: Nouveau packaging et logo pour un film Fuji.
Strategy: The logo is inspired by a Japanese character. The packaging is designed with a triangular shape to distinguish it from competitors and suggests a connection with Fuji mountain. The packaging for the different speeds of the film have different color themes. The packages are easy to stack.
Strategie: Das Logo wurde von einem japanischen Schriftzeichen inspiriert. Die Dreiecksform ist einerseits auffällig, andererseits ist sie eine Anspielung an den Berg Fuji. Farbkodierungen erleichtern die Unterscheidung der verschiedenen Filme. Die Verpackungen lassen sich problemlos stapeln.
Stratégie: Le logo s'inspire d'un caractère japonais. La forme triangulaire du packaging vise à le démarquer des produits concurrents et suggère le mont Fuji. Les codes couleur aident à différencier les types de film. Les packagings peuvent être facilement empilés.
Medium, Materials: Uncoated card with watercolor texture.

Pages 166, 167
Student: Chris Panagakis / College: School of Visual Arts
Department: Photography / Department Chair: Eve Sonneman
Class: Independent Study / Instructor: Algis Balsys
Project: The independent study focused on creating clear, straightforward portraits.
Projekt: Klare Photoporträts mit den einfachsten, direktesten Mitteln.
Projet: Créer des portraits d'une grande netteté avec les moyens les plus simples et les plus directs.

Pages 168, 169
Student: Damian Heinisch / College: GH Essen, Folkwang
Dean: Grün / Department: Kommunikations-Design, Folkwang
Class: Photo-graphy, Typography / Instructor: Erich von Endt
Project: Color and black-and-white still-life photos, panorama shots in color of ski lifts.
Projekt: Stilleben in Farbe in Schwarzweiss. Panoramaaufnahmen in Farbe von Skiliften.
Projet: Natures mortes en couleur et en noir et blanc, prises de vues panoramiques en couleur de télésièges.
Strategy: Try to isolate the subjects from their original surrounding/meaning.
Strategie: Ein Versuch, die Gegenstände aus ihrem ursprünglichen Bedeutungszusammenhang zu isolieren.
Stratégie: Essayer d'isoler les objets de leur environnement traditionnel et oublier ce qu'ils évoquent.

Page 170
Student: Christine Capps / College: Art Institute of Atlanta
Dean: Carol Lafayette / Department: Photographic Imaging
Department Chair: Phil Bekker / Class: Portfolio
Instructor: Phil Bekker
Project: Portfolio category—free choice theme.
Projekt: Freie Projekte für die Arbeitsmappe.
Projet: Création d'un portfolio – sujets à choix.
Medium, Materials: Photography

Page 171
Student: Alfeo Dixon / College: Portfolio Center
Department: Photography / Department Chair: Ray Ellis
Class: People and Portrait / Instructor: Gemma Gatti
Project: Period piece.

Page 172
Student: Ryan Smith / College: Art Institute of Atlanta
Dean: Carol Lafayette / Department: Photographic Imaging
Department Chair: Phil Bekker / Class: Portfolio
Instructor: Phil Bekker
Project: Exterior location—infrared.
Projekt: Infrarot-Aufnahmen im Freien.
Projet: Prises de vues infrarouges en extérieur.
Medium, Materials: Infrared photography

Page 173
Student: Lori K. Sapio / College: Northern Illinois University
Department: Design / Department Chair: John Delilo
Class: Independent Study / Instructor: Phil Melnick
Project: Independent project showing the saturation of color in found objects.
Projekt: Freies Projekt, bei dem es um die Intensität von Farben geht.
Projet: Sujet libre devant mettre en évidence la saturation des couleurs.
Strategy: The student photographed at concerts, in the streets of Chicago and at Disney World to play off the saturation of color materials.
Strategie: Die Aufnahmen entstanden bei Konzerten, in den Strassen von Chicago und in Disneyworld, jeweils im Hinblick auf die Farbintensität.
Stratégie: Les photographies ont été prises lors de concerts, dans les rues de Chicago et à Disney World.
Medium, Materials: Agfa color negative film and Kodak Supra II paper

Page 174
Student: Geoffrey Wells / College: Portfolio Center
Department: Photography / Department Chair: Ray Ellis
Class: Art Direction and Photography
Instructors: Ray Ellis, Grady Phelan / Art Director: Mary Bennett
Project: "It fell to earth."
Projekt: «Es fiel auf die Erde.»
Projet: «C'est tombé sur la terre.»

Page 175
Student: Melissa Maciag / College: School of Visual Arts
Department: Photography / Department Chair: Eve Sonneman
Instructor: Elaine Matezk
Project: "Spitting in the face of traditional fashion photography."
Projekt: «Eine Ohrfeige für die traditionelle Modephotographie.»
Projet: Prendre le contre-pied de la photographie de mode.

Page 176
Student: Dominic Trautvetter / College: Fachhochschule Dortmund
Dean: Dr. Kottmann / Department: Design / Department Chair: H. Mante / Class: Conceptual Layout
Instructor: Dieter Ziegenfeuter
Project: Call-for-entries poster for a photo competition with the theme of "Wunschmaschine," or "wish machine." The competition is part of "Focus '96," an event organized by students in the design department.
Projekt: Plakat für einen Photowettbewerb mit dem Thema «Wunschmaschine». Der Wettbewerb fand im Rahmen von «Focus '96» statt, einer Veranstaltung des Studienganges Graphik-Design.
Projet: Affiche pour un concours de photographie ayant pour thème: «Machine de rêve». Ce concours s'est déroulé dans le cadre de «Focus 96», une manifestation organisée pour des étudiants en design graphique.
Strategy: The black surface of the poster avoids influencing competitors, but offers a surface on which they can project their imagination.
Strategie: Die schwarze Oberfläche des Plakates vermeidet jegliche Beeinflussung der Wettbewerbsteilnehmer, während sie gleichzeitig Raum für ihre Phantasie lässt.
Stratégie: Le fond noir de l'affiche évite d'influencer les étudiants en lice et laisse le champ libre à leur imagination.
Medium, Materials: Photoshop, Quark Xpress. Offset on paper.

Page 177
Student: Xun-Lei Sheng / College: School of Visual Arts
Department: Graphic Design / Department Chair: Richard Wilde
Class: Senior Portfolio / Instructor: Paula Scher
Project: Knoll.
Projekt: Knoll-Möbel.
Projet: Meubles Knoll.
Strategy: Keeping the Knoll logo, while giving it new meaning.
Strategie: Die Lösung besteht in einer neuen Aussage des vorhandenen Logos.
Stratégie: Solution: même logo avec une nouvelle signification.

Page 178
Student: Yim Cheng / College: School of Visual Arts
Department: Advertising and Graphic Design
Department Chair: Richard Wilde / Class: Graphic Design Portfolio
Instructor: Carin Goldberg
Project: Edible architecture, delicious designs.
Projekt: Essbare Architektur, köstliche Designs.
Projet: Architecture comestible, designs succulents.
Strategy: Using architectural planning, "build" a cake or pie.

Strategie: Der «Bau» eines Kuchens mit architektonischer Planung.
Stratégie: «Construire» un gâteau sur la base de plans architectoniques.
Medium, Materials: Illustrator

Page 179
Student: Ben Poston / College: Oregon State University
Dean: Kay Schaffer / Department: Art / Department Chair:
David Hardesty / Class: Advanced Typography
Instructor: Andrea Marks
Photographer and Copywriter: Ben Poston
Project: Utilizing a large format, research object and design a poster
which conveys the essence of that object.
*Projekt: Gestaltung eines Plakates, welches das Wesen des gewählten
Gegen-standes zum Ausdruck bringt.*
Projet: Etude d'un objet et création d'une affiche qui en reflète l'essence.

Page 180
Student: James Tung / College: School of Visual Arts
Department: Graphic Design / Department Chair: Richard Wilde
Class: Typography / Instructor: Richard Poulin
Medium, Materials: Digital output, Iris print

Page 181 top
Student: Fons M. Hickmann / College: Bugh Wuppertal
Dean: Bazon Brock / Department: Kommunikations Design
Class: Uwe Loesch / Instructor: Bazon Brock
Photographer: Frank Goldner
Project: Poster for design seminar dealing with objects for museums
shops. The title is a play on words in German: "Warenwunder" means
objects with commercial success but phonetically it is the same as
"real miracles"—the claim is that objects in museum shops sell well.
*Projekt: Poster für Design-Seminare für Museumsshop-Objekte: «Die
Waren-wunder tut die Madonna erst im Museum.»*
*Projet: Affiche pour un séminaire de design destinée à une boutique de musée.
L'accroche de l'affiche est un jeu de mots qui signifie à la fois: «La Madonne
ne fait de vrais miracles que dans les musées» ou «La Madonne ne nous
offre les objets du miracle que dans les musées».*

Page 181 bottom
Student: Claudia Oelert / College: Academy of Fine Arts
Dean: Olaf Schwencke / Department: Graphic Design
Instructor: Holger Matthies
Project: Presentation of the Palucca School, a dance academy in
Dresden, Germany.
Projekt: Darstellung der Palucca-Tanzakademie in Dresden.
Projet: Présentation de l'Académie de danse de Dresde.
Strategy: The posters represent the dance styles practiced at the
Palucca School—classical, ballet, contemporary and Spanish dance.
*Strategie: Die Plakate beziehen sich auf die verschiedenen Arten des Tanzes
die an der Akademie gelehrt werden.*
*Stratégie: Les affiches se réfèrent aux différents styles de danse enseignés
dans l'école Palucca.*

Page 182
Student: Benoit Jeay / College: ESAG
Department: Graphic Design
Instructors: Michel Bouvet, Costanza Matteucci (assistant)
Project: Think about the notions of tolerance and intolerance
through the subject of racism.
Projekt: Rassismus und die Auffassung von Toleranz und Intoleranz.
*Projet: Réflechir, à travers le thème du racisme, sur les notions de tolérance et
d'intolérance.*
Strategy: Each student expressed these two notions in two images that
are at the same time different and complementary.
*Strategie: Jeder Student gab diesen beiden Begriffen in zwei Bildern
Ausdruck, die sich voneinander unterscheiden, aber auch ergänzen.*
*Stratégie: Chaque étudiant a exprimé ses notions dans deux images à la fois
différentes et complémentaires.*

Page 183 left
Student/Photographer: Amanda Barile / College: Pennsylvania
State University / Dean: Neil Porterfield / Department: Graphic
Design / Department Chair: Jim Stephenson / Class: Photgraphy
Instructor and Art Director: Kristin Breslin Sommese
Project: Design a poster for Women's Awareness Week at
Penn State University.
Projekt: Plakat für eine Frauenwoche an der Penn State University.
Projet: Affiche consacrée à la «Semaine de la Femme» à l'Université Penn State.
Strategy: The design is meant to encourage women to speak out. The
words "if you allow fear to bind you in silence you will soon fade
away" run down the center of the body, binding the woman's mouth
and hands.
*Strategie: Die Frauen sollen ermuntert werden, ihre Meinung zu sagen. Die
Worte «Wenn du es zulässt, dass die Angst dir zu Kehle zuschnürt, wird
bald nichts mehr von dir da sein» laufen am Körper herunter und knebeln
Mund und Hände.*

*Stratégie: Les femmes sont encouragées à dire leur opinion. Les mots de la
phrase «Si tu laisses la peur te clouer au silence, tu ne seras bientôt plus que
l'ombre de toi-même» descendent le long du corps de la femme et bâillonnent
sa bouche et ses mains.*
Medium, Materials: Black-and-white 16" x 20" self-portrait.

Page 183 right
Student: Triton Keugh / College: The Advertising Arts
Dean: Larry Lewis / Class: Special Studies III / Instructor: Vicki Eddy
Project: Poster designed as a public service for MADD (Mothers
Against Drunk Driving) meant to appeal to youth.
*Projekt: Plakat für MADD (Mütter gegen Alkohol am Steuer), das sich an
die Jugend wendet.*
*Projet: Affiche pour MADD (Mères contre l'alcool au volant) s'adressant
aux jeunes.*

Page 184 top
Student: Peter Vajda / College: Hungarian Academy of Fine Arts
Department: Graphic Design / Department Chair: Kalman Molnar
Instructor: Tamas Felsmann
Project: Nike poster.
Projekt: Plakat für Nike.
Projet: Affiche Nike.

Page 184 middle
Student: Nathan Savage / College: Southwest Texas State University
Dean: Richard Cheatham / Department: Art / Department Chair:
Brian Row / Class: Ad and Design I / Instructor: Bill Meek
Project: Design a poster for Earth Day '97 in New York.
Projekt: Entwurf eines Plakates für «Earth Day '97» in New York.
Projet: Affiche pour le «Jour de la Terre 97» à New York.
Strategy: A graffiti-marked subway sign for Bleeker Street plays on
the name, changing it to "Bleaker" street.
*Strategie: Aus dem U-Bahnschild für die Bleeker Street, mit Graffitis
versehen, wird «Bleaker» Street, was soviel wie trostlose Strasse bedeutet.*
*Stratégie: Jeu de mots avec l'écriteau de la bouche de métro de Bleeker Street,
recouvert de graffiti: le nom de la rue a été changé en «Bleaker» Street (rue morne).*
Medium, Materials: Silkscreen printed on scratchboard

Page 184 bottom
Student: Hye Won Chang / College: School of Visual Arts
Department: Graphic Design / Department Chair: Richard Wilde
Class: Senior Portfolio / Instructor: Carin Goldberg
Medium, Materials: Photoshop Illustrator

Page 185
Student: Jon Sueda / College: California College of Arts and Crafts
Dean: Michael Vanderbyl / Department: Graphic Design Department
Chair: Leslie Becker / Class: Graphic Design III
Instructors: Neal Zimmermann, Dennis Crowe
Project: Design a poster to announce the opening of the
Buckminster Fuller Museum. Emphasize clear communication of
visual information.
*Projekt: Ein Plakat für die Eröffnung des Buckminster-Fuller-Museums,
mit klarer Information.*
*Projet: Affiche informative annonçant l'inauguration du musée
Buckminster Fuller.*
Strategy: The student highlights Buckminster Fuller's invention of the
"dymaxion" car, and his discovery that a car would be more efficient if
it could steer from the back wheel and propel itself from the front,
much as a fish swims. With this modification, one-move parallel parking
and a sharper turn radius were possible. The student combines an automobile from the 1930s with a fish to represent Fuller's thinking process.
*Strategie: Herausgestellt wird Buckminster Fullers Erfindung: das «Dymaxion»-
Auto. Er hatte entdeckt, dass die Steuerung eines Autos durch die hinteren Räder
und der Antrieb durch die Vorderräder, ähnlich wie beim Fisch, vorteilhafter ist.
Hier wurde deshalb ein Auto aus den 30er Jahren mit einem Fisch kombiniert.*
*Stratégie: L'accent est mis sur l'invention de Buckminster Fuller: la voiture
«dymaxion». Fuller avait découvert que la conduite d'une voiture est plus
facile si la traction se fait depuis les roues arrière et la propulsion, depuis les
roues avant, à l'image des mouvements d'un poisson. Pour cette raison, l'étudiant à intégré un poisson à cette automobile datant des années 30.*

Page 186
Student: Matthew Staab / College: The Creative Circus
Department: Design / Department Chair: Rob Lawton
Class: Design / Instructor: Rob Lawton
Strategy: Poster for an Alfred Hitchcock film festival.
Strategie: Plakat für ein Alfred-Hitchcock-Filmfestival.
Stratégie: Affiche pour un festival du film consacré à Alfred Hitchcock.
Medium, Materials: Cut paper

Page 187 top left
Student: Dong-Hyun Kim / College: School of Visual Arts
Department: Graphic Design / Department Chair: Richard Wilde
Class: Design with Type / Instructor: Henrietta Condak

Project: Bauhaus 1.
Projekt: Das Bauhaus.
Projet: Le Bauhaus.
Strategy: Collage of images from Weimar and Dessau period. Red and blue type are integral to the design.
Strategie: Collage von Bildern aus der Weimarer und Dessauer Zeit.
Stratégie: Collage d'images datant de l'époque de Weimar et de Dessau.
Medium, Materials: Photoshop, Illustrator

Page 187 top right
Student: Peter Vajda / College: Hungarian Academy of Fine Arts
Department: Graphic Design / Department Chair: Kalman Molnar
Instructor: Tamas Felsmann
Project: Orkeny Totek theater poster.
Projekt: Entwurf eines Theaterplakates.
Projet: Création d'une affiche de théâtre.
Strategy: Poster for a grotesque drama taking place at time of World War II. A dead soldier's family members produce paper boxes at the instructions of their guest, a lunatic sergeant.
Strategie: Es handelt sich um eine Groteske, die zur Zeit des zweiten Weltkriegs spielt. Die Familien-angehörigen eines gefallenen Soldaten produzieren auf Weisung ihres Gastes, eines verrückten Feldwebels, Papierboxen.
Stratégie: Affiche pour un drame grotesque qui se déroule durant la Seconde Guerre mondiale. Les membres de la famille d'un soldat mort durant la guerre fabriquent des boîtes en papier sur ordre de leur hôte, un sergent lunatique.

Page 187 bottom left
Student: Regina Krutoy / College: School of Visual Arts
Dean: David Rhodes / Department: Graphic Design
Department Chair: Richard Wilde / Class: Portfolio
Instructor: Paula Scher
Project: Champion poster.
Projekt: Gestaltung eines Plakates für ein Sportgeschäft.
Projet: Conception d'une affiche pour un magasin de sports.
Strategy: The student's choice of imagery was to show that a real champion does not quit.
Strategie: Die Aussage dieses Plakates: ein wirklicher Champion gibt nicht auf.
Stratégie: Message véhiculé par cette affiche: «Un vrai champion n'abandonne jamais.»
Medium, Materials: QuarkXpress, Adobe Illustrator, Adobe Photoshop

Page 187 bottom right
Student: Hitomi Sato / College: School of Visual Arts
Department: Graphic Design / Department Chair: Richard Wilde
Class: Graphic Design Portfolio / Instructor: Paula Scher
Project: Poster for the "50th on 5th" anniversary celebration of the Jewish Museum.
Projekt: Plakat zum 50 jährigen Bestehen des Jüdischen Museums an der 5th Avenue.
Projet: Affiche commémorant les 50 ans du Musée Juif.
Strategy: The student used architectual plans and maps of the museum as graphic elements in the design.
Strategie: Architektonische Zeichnungen und Pläne des Museums dienen als graphische Elemente.
Stratégie: Dessins architectoniques et plans du musée constituent les principaux éléments graphiques.
Medium, Materials: Computer

Page 188 top
Student: Arsendio Garcia-Monsalve / College: Art Center College of Design / Department: Product Design / Department Chair: Martin Smith / Class: Environmental Studio Seminar, Furniture Design
Instructor: David Mockarski / Photographer: Steve Heller
Project/Assignment: "Guadiana," a chair designed to be used in a cafeteria.
Projekt: «Guadiana», ein Stuhl für Cafés.
Projet: «Guadiana», chaise de café.
Strategy: The student wanted to design a chair that solves the problem of having no safe place to put your bags when you arrive at a cafe.
Strategie: Dem Studenten ging es um einen Stuhl, der das Problem eines sicheren Abstellplatzes für Taschen in Cafés löst.
Stratégie: L'étudiant voulait concevoir une chaise qui offre un endroit sûr aux clients pour déposer leur sac.
Medium, Materials: Birch plywood, stainless steel square tube.
Birke (Sperrholz), Edelstahlrohr.
Bouleau contreplaqué, tube en acier inoxydable.

Page 188 middle
Student: Travis Rogers / College: Rhode Island School of Design
Department: Industrial Design / Class: 3D Design
Instructor: Debby Coolidge

Page 188 bottom
Student: Michelle Chong / College: Art Center College of Design
Dean and Department Chair: Patricia Belton Oliver / Department: Environmental Design / Class: Environmental Design Topic Studio:

Furniture Design / Instructor: David Mockarski
Project: "Note," a stool for a music store.
Projekt: «Note», ein Stuhl für einen Musikladen.
Projet: «Note», chaise destinée à un magasin de musique.
Strategy: In this class assignment on seating, students focused on linking the conceptual development of the piece to the emotional qualities expressed by the final product. The design for this stool is inspired by a guitar and a musical note.
Strategie: Bei diesem Stuhlprojekt für eine Klasse konzentrierten sich die Studenten auf die Entwicklung eines von emotion-alen Eigen-schaften geprägten Produktes. Ausgangspunkt für das Design dieses Stuhls sind eine Gitarre und eine Note.
Stratégie: Dans le cadre de ce projet, les étudiants ont mis l'accent sur les qualités émotionnelles du produit. Le design s'inspire d'une guitare et d'une note de musique.
Medium, Materials: Aluminum frame, purple heart seat

Page 189
Student: Peter Benarcik / College: Art Center College of Design
Department Chairs: Richard Hertz, Steve Diskin / Department: Graduate Environmental Design / Class: Furniture Design—Urban Pairings / Instructor: David Mockarski / Photographer: Steven Heller
Project: "Adam & Eve" cabinets.
Projekt: «Adam & Eva»-Schränke.
Projet: «Adam & Eve», armoires.
Medium, Materials: Birch plywood, rock maple, cherry veneers, aluminum stock (leg members).

Page 190 top
Student: Terry Allan Shigemitsu / College: Art Center College of Design / Department Chair: Martin Smith / Department: Product Design, Computer Animation / Class: Furniture Design—Urban Pairings / Instructor: Imre Molnar / Photographer: Steven Heller
Project: Stovetop espresso maker.
Projekt: Espresso-Maschine.
Projet: Machine à express.
Strategy: High-end functional kitchen art piece inspired by Philippe Starck. Design cues taken from Starck's use of soft edges and whimsy.
Strategie: Ein von Philippe Starck inspirierter, funktionaler Kunstgegenstand für die Küche.
Stratégie: Objet artistique et fonctionnel pour la cuisine, inspiré des créations de Philippe Starck.
Medium, Materials: Sand-cast aluminum, black walnut, glass.

Page 190 middle
Student: Peter Streckfuss / College: Rhode Island School of Design
Department: Industrial Design / Department Chair: Mickey Ackerman / Class: Metal II / Instructor: Dick Ramspot
Photographer: Mark Johnston

Page 190 bottom
Student: Roosevelt Brown / College: Art Center College of Design
Department Chair: Martin Smith / Department: Product Design
Class: Sixth-Term Package Design / Instructor: Norm Sherman
Project: Stovetop espresso maker.
Projekt: Espresso-Maschine.
Projet: Machine à express.
Strategy: High-end functional kitchen art piece inspired by Philippe Starck. Design cues taken from Starck's use of soft edges and whimsy.
Strategie: Ein von Philippe Starck inspirierter, funktionaler Kunstgegenstand für die Küche.
Stratégie: Objet artistique et fonctionnel pour la cuisine, inspiré des créations de Philippe Starck.
Medium, Materials: Sand-cast aluminum, black walnut, glass.

Page 191
Student: Gerard Thomas / College: Art Center College of Design
Class: Independent Study Project
Project: Motorcycle

Page 192 top
Student: Yuki Midorikawa Haelters / College: Rhode Island School of Design Department: Industrial Design / Department Chair: Mitchell Ackerman / Class: Chair Design Studio
Instructor: Seth Stem / Photographer: Mark Johnston

Page 192 bottom
Students: Arsenio Garcia-Monsalve, Cecilia Vitas-Volcoff
College: Art Center College of Design / Department: Environmental & Product Design / Department Chair: Patricia Oliver
Class: Environmental Studio / Seminar: Furniture Design
Instructor: David Mocarski / Photographer: Steven Heller
Project: Vivace, "the new conference chair."
Projekt: «Vivace», ein neuer Konferenzstuhl.
Projet: «Vivace», chaise pour une salle de conférences.
Strategy: The goal was to design a chair which could stack or

fold, would have a writing surface and be suited for an educational environment.
Strategie: Das Ziel war der Entwurf eines Stuhles, der sich stapeln oder zusammenlegen lässt. Zudem sollte er eine Schreibfläche haben und sich für Schulungsräume eignen.
Stratégie: L'objectif était de créer une chaise qui se laisse à la fois plier et empiler. En outre, celle-ci devait présenter une surface pour écrire et être adaptée aux salles de cours.
Medium, Materials: Polypropylene and steel rod.

Page 193 top
Student: Dario Antonioni / College: Art Center College of Design
Department: Environmental Design / Department Chair: Patricia Belton Oliver / Class: Environmental Design Topic Studio: Furniture Design / Instructor: David Mocarski
Project: "Praying Mantis," home office workstation.
Projekt: «Gottes-anbeterin», ein Arbeitsplatz für das Büro zu Hause.
Projet: «Mante religieuse», poste de travail domestique.
Strategy: Designed for a studio titled "Pairs/Parallels," this project is visually inspired by the praying mantis. It is designed to be easily moved and adjustable to any environment. The use of metal is minimized to make it seem warmer and lighter.
Strategie: Dieser Entwurf wurde von einer Gottesanbeterin inspiriert. Er lässt sich leicht bewegen und jeder Umgebung anpassen. Der Einsatz von Metall wurde auf ein Minimum reduziert, um alles wärmer und leichter wirken zu lassen.
Stratégie: Inspiré d'une mante religieuse, ce design a été conçu pour s'adapter à n'importe quel environnement. Le métal a été réduit au minimum pour rendre l'ensemble plus léger, plus «chaleureux».
Medium, Materials: Ash and birch wood, glass, steel, automotive paint finish on the steel. Dimensions: 4' x 9' x 7'.

Page 193 bottom
Student: Dario Antonioni / College: Art Center College of Design
Department: Environmental Design / Department Chair: Patricia Belton Oliver / Class: Environmental Design
Topic Studio: Furniture Design / Instructor: David Moçarski
Project: The home office. Students were asked to explore the relationship between concept, content, form and materials. Attention was given to connections, finish and choice of materials. Emphasis was placed on convenience, flexibility and function.
Projekt: Das Büro zu Hause. Die Studenten waren aufgefordert, sich mit der Beziehung von Konzept, Inhalt, Form und Material zu befassen. Wichtig waren die Kombinationen, Wahl und Verarbeitung des Materials. Das Hauptgewicht lag auf Bequem-lichkeit, Anpassungsfähigkeit und Funktion.
Projet: Le bureau domestique. La tâche des étudiants consistait à explorer la relation entre concept, contenu, forme et matériaux. Le design devait remplir les critères suivants: confort, flexibilité et fonctionnalité.
Strategy: The student tried to make the desk "inviting," to entice the user into working. The primary dialogue between "home" and "office" is achieved through the use of materials: cool steel and glass associated with the corporate world, and hand-hewn, tactile, warm woods more often found in the home. The piece rides on inconspicuous rolling casters allowing easy mobility.
Strategie: Ein «einladender» Schreibtisch. Der Dialog zwischen der Vorstellung von Büro und privaten Wohnräumen wird durch das Material erreicht: Stahl und Glas lassen an die Geschäftswelt denken, während von Hand bearbeitetes, warm wirkendes Holz das Material zum Wohnen ist.
Stratégie: L'étudiant a voulu créer un bureau séduisant, qui invite au travail. Les caractéristiques propres à un bureau et à un intérieur privé sont rendues ici par le biais des matériaux utilisés: l'acier et le verre recréent l'atmosphère d'un bureau tandis que le bois, travaillé à la main, confère une touche chaleureuse.
Medium, Materials: Plywood inner support covered with 1/8" poplar. This is finished with maple and mahagony veneers and hardwoods, oiled and sealed. Steel frame. Dimensions: 3'9" x 4' x 7'

Page 194
Student: Dario Antonioni / College: Art Center College of Design
Department: Environmental Design / Department Chair: Patricia Belton Oliver / Class: Environmental Design Topic Studio: Furniture Design / Instructor: David Mocarski
Project: Anthropometrics. Folding chair. Students were asked to design a piece of furniture to be used in the Zenobio Institute in Venice, Italy. Emphasis was placed on comfort, reliabiltiy, and mass production methods.
Projekt: Klapp-stuhl. Entwurf eines Stuhls für das Zenobio Institut in Venedig. Es ging vor allem um Bequemlichkeit, Stabilität und die Eignung für eine industrielle Produktion.
Projet: Chaise pliante. Design d'un meuble destiné à l'institut Zenobio à Venise. Les principaux critères de design étaient: confort, stabilité et production industrielle.
Strategy: The design is influenced by the Venetian Gondola. Focusing on the skewed keel of the gondola, the student's design centered on the idea of the curve. The challenge was to create a curve that would accomodate the requirements of a folding chair.

Strategie: Der Entwurf wurde von einer venezianischen Gondel inspiriert. Der Kiel der Gondel veranlasste den Studenten, sich auf eine Wölbung zu konzentrieren. Die Schwierigkeit lag darin, eine Wölbung zu schaffen, die sich für einen Klappstuhl eignet.
Stratégie: Chaise inspirée d'une gondole vénitienne. Pour l'étudiant, qui souhaitait reprendre la forme de la quille, la principale difficulté fut de concevoir une courbure qui se prête à une chaise pliante.
Medium, Materials: CNC milled aluminum, finely-brushed aluminum sheet, rubber, African striped mahogany.
Dimensions: 3' x 19' x 28'

Page 195
Student: Scott Pitters / College: Art Center College of Design
Department: Environmental Design / Instructor: David Mocarski
Project: "NOBI": Design a piece of furniture for the Zenobio Institute in Venice, Italy.
Projekt: «NOBI», Entwurf eines Möbels für das Zenobio Institut in Venedig.
Projet: «NOBI», design d'un meuble destiné à l'institut Zenobio à Venise.
Strategy: When the chair is collapsed, the form recalls the initial curves of the gondola which inspired it. It was important that the chair have a contemporary look, be made from non-traditional materials and respond to practical considerations of storage and portability.
Strategie: Zusammengelegt erinnert die Form an eine Gondel. Wichtig war, dass der Stuhl zeitgemäss wirkt, aus neuen Materialien hergestellt ist und sich leicht lagern und transportieren lässt.
Stratégie: La courbure de la chaise une fois pliée fait penser à une gondole. La chaise devait être moderne, fabriquée avec des matériaux nouveaux, facile à transporter et à ranger.

Page 196
Student: Sharon Slaughter / College: Portfolio Center
Department: Design / Department Chair: Hank Richardson
Class: Advanced Packaging / Instructor: Michael Bergeron
Project: Lumipack lantern.
Projekt: Lumipack-Lampe.
Projet: Lampe de poche surdimensionnée.

Page 197 top
Student: Jake Rivas / College: California College of Arts and Crafts
Department Chair: Steven Skov Holt / Instructor: Paul Braund
Photographer: Mark Serr
Project: Recycled modular sneakers.
Projekt: Sportschuhe aus wiederverwertetem Material.
Projet: Sneakers réalisé avec du matériel recyclé.

Page 197 middle
Student: Page Hadden / College: California College of Arts and Crafts / Department Chair: Steven Skov Holt / Instructor: Paul Braund / Photographer: Mark Serr
Project: "Zecta" two-way adjustable children's bicycle.
Projekt: «Zecta»—ein verstellbares Kinder-Fahrrad.
Projet: «Zecta»—un cycle pour enfants ajustable.

Page 197 bottom
Student: Kubo / College: California College of Arts and Crafts
Department Chair: Steven Skov Holt / Instructor: Paul Braund
Project: Motorcycle helmet.
Projekt: Motorradhelm.
Projet: Casque de moto.

Page 198
Student: Bill Burns / College: California College of Arts and Crafts
Department: Industrial Design
Department Chair: Steven Skov Holt / Instructor: Paul Braund
Photographer: Mark Serr
Project: Communal table.
Projekt: Ein grosser Küchen-tisch.
Projet: Grande table collective.

Page 199
Student: Zita Watkins / College: The Swinburne School of Design
Dean: Helmut Lueckenhausen / Department: Industrial Design
Department Chair: Lyndon Anderson / Class: Industrial Design, Fourth-Year Honors / Instructor: Barry Quantrell
Project: "Princess" lamp. Princess is made from poly-propylene and is available in four colours. Her form is the result of functional requirements; no added parts are needed and nothing ishid-den or disguised.
Projekt: «Princess»-Leuchte. «Princess» wurde aus Polypropylen gefertigt und ist in vier Farben erhältlich. Ihre Form ist ganz auf die Funktion ausgerichtet; es sind weder zusätzliche Teile nötig, noch ist etwas versteckt oder verdeckt.
Projet: Luminaire «Princess» composé de polypropylène et disponible en quatre coloris. La forme suit la fonction: aucun élément supplémentaire n'est nécessaire et rien n'est caché ou déguisé.

Page 200
Student: Elizabeth A. Devries / College: Hamline University
Dean: Gerry Greiner / Department: Art
Department Chair: Leo Lasansky / Class: Problems in 3D and Design
Instructor: Debbie Sigel
Project: Using cardboard and glue, construct a chair able to support a person's weight.
Projekt: Gestaltung eines Stuhles aus Pappe und Klebstoff, der das Gewicht einer Person tragen kann.
Projet: Création d'une chaise en carton avec de la colle devant supporter le poids d'une personne.
Strategy: The student wanted to create movement in the design without losing the integrity of the cardboard.
Strategie: Ohne den Charakter des Materials zu leugnen, sollte Bewegung in das Design kommen.
Stratégie: L'étudiante a imprimé une forme de mouvement à son design tout en conservant les spécificités du matériau utilisé.
Medium, Materials: Cardboard, wood glue, hot glue

Page 201
Students: Elliott Hsu, Jim Doan, Victor Fernandez
College: University of Illinois / Dean: Dean Moyer
Department: Industrial Design
Department Chair: Andrzej Wroblewski / Instructor: Surya Vanka
Project: Product name: Aerio timepiece. The design team was given a set of analog clock mechanisms and was told to design a clock that incorporates form and function.
Projekt: Ein Chronometer namens «Aerio». Das Design-Team erhielt ein Uhrwerk, um daraus eine Uhr zu machen, wobei Form und Funktion den gleichen Stellenwert haben sollten.
Projet: Un chrono-mètre intitulé «Aerio». L'équipe de designers a reçu le mécanisme d'une montre comme objet de base. La forme et la fonction de la montre devaient avoir la même importance.
Strategy: The idea behind Aerio is to give the user something more than just the time. This design mimics the movement of a flower toward light. A slightly weighted minute hand and a ball bearing with a track allows it to sway as the time changes.
Strategie: Aerio soll ihrem Besitzer mehr als nur die Zeit angeben. Das Design imitiert die Bewegung einer Blume hin zum Licht. Der mit einem kleinen Gewicht versehene Minutenzeiger und ein Kugellager mit einer Schiene sorgen für die Bewegung.
Stratégie: Aerio ne se limite pas à un instrument pour mesurer le temps. Son design imite l'orientation d'une fleur vers la lumière. La trotteuse, pourvue d'un petit poids, et un roulement à billes créent le mouvement.
Medium, Materials: Aluminum, graphite, steel ball bearing, analog clock

Page 202, 203
Student: Rudy Widiaman / College: Art Center College of Design
Photographer: Steven Heller / Department: Product Design
Department Chair: Martin Smith / Class: Product Design
Instructors: Norman Schureman, Daniel Packman

Page 204
Student: Brett Nystul / College: Art Center College of Design
Photographer: Steven Heller

Page 205
Student: Grant Delgatty / College: Art Center College of Design
Photographer: Steven Heller

Page 206
Students: Jeff Phillips, Scott Chandler / College: Virginia Tech
Dean: David Crane / Department Chair: Robert Fields
Class: Advanced Visual Communications / Instructor: Scott Chandler
Project: Develop CD promotional piece to display portfolio.
Projekt: Entwicklung einer CD-Promotion als Teil der Arbeitsmappe der Studenten.
Projet: Créer une promotion de CD destinée au portfolio des étudiants.
Strategy: The high-tech appearance and technical expertise convey creative skills.
Strategie: Der High-tech-Look zeigt das Geschick und das technische Können.
Stratégie: Le look high-tech témoigne de l'habileté et du savoir-faire technique.
Medium, Materials: Circuit boards, Free-hand, Photoshop, Director

Page 207
Student: Richard Vasquez / College: California State University Long Beach / Department: Art and Visual Communication
Class: Visual Communication / Instructor: Archie Boston
Illustration: Richard Vasquez
Project: "Stinking Rose" restaurant promotions.
Projekt: Werbemittel für ein Restaurant namens «Stinking Rose».
Projet: Matériel promotionnel pour le restaurant «Stinking Rose».
Strategy: Menu, bag and coaster design for a restaurant specializing in garlic dishes.
Strategie: Gestaltung der Speisekarte, der Tragtasche und Untersätze für ein Restaurant, das sich auf Knoblauch-Gerichte spezialisiert hat.
Stratégie: Conception de la carte, d'un sac et des sets de table d'un restaurant proposant des spécialités à l'aïl.
Medium, Materials: Pastels, pastel pencils, ink, Photoshop, Quark Xpress

Pages 208, 209
Student: Angela Perez-Charneco / College: Pennsylvania State University / Dean: Neil Porterfield / Department: Graphic Design
Department Chair: Jim Stephenson / Class: Packaging / Instructor: Kristin Breslin Sommese / Photographer: Dwain Harbst
Art Director: Kristin Sommese
Project: Create a series of shopping bags for a women's clothing store.
Projekt: Eine Reihe von Tragtaschen für ein Damenmodegeschäft.
Projet: Série de sacs pour une boutique de mode.
Strategy: The student wanted the packaging to reflect the elegant and classic nature of the clothing. She incorporated pin striping and color combinations of the clothes. The "C" of the store's name is reflected in the shape of the handle of the bag.
Strategie: Eine Verpackung, die dem eleganten, klassischen Stil der Kleidung entspricht. Die Studenten liessen sich von der Kleidung inspirieren, indem sie Nadelstreifen und verschiedene Farben in ihr Design aufnahmen. Das «C» des Namens des Geschäftes wird durch den Henkel der Tasche geformt.
Stratégie: Les sacs reflètent le raffinement et l'élégance de la ligne de vêtements. L'étudiante s'est inspirée des vêtements en intégrant divers coloris et de fines rayures au design. Le «C» du nom du magasin forme la anse du sac.
Medium, Materials: Glass bottles, black spray paint, colored paper

Page 210 top
Student: James Shun / College: School of Visual Arts
Department: Graphic Design / Department Chair: Richard Wilde
Class: Senior Portfolio / Instructor: Carin Goldberg

Page 210 bottom
Student: Yim Cheng / College: School of Visual Arts
Department: Advertising and Graphic Design
Department Chair: Richard Wilde / Class: Portfolio, Graphic Design
Instructor: Carin Goldberg

Page 211
Student: Lloyd Rodriues / College: School of Visual Arts
Department: Graphic Design / Department Chair: Richard Wilde
Class: Typography / Instructor: Carin Goldberg

Page 212 top
Student: Maureen Meyer / College: Pennsylvania State University
Dean: Neil Porterfield / Department: Graphic Design
Department Chair: Jim Stephenson / Class: Packaging / Instructor: Kristin Breslin Sommese / Photographer: Dave Shelly
Art Director: Kristin Sommese
Project: Design a shopping bag for a bakery specializing in desserts.
Projekt: Tragtasche für eine Konditorei, die sich auf Desserts spezialisiert hat.
Projet: Sac pour une pâtisserie fine spécialisée dans les desserts.
Strategy: The student chose to represent desserts with a cherry. The die-cut of the cherry enables the purchaser to see the contents of the bag. The stem forms the handle of the bag.
Strategie: Eine Kirsche dient als Symbol für Desserts. Die Ausstanzung ermöglicht dem Käufer, den Inhalt zu betrachten. Der Stil der Kirsche wird zum Griff.
Stratégie: Une cerise symbolise les desserts. L'estampe en forme de cerise permet au consommateur de voir le contenu du sac. La tige forme la anse du sac.
Medium, Materials: Wrapping paper, floral wire, archival white paper

Page 212 middle
Student: Mieko Kojima / College: School of Visual Arts
Department: Graphic Design / Department Chair: Richard Wilde
Class: Portfolio / Instructor: Carin Goldberg
Project: Create identity of company with unique logo to get attention of customer.
Projekt: Entwicklung eines Firmenerscheinungs-bildes mit einem einzigartigen Logo.
Projet: Création d'une identité visuelle pour une société, comprenant des sacs et un logo.

Page 212 bottom
Student: Amanda Barile / College: Pennsylvania State University
Dean: Neil Porterfield / Department: Graphic Design
Department Chair: Jim Stephenson / Class: Packaging
Instructor: Kristin Breslin Sommese / Photography of Bags: Amanda Barile / Photographer: Dwaine Harbst
Art Director: Kristin Breslin Sommese
Project: Design a shopping bag for a gourmet cooking store named Capa.
Projekt: Entwurf einer Tragtasche für einen Delikatess-Laden, der Capa heisst.

Projet: Création d'un sac pour le traiteur Capa.
Strategy: The herbs and spices on the bag show what is sold in the store. The different sides of the bag show a decrease in the herbs and spices as they are used by the customer.
Strategie: Die Kräuter und Gewürze auf der Tragtasche zeigen, was in dem Laden verkauft wird. Auf den verschiedenen Seiten der Tasche sind immer weniger Kräuter und Gewürze zu sehen, so als habe sie der Käufer allmählich verbraucht.
Stratégie: Les épices et les herbes aromatiques figurant sur le sac illustrent les produits vendus dans le magasin. Les différents côtés du sac présentent de moins en moins d'herbes et d'épices comme si le consommateur les avait utilisées au fur et à mesure.
Medium, Materials: Color photography, wire

Page 213
Student: Hiro H. Westdorp / College: Pasadena City College
Department: Art / Department Chair: Linda Malm / Class: Product Design, Craft and Jewelry / Instructors: Stan Kong, Kay Yee
Project: Using industrial or recycled materials, make fashion accessories.
Projekt: Einsatz von Industrie- oder wieder-verwertetem Material für ModeAccessoires.
Projet: Création d'accessoires de mode à partir de matériaux industriels ou recyclés.
Strategy: The student is interested in recycled aluminum. He cut out soda cans, riveted them to a sheet and covered it with a window screen.
Strategie: Der Student entschied sich für Aluminium. Er zerschnitt Getränkedosen, nietete sie auf eine Platte und bedeckte diese mit einem Fliegenfenster.
Stratégie: L'étudiant a porté son choix sur de l'aluminium. Il a découpé des canettes de soda, les a rivées pour en faire une plaque qu'il a recouverte avec une fenêtre grillagée.
Medium, Materials: Aluminum, electric wire, plastic, steel, nylon

Page 214
Student: Matthew Smith / College: Mon-mouth University
Dean: Stunkel / Department: Art / Department Chair: Dimattio
Instructor: Pat Cresson
Medium, Materials: Iris print illustrator

Page 215
Student: Ross Morgan / College: University of Ballarat
Instructor: David O'Calligan
Project: Design four stamps and point-of-sale wallet or booklet.
Projekt: Entwurf von vier Briefmarken und einer Broschüre für den Laden.
Projet: Création de quatre timbres et d'une brochure pour un magasin.
Strategy: The student chose to portray design and innovation of the 30s art deco era.
Strategie: Das Thema ist die Art-deco-Periode in den dreissiger Jahren.
Stratégie: Thème: les années 30, l'art déco.
Medium, Materials: Scoured photos from the 30s, airbrushed and enhanced in Photoshop, assembled in Illustrator 5.5.

Page 216
Student: Mary Belibasakis / College: School of Visual Arts
Dean: David Rhodes / Department: Graphic Design
Department Chair: Richard Wilde / Class: Portfolio
Instructor: Carin Goldberg
Project: Design a typeface.
Projekt: Entwurf einer Schrift.
Projet: Création d'une famille de caractères.
Strategy: The student used bright lights and colorful liquid to create "drivel."
Strategie: Die Studentin benutzte helles Licht und farbige Flüssigkeiten.
Stratégie: L'étudiante a opté pour un éclairage lumineux et des liquides colorés.

Page 217
Student: Blake Tannery / College: The Creative Circus
Department: Design / Department Chair: Rob Lawton
Class: Lettering Instructor: Rob Lawton
Project: Hand-lettering for an Anna Colgan design.
Projekt: Handschrift für ein Anna-Colgan-Design.
Projet: Calligraphie pour un design d'Anna Colgan.
Strategy: Pretty girl, pretty script.
Strategie: Hübsches Mädchen, hübsche Schrift.
Stratégie: Belle fille, belle écriture.
Medium, Materials: Ink and paper hand-lettering
Handschrift, Tinte und Papier
Encre, papier et calligraphie

Page 218
Student: Surasak Luengthaviboon/ College: Savannah College
Dean: Catherine Mark / Department: Graphic Design
Department Chair: Danial Fantauzzi / Class: Computer Typography
Instructor: Amy Kern
Medium, Materials: Freehand

Page 219
Student: Regina Krutoy / College: School of Visual Arts
Department: Graphic Design / Department Chair: Richard Wilde
Class: Typography / Instructor: Richard Poulin
Medium, Materials: Illustrator, plexiglass, illustration board and scale figures.

Page 220
Student: Frank Anselmo / College: School of Visual Arts
Dean: David Rhodes / Department: Advertising and Graphic Design
Department Chair: Richard Wilde / Class: Typography
Instructor: Sara Giovanitti
Medium, Materials: Power Mac

Page 256
Student: John Grande / College: School of Visual Arts
Department: Illustration & Cartooning
Department Chair: Jack Endewelt

Index **Verzeichnisse** Index

Index **Verzeichnisse** Index

Students Studenten Etudiants

Professors Professoren Professeurs

Schools Universitäten Universités

Graphis Magazine

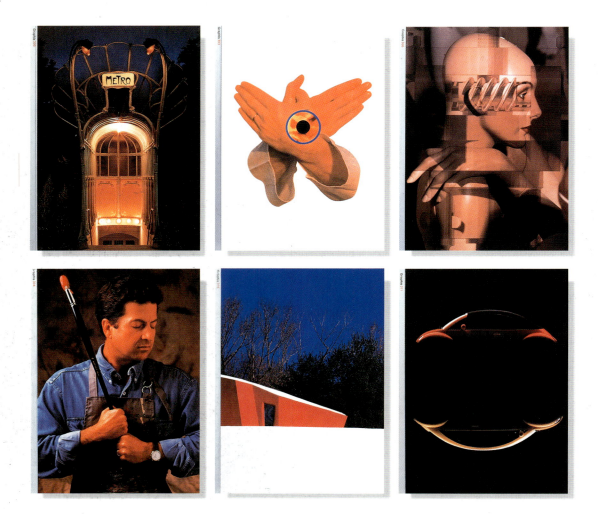

Graphis Books

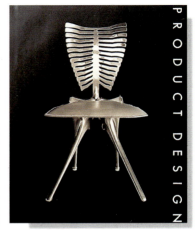

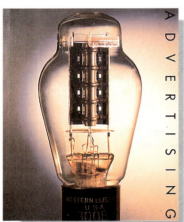

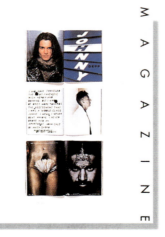

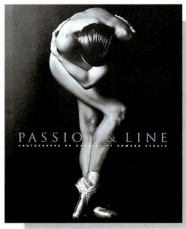